Responses to Economic Change

This is Volume 27 in the series of studies commissioned as part of the research program of the Royal Commission on the Economic Union and Development Prospects for Canada.

The studies contained in this volume reflect the views of their authors and do not imply endorsement by the Chairman or Commissioners.

Responses to Economic Change

DAVID LAIDLER
Research Coordinator

Published by the University of Toronto Press in cooperation with the Royal Commission on the Economic Union and Development Prospects for Canada and the Canadian Government Publishing Centre, Supply and Services Canada

University of Toronto Press
Toronto   Buffalo   London

Grateful acknowledgment is made to the following for permission to reprint previously published and unpublished material: California Tax Foundation.

©Minister of Supply and Services Canada 1986

Printed in Canada
ISBN 0-8020-7270-4
ISSN 0829-2396
Cat. No. Z1-1983/1-41-27E

CANADIAN CATALOGUING IN PUBLICATION DATA

Main entry under title:
Responses to economic change

(The Collected research studies / Royal Commission on the Economic Union and Development Prospects for Canada,
ISSN 0829-2396 ; 27)
Includes bibliographical references.
ISBN 0-8020-7270-4

1. Canada — Economic conditions — 1971–   — Addresses, essays, lectures.
2. Canada — Economic policy — 1971–   — Addresses, essays, lectures. 3. Industry and state — Canada — Addresses, essays, lectures. I. Laidler, David, 1938–
II. Royal Commission on the Economic Union and Development Prospects for Canada.
III. Series: The Collected research studies (Royal Commission on the Economic Union and Development Prospects for Canada) ; 27.

HC115.R47 1985   338.971   C85-099249-4

PUBLISHING COORDINATION: Ampersand Communications Services Inc.
COVER DESIGN: Will Rueter
INTERIOR DESIGN: Brant Cowie/Artplus Limited

CONTENTS

FOREWORD *ix*
INTRODUCTION *xi*
PREFACE *xv*
ACKNOWLEDGMENTS *xix*

1. **Resources and Economic Development in Historical Perspective**
   C. Knick Harley
   Introduction *1*
   Long-Term Relationships between Population and the
     Standard of Living *3*
   Resource Abundance and North American Growth *8*
   Organized Concern for Conservation *16*
   Resource Use Projections over a Century of Experience *19*
   Property Rights and Resources *21*
   Conclusion: Resource Shortage and the Market
     in Historical Perspective *26*
   Notes *29*
   Bibliography *30*

2. **Entrepreneurship, Innovation and Economic Change**
   David W. Conklin
   Some Aspects of Entrepreneurship *33*
   Innovation and Economic Change *40*
   The Role of Government *52*
   Notes *71*
   Bibliography *71*

3. **Rules versus Discretion in Constitutional Design**
   Charles K. Rowley
   Introduction   *75*
   The Reason of Rules   *76*
   Voter Power   *84*
   Incumbent Governments   *87*
   Canadian Constitutional Design   *93*
   Notes   *103*
   Bibliography   *103*

4. **The Growth of the Public Sector in Canada**
   Dan Usher
   Explaining the Growth of Government   *107*
     Rational Self-Interest Theories   *108*
     Conspiracy Theories   *117*
   Measuring the Growth of Government Involvement in
     the Economy   *119*
   Conclusions
   Appendix: The Price of Government Output and the
                 Measurement of the Share of the Public
                 Sector in the Economy   *123*
   Notes   *132*
   Bibliography   *133*

5. **Economic Rationality and the Political Behaviour of Canadians**
   Claude Montmarquette
   Introduction   *135*
   The Concept of the Political Market   *138*
   The Functioning of the Canadian Political Market   *140*
   The Pressure Group Model   *140*
   The Median-Voter Model   *141*
   The Consensus Calculation Model   *143*
   Conclusion   *145*
   Notes   *148*
   Bibliography   *149*

6. **Government, Special Interest Groups and Economic Growth**
   André Blais and John McCallum
   Introduction   *153*
   Overview of the Facts   *155*
   Why Growth Rates Differ: Analytical Framework   *161*
   Empirical Implementation   *167*
   Empirical Results   *173*
   Interpretation of the Results   *178*
   APPENDIX A: Economic Growth in Historical Perspective,
                   Canada and the United States   *186*

APPENDIX B: Theoretical Model   *188*
APPENDIX C: Definitions of Variables   *190*
APPENDIX D: Regression Results   *192*
Notes   *199*
Bibliography   *200*

7. **Improving Productivity in the Government Sector:
The Role of Contracting Out**
Robert L. Bish
Introduction   *203*
Separating Demand and Supply   *205*
The Nature of Government Services and
   Bureaucratic Production   *205*
Contracting   *208*
Adapting to the Future   *229*
Conclusions and Observations   *231*
Notes   *233*
Bibliography   *235*

ABOUT THE CONTRIBUTORS   *239*

When the members of the Rowell-Sirois Commission began their collective task in 1937, very little was known about the evolution of the Canadian economy. What was known, moreover, had not been extensively analyzed by the slender cadre of social scientists of the day.

When we set out upon our task nearly 50 years later, we enjoyed a substantial advantage over our predecessors; we had a wealth of information. We inherited the work of scholars at universities across Canada and we had the benefit of the work of experts from private research institutes and publicly sponsored organizations such as the Ontario Economic Council and the Economic Council of Canada. Although there were still important gaps, our problem was not a shortage of information; it was to interrelate and integrate — to synthesize — the results of much of the information we already had.

The mandate of this Commission is unusually broad. It encompasses many of the fundamental policy issues expected to confront the people of Canada and their governments for the next several decades. The nature of the mandate also identified, in advance, the subject matter for much of the research and suggested the scope of enquiry and the need for vigorous efforts to interrelate and integrate the research disciplines. The resulting research program, therefore, is particularly noteworthy in three respects: along with original research studies, it includes survey papers which synthesize work already done in specialized fields; it avoids duplication of work which, in the judgment of the Canadian research community, has already been well done; and, considered as a whole, it is the most thorough examination of the Canadian economic, political and legal systems ever undertaken by an independent agency.

The Commission's research program was carried out under the joint direction of three prominent and highly respected Canadian scholars: Dr. Ivan Bernier (*Law and Constitutional Issues*), Dr. Alan Cairns (*Politics and Institutions of Government*) and Dr. David C. Smith (*Economics*).

Dr. Ivan Bernier is Dean of the Faculty of Law at Laval University. Dr. Alan Cairns is former Head of the Department of Political Science at the University of British Columbia and, prior to joining the Commission, was William Lyon Mackenzie King Visiting Professor of Canadian Studies at Harvard University. Dr. David C. Smith, former Head of the Department of Economics at Queen's University in Kingston, is now Principal of that University. When Dr. Smith assumed his new responsibilities at Queen's in September 1984, he was succeeded by Dr. Kenneth Norrie of the University of Alberta and John Sargent of the federal Department of Finance, who together acted as Co-directors of Research for the concluding phase of the Economics research program.

I am confident that the efforts of the Research Directors, research coordinators and authors whose work appears in this and other volumes, have provided the community of Canadian scholars and policy makers with a series of publications that will continue to be of value for many years to come. And I hope that the value of the research program to Canadian scholarship will be enhanced by the fact that Commission research is being made available to interested readers in both English and French.

I extend my personal thanks, and that of my fellow Commissioners, to the Research Directors and those immediately associated with them in the Commission's research program. I also want to thank the members of the many research advisory groups whose counsel contributed so substantially to this undertaking.

DONALD S. MACDONALD

INTRODUCTION

At its most general level, the Royal Commission's research program has examined how the Canadian political economy can better adapt to change. As a basis of enquiry, this question reflects our belief that the future will always take us partly by surprise. Our political, legal and economic institutions should therefore be flexible enough to accommodate surprises and yet solid enough to ensure that they help us meet our future goals. This theme of an adaptive political economy led us to explore the interdependencies between political, legal and economic systems and drew our research efforts in an interdisciplinary direction.

The sheer magnitude of the research output (more than 280 separate studies in 70 + volumes) as well as its disciplinary and ideological diversity have, however, made complete integration impossible and, we have concluded, undesirable. The research output as a whole brings varying perspectives and methodologies to the study of common problems and we therefore urge readers to look beyond their particular field of interest and to explore topics across disciplines.

The three research areas, — *Law and Constitutional Issues*, under Ivan Bernier; *Politics and Institutions of Government*, under Alan Cairns; and *Economics*, under David C. Smith (co-directed with Kenneth Norrie and John Sargent for the concluding phase of the research program) — were further divided into 19 sections headed by research coordinators.

The area *Law and Constitutional Issues* has been organized into five major sections headed by the research coordinators identified below.

- Law, Society and the Economy — *Ivan Bernier and Andrée Lajoie*
- The International Legal Environment — *John J. Quinn*
- The Canadian Economic Union — *Mark Krasnick*

- Harmonization of Laws in Canada — *Ronald C.C. Cuming*
- Institutional and Constitutional Arrangements — *Clare F. Beckton and A. Wayne MacKay*

Since law in its numerous manifestations is the most fundamental means of implementing state policy, it was necessary to investigate how and when law could be mobilized most effectively to address the problems raised by the Commission's mandate. Adopting a broad perspective, researchers examined Canada's legal system from the standpoint of how law evolves as a result of social, economic and political changes and how, in turn, law brings about changes in our social, economic and political conduct.

Within *Politics and Institutions of Government*, research has been organized into seven major sections.

- Canada and the International Political Economy — *Denis Stairs and Gilbert Winham*
- State and Society in the Modern Era — *Keith Banting*
- Constitutionalism, Citizenship and Society — *Alan Cairns and Cynthia Williams*
- The Politics of Canadian Federalism — *Richard Simeon*
- Representative Institutions — *Peter Aucoin*
- The Politics of Economic Policy — *G. Bruce Doern*
- Industrial Policy — *André Blais*

This area examines a number of developments which have led Canadians to question their ability to govern themselves wisely and effectively. Many of these developments are not unique to Canada and a number of comparative studies canvass and assess how others have coped with similar problems. Within the context of the Canadian heritage of parliamentary government, federalism, a mixed economy, and a bilingual and multicultural society, the research also explores ways of rearranging the relationships of power and influence among institutions to restore and enhance the fundamental democratic principles of representativeness, responsiveness and accountability.

Economics research was organized into seven major sections.

- Macroeconomics — *John Sargent*
- Federalism and the Economic Union — *Kenneth Norrie*
- Industrial Structure — *Donald G. McFetridge*
- International Trade — *John Whalley*
- Income Distribution and Economic Security — *François Vaillancourt*
- Labour Markets and Labour Relations — *Craig Riddell*
- Economic Ideas and Social Issues — *David Laidler*

Economics research examines the allocation of Canada's human and other resources, the ways in which institutions and policies affect this allocation, and the distribution of the gains from their use. It also considers the nature of economic development, the forces that shape our regional and industrial structure, and our economic interdependence with other countries. The thrust of the research in economics is to increase our comprehension of what determines our economic potential and how instruments of economic policy may move us closer to our future goals.

One section from each of the three research areas — The Canadian Economic Union, The Politics of Canadian Federalism, and Federalism and the Economic Union — have been blended into one unified research effort. Consequently, the volumes on Federalism and the Economic Union as well as the volume on The North are the results of an interdisciplinary research effort.

We owe a special debt to the research coordinators. Not only did they organize, assemble and analyze the many research studies and combine their major findings in overviews, but they also made substantial contributions to the Final Report. We wish to thank them for their performance, often under heavy pressure.

Unfortunately, space does not permit us to thank all members of the Commission staff individually. However, we are particularly grateful to the Chairman, The Hon. Donald S. Macdonald; the Commission's Executive Director, J. Gerald Godsoe; and the Director of Policy, Alan Nymark, all of whom were closely involved with the Research Program and played key roles in the contribution of Research to the Final Report. We wish to express our appreciation to the Commission's Administrative Advisor, Harry Stewart, for his guidance and advice, and to the Director of Publishing, Ed Matheson, who managed the research publication process. A special thanks to Jamie Benidickson, Policy Coordinator and Special Assistant to the Chairman, who played a valuable liaison role between Research and the Chairman and Commissioners. We are also grateful to our office administrator, Donna Stebbing, and to our secretarial staff, Monique Carpentier, Barbara Cowtan, Tina DeLuca, Françoise Guilbault and Marilyn Sheldon.

Finally, a well deserved thank you to our closest assistants: Jacques J.M. Shore, *Law and Constitutional Issues*; Cynthia Williams and her successor Karen Jackson, *Politics and Institutions of Government*; and I. Lilla Connidis, *Economics*. We appreciate not only their individual contribution to each research area, but also their cooperative contribution to the research program and the Commission.

IVAN BERNIER
ALAN CAIRNS
DAVID C. SMITH

The thirteen essays contained in this volume and its companion are the product of the Commission's research program in "Economic Ideas and Social Issues." Taken together, these two volumes make up what I hope will be judged a balanced account of the current state of economists' thinking about certain aspects of the theory of economic policy. Their coverage is not, of course, comprehensive. Some topics which would certainly have merited one or more essays, had these two volumes been conceived of in isolation, were of such importance to the Commission's work that whole volumes, or even sets of volumes, are devoted to them elsewhere in its research output. Thus, though matters of macro-economic policy, trade policy, industrial policy, the labour market, income security, the conduct of policy in a federal state, and so on, are all touched on here, and some of them quite heavily, their treatment does not purport to be complete.

These two volumes concentrate on such matters as the meaning of economic well-being and the way in which social and political organiza-tion impinges upon a society's ability to achieve and sustain it. In particular they discuss the consequences of the private pursuit of indi-vidual well-being for society as a whole, and consider the extent to which collective action, organized through government, is a desirable supplement to, or indeed substitute for, such private activity. Thus, the problems addressed here overlap not just with issues studied elsewhere in the Economics research program, but also in the Law and Institutions programs. The perspective of our studies is nevertheless that of the economist. Good interdisciplinary research occurs, not when an econo-mist plays amateur lawyer and political scientist, but when specialists from various disciplines study a common set of problems, each one bringing to that study the special insights of their own areas. None of the contributors to these volumes, therefore, claims a monopoly of expertise on the issues studied, but each could claim, quite rightly, that economic analysis provides a powerful tool with which to study them. Economics does not have all the answers, but it does have some of the questions.

At the risk of considerable oversimplification, it is possible to distinguish two distinct strands in economists' thinking about the theory of policy, one associated with so-called "welfare economics," and the other with "public choice theory." The former concentrates on questions about the nature of economic well-being, and what individuals and their governments ought to do to achieve it. The latter, building upon the economist's insight, limited no doubt, but valuable for all that, that individuals tend to look after themselves first and the rest of society later, asks questions about the way in which legal and political institutions affect individuals' behaviour, and about how those institutions can be designed to minimize the degree of conflict between public and private goals. Moreover, "welfare economics" traditionally assumed a rather stable economic environment in developing its theorems. Economists working in the "public choice" tradition are more inclined to take a changing and uncertain environment as the norm.

These two broad themes are by now so intertwined in the literature on the theory of economic policy that it has become impossible to invoke one of them without also referring to the other. Nevertheless, our two volumes may be distinguished in a rough and ready way by the relative emphasis which they give to these two strands of thought. The first of them, which begins with an overview essay designed to place the individual contribution to both volumes in a common perspective, thereafter concentrates on the nature of well-being and the role of government in providing for it through the welfare state, the tax system, and in measures designed to deal with failures of the market mechanism properly to utilize society's scarce resources. The second, beginning as it does with a study of the history of certain types of market failure, and political attempts to deal with them, concentrates more heavily upon the way in which legal and political constraints influence the attempts of individuals, both as private economic agents, but also as political beings, to deal with their own and their society's constantly evolving economic problems.

The differences here are matters of emphasis, however. When all is said and done, the fact that the results of our research on "Economic Ideas and Social Issues" have been divided into two volumes of roughly equal length has more to do with the physical problems of printing and bookbinding than with any sharp intellectual division in their subject matter. Though each essay may be read as an entity in its own right, and though I hope that readers will find each of these two volumes worthwhile in and of itself, it is nevertheless the case that, when this research program was planned, it was hoped that its results would be sufficiently well integrated to stand as a single collection. How well we have succeeded in achieving that goal must be left to the reader to judge.

DAVID LAIDLER

ACKNOWLEDGMENTS

To edit the collection of essays contained in this volume and its companion was an intellectually rewarding and challenging task, but I could not have carried it out alone. At every stage in the endeavour invaluable help was available from a research advisory group whose members included: Thomas J. Courchene, University of Western Ontario; H. Scott Gordon, Queen's University and Indiana University; C. Knick Harley, University of Western Ontario; William Schworm, University of British Columbia; Dan Usher, Queen's University; Michael Walker, Fraser Institute; and Lars Osberg, Dalhousie University.

D.L.

Resources and Economic Development in Historical Perspective

C. Knick Harley

Introduction

Fixed resources have long been seen as a potential limit on economic growth. Despite the rapid economic growth of the West during the last two hundred years, concern about this limit attracts attention at regular intervals, usually at times when economic performance falls short of expectations. Many projections in the early 1980s contain predictions of severe global problems of shortages and pollution in the near future.[1] It is certainly inappropriate for an economist to ignore scarcity, and only a fool would ignore the finiteness of the physical world. Nonetheless it is appropriate to look at current neo-Malthusian predictions within a broader context that includes both the history of ideas and the predictive power that these ideas have exhibited in the past.

The historical record indicates that resource availability, or lack of it, has generally not limited growth in market economies. These economies have generated technological change at a sufficiently rapid rate to create, in effect, new resources. The mechanism of the market has successfully allocated scarce resources so that changing supply and demand has been accommodated. When direct regulation has been attempted, the effect has often been the introduction of problems similar to those the regulations were aimed at preventing.

Malthus' name has become associated with concerns about increasing scarcity. He himself seems to have stood at a watershed in history. His ideas had striking relevance to the period in which he wrote and to most of previous human history. Thereafter, although concern that growth was threatened by impending exhaustion of various natural resources remaining, both population and standards of living have expanded apace. This is particularly true in Western Europe and its overseas offshoots, but it seems also to hold in a less dramatic form even for the less developed economies.

In a short study, examination of Malthusian ideas must be selective. Malthus' appreciation of the effect of increasing population on average output and wages and Ricardo's contemporaneous development of the theory of rent provided the analytical foundations of modern economics. The classical economists expected resource limitations to constrain economic growth, probably within their own lifetimes. Until late in the 19th century only Marx, of the leading economic thinkers, viewed the productive capacity of the economy as potentially unlimited and appreciated the enormous increase in population and per capita income of his own time. The ideas of diminishing returns and marginal productivity continue to dominate economic thinking in our own time. They have been very powerful tools in gaining understanding of major aspects of the behaviour of market economies. It is interesting, however, to notice that this line of thinking has not been exceptionally helpful in understanding the simultaneous rapid growth of both population and output that has been the most striking feature of the last 150 years in the West.

The influence of Malthus on economic thought has not been confined to the theory of prices but also loomed large in John Maynard Keynes' thinking as he developed modern macroeconomics. Keynes became convinced, at least as early as the years immediately following World War I, that the 19th century growth of both population and per capita income had been a temporary effect of the expansion of the world economy into previously sparsely settled continental areas. He shared the classical economists' expectation of an imminently approaching steady-state economy. The low and falling rate of return on investment that this implied would be a powerful depressant on investment and hence a primary cause of what he saw as a persistent shortfall of aggregate demand. This belief in turn underlay his perception of the high levels of unemployment, particularly in Britain, during the inter-war years, and was the keystone of his analysis in *The General Theory* and the subsequent development of macroeconomics.

From the North American perspective resource constraint was long viewed by contemporaries and subsequently by historians from the opposite perspective to that of the Malthusians. Here the abundance of resources represented by the "frontier" was seen as the source of prosperity for the United States until the end of the 19th century. In Canada, this view has become enshrined in the "staple thesis" of Canadian development. Early growth is seen as having been generated by the resources of fish and fur; British policies created markets for Canadian timber and wheat and thus supported growth. The absence of the active frontier from the 1870s to the 1890s is seen as a cause of economic stagnation. With the twentieth century, the return of the resource frontier, the "wheat boom," is generally seen as a rescue from that stagnation, and expanded resources as the source of prosperity. Careful examination of the historical record, however, reveals that most growth was unaffected by the frontier and that the frontier was not, in a static sense, a pool of resources waiting to be tapped. Rather, the development of resources depended on the very technological change that everywhere confounded Malthusian prediction. It was transportation improvements that provided falling food prices for most consumers and, at the same time, gave value to the resources of the frontier and allowed these resources to support further growth.

The passing of the frontier set in motion an influential school of thought, particularly in the United States, that was essentially Malthusian. This was the Conservation Movement that formed part of the Progressive Movement at the beginning of this century. Its premise was that resources had been wasted in the days of the frontier and, even more inappropriately, were still being wasted. Wise management incorporating active government involvement was necessary to preserve a heritage for future generations. This body of thought generated considerable accomplishments, chief among them the great wilderness parks of the continent and an ecological concept of resources. Nonetheless, their prognosis for resource exhaustion was not confirmed by subsequent history.

Recent discussion of increasing resource scarcity has evolved from the environmental concerns of the early 20th century. For an economist this literature is best viewed from two perspectives. The first, the Malthusian issue, is that of limits to expansion because of decreasing returns when some resources are strictly limited in quantity. The second is often termed the problem of the commons. Most simply put, this is the observation that a scarce resource will be overused if access to it is free or, more generally, priced below its scarcity value. The most obvious current example is the issue of pollution where individuals use clean air or water for waste disposal at little or no cost. The same issue enters into many current and historical issues of resource use and depletion: in land use and disposition, the rate of exploitation of forests, the use of water in the American West, and the pricing of oil and gas. In such situations the issue of the limited stock of a resource must be distinguished from that overuse because its nature (e.g., air) or because policy, (e.g., water in the American West) precludes pricing the resource at its scarcity value.

Long-Term Relationships between Population and the Standard of Living

Assessment of Malthusian ideas in understanding the human experience begins appropriately with the historical record. Such an exercise is, of course, a highly fallible guide to the future. Conditions change and

FIGURE 1-1 Real Wages and Population in England, 1300–1980

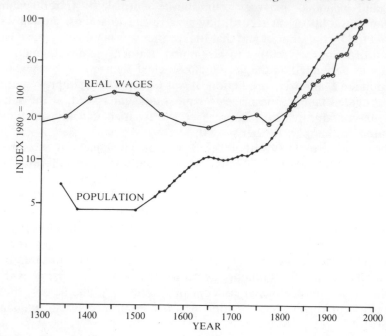

historians are understandably reluctant to claim that their craft provides predictions. Nonetheless, studying what has occurred helps to delineate questions to ask and to discipline extreme speculation.

The relationships among the size of the human population, the environment and standard of living over several centuries seem to provide an appropriate beginning for a study of man and his environment. The ecological processes that are involved presumably work themselves out in a time dimension best measured in generations.

We have data from the Middle Ages on population and the standard of living for Britain. From the records of the colleges of Oxford, data have been compiled on the wages received by building craftsmen and labourers, and on the prices of principal consumer goods since the beginning of the 14th century.[2] Population estimates must be relied on for periods prior to systematic censuses. Two Cambridge scholars have provided reliable demographic data for England, compiled from parish church records, back to the mid-16th century.[3] Prior to that, the data on population are much more speculative but there is broad agreement regarding general trends. The wage and population information is presented in Figure 1-1.

The graph shows two time periods when relationships between the standard of living and population differed. Curiously enough, the change from the earlier relationship to the later appears to have occurred during

Malthus' lifetime (1766–1834). Before the late 18th century, the relationship may be called Malthusian.[4] The demographic catastrophe of the middle of the 14th century — the Black Death, broadly considered — reduced the population of England by approximately a third. This decline was accompanied by an equally dramatic increase in the real wages of Oxford builders. Between the middle of the 14th and the mid-15th century their real wages rose by 50 percent, attaining a level unequalled again until the middle of the 19th century. Population remained at about the post-crisis level until the early 16th century, when it began to rise again at, for that period, a rapid rate of about half a percent annually until the middle of the 17th century. Rising population was accompanied by a steady decline in real wages to approximately the level that had prevailed in the years before the Black Death. In the following century population growth practically ceased and real wages again began to grow slowly. Finally, at the end of the 18th century, population growth again accelerated and real wages appear to have fallen.[5]

Since the early 19th century the relationship between population and real wages shows no trace of the earlier Malthusian decline in wages produced by population pressure on resources. Population grew throughout the 19th century at an unprecedented annual rate that exceeded 1.25 percent as the death rate fell and the birth rate rose. At the same time, real wages began the sharp upward trend that has been maintained until the present.

Other countries of northwestern Europe, together with North America and Australasia, have shared this British experience, i.e., Malthusian population pressure acted as the principal determinant of real wages until the 19th century ushered in unprecedented increases in both real wages and population growth. In fact, within this group the British growth of real wages appears moderate; a graph of any other country's real wage growth would show a steeper climb than that in Figure 1-1. Thus, the basic evidence regarding the relationship between human population and the environment provides no indication of an impending crisis.

Food production then has not in fact emerged as the constraint on economic growth that Malthus and the classical economists of the early 19th century had expected. Agricultural production has declined continuously in importance relative to total economic activity in all the advanced economies even while per capita food consumption has increased. In this process land rent, which in the classical growth model was to grow in importance as scarcity became more severe, has declined to insignificance. Again the long-term data from the British economy illustrate what has happened most dramatically. In the late 17th century some two-thirds of all economic activity was agricultural production and approximately a quarter of all income accrued to land rents. By the early

19th century agriculture had decreased to less than half of income and land rents to about 15 percent of income. This trend continued into the 20th century and by the inter-war period agriculture was less than five percent of income and agricultural rents were insignificant at less than one half of one percent of income.[6] In all the advanced economies agricultural rent is entirely overshadowed by urban site rent. For example, Kuznets in his pioneering estimates of U.S. national income produced in the 1940s decided that agricultural rent was too insignificant to warrant independent estimation.[7]

The combined growth of population and real wages has been most pronounced in the developed economies but has also extended to less developed economies. To be sure the process started later and the growth of real wages has been slower in the less developed economies with the result that the income gap between the world's rich and poor countries has widened over the last 150 years. Nonetheless, the relationship between population and income indicates that diminishing returns in resources are not the determinant of trend in per capita income.

The data for the underdeveloped economies are much weaker than for the developed economies both for income and population. Of the underdeveloped economies, India is both one of the most important and among the best studied. A brief outline of its long-run trends is indicative of the experience of the less developed economies. Figure 1-2 illustrates estimates of the Indian population for approximately two centuries and per capita national income for a century. These data are imperfect but they indicate that, during the half century before World War I, population increased by about a fifth while per capita income increased by a third. From World War I until independence, per capita income appears to have stagnated, remaining generally unchanged. This cannot really be interpreted as a truly Malthusian episode, however, since it was accompanied by a tripling of the rate of population growth. By the end of these 30 years the environment was supporting a population 50 percent larger at the same average level. Since independence, population growth has again doubled (to an annual rate of about 2.3 percent) but per capita income has increased by some 50 percent.[8]

Certainly the arithmetical results of projecting this recent population and income growth are shocking. At the end of a century, population would have increased to ten times its current level and the level of output would have increased some 18 times. While such figures immediately bring to mind Malthus' contrast between exponential growth of population and the limited possible expansion of resources, there is nothing in recent history to show that positive checks are coming into play. It may in fact be more fruitful at this point to look at the evidence of demographic history than to speculate on the effects of blind extrapolation of trends.

FIGURE 1–2 Per Capita Income and Population in India 1750–1980

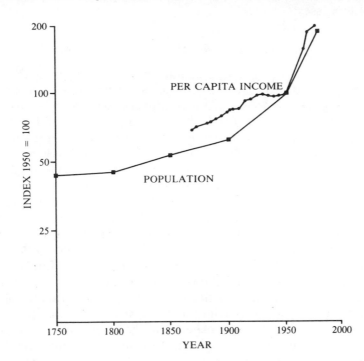

There is ample evidence from the demographic history of north-western Europe that population size has, since at least late medieval times, been heavily influenced by active control of age of marriage and family size, what Malthus called "moral restraint," and not by the biological possibility of exponential growth restrained by the "vice and misery" of poverty and an associated high death rate. The clearest indication of this appears in the evidence on marriage. The typical European remained unmarried well into the child-bearing years; women (whose age is of importance in fertility) married in their mid-twenties. Such a relative delay of marriage would decrease the number of births per woman by two or three over an unrestrained fertility situation. There is also some evidence in the form of the spacing of births, particularly of last children, indicating that fertility was limited within marriage. This long historical experience, and the dramatic reduction in birth rates and population growth over the last century, provide clear evidence that in some societies population is regulated by decisions, embodied in both social custom and individual choice, rather than by a mechanistic process such as Malthus supposed. To what degree the European experience can be extended to other societies is an important but open question. Certainly many societies have not exhibited fertility limitations of the European type. Nonetheless, population dynamics certainly involves an interaction among social and individual decisions and biological processes.[9]

Resource Abundance and North American Growth

By the last quarter of the 19th century it became apparent that the economy was supporting both a growing population and a rising standard of living. The obvious reaction of British observers was to point to increasing supplies of overseas food, most particularly from the United States, as the cause of postponement of the application of the Malthusian logic. The settlement of the American West and the Russian steppes could be seen as a dramatic increase in the land available to the European economy, delaying the inevitable onset of diminishing returns. At the same time American historiography became dominated by the idea that the American experience was powerfully conditioned by the existence of a frontier of free land. The emergence and popularization of this view may be attributed to the work of the historian Frederick Jackson Turner in the last decade of the nineteenth century.[10] While Turner's own work and that of most of his followers concentrated on the role of free land in shaping the political institutions and the social attitudes of the United States, explicit in the Turner thesis was a belief that the "free land" of the frontier offered prosperity to the ambitious and the hard working even if they lacked capital. This abundance that freed the average American from the tyranny of capital also ensured high wages and general prosperity to the country. This view of growing prosperity as a product of the gradual incorporation of abundance into the national economy has subsequently found wide acceptance as an interpretation of the prosperity and growth of the United States. Underlying this interpretation is, of course, the Malthusian model of economic change where prosperity is determined by the ratio of resources to population; but here is a historical anomaly in which resources were not fixed but were growing more rapidly than population as the continent was opened up.

This idea that abundant resources were the key to the growth in North America appears widely in historical interpretation, but nowhere more explicitly than in the "staple thesis" interpretation of growth which is usually attributed to Harold Innis and W.A. Mackintosh.[11] This view has dominated interpretations of Canadian economic history for at least a half century and has found important expression in the interpretation of the economic history of the United States and other areas of recent settlement. Growth and prosperity are linked to the discovery or development of a staple commodity that is in wide demand in older settled regions — Europe in this context. The sale of the staple itself generates income and it also generates "linkages" that lead to the growth of a more diversified economy. These linkages are of three types. "Backward linkages" create a direct demand for activities that are necessary for the economic production of the staple. An example is the building of railroads for the export of Prairie wheat. "Forward linkages" arise from the fact that in the region exporting the staple, the staple product will be inexpensive. This presence of inexpensive raw materials will attract industries that use the raw material. "Final demand linkages" arise from the demand for consumer goods that is created by income from staple production and its linkages. In successful staple-led growth the linkages are seen to be powerful enough to create a diversified economy that can grow independently of the staple. Staple-based growth may, however, create problems if it fails to generate an adequate demand for domestic diversification but rather encourages dependence on institutions directed to export production.

Canadian economic history has been written around this view.[12] The success or failure of various periods has been judged on the strength of the growth of staple exports and on the character of the linkages that could be attributed to various staples. Thus Canadian economic history has been a chronology of staples or their absence. The texture of the narrative is enriched by consideration of a staple's nature and its linkages and by analysis of progress toward an independent economy. The earliest period is seen in terms of the cod fisheries and the fur trade. Both led to some settlement and local economic activity but neither was a successful engine of independent growth. The period following the American Revolution is seen first from the perspective of the Maritimes as an attempt to create, with the assistance of imperial navigation laws, a shipping industry and a staple trade in foodstuffs with the sugar colonies of the West Indies. This trade would emulate the basis of New England's prosperity, with linkages to the sugar staple of the islands. Simultaneously the British instituted differentially higher duties on Baltic timber than on colonial wood and created an important timber industry in the Maritimes and Quebec. These staples generated acceptable growth and prosperity in the region but the decline of the industries after Confederation has raised questions of their adequacy as a basis of economic independence. The settlement, growth and prosperity of Upper Canada appear to be driven by a successful wheat staple export trade to Britain under the special provisions of the Corn Laws. Wheat is regarded as a particularly desirable staple because it is seen as possessing extensive linkages and as creating the kind of enterprising society that was associated with Turner's American frontier.

In Canada, the staple thesis predicts relative failure as well as success. In the years just preceding the mid-19th century, the British moved toward free trade and removed the special treatment that had supported Canadian wheat and timber in British markets. Initially, the story goes, the shock was cushioned by the Reciprocity Treaty with the United States (1854) that created an alternative market by allowing Canadian raw materials free access to American markets. American unwillingness to extend the treaty in 1864, combined with the rapid disappearance of the frontier of free land in Upper Canada inaugurated a long period of relative stagnation due to the lack of the dynamics of an active staple. The settlement of the Prairies that accompanied the recovery of wheat prices after 1896 created Canada's greatest period of prosperity. The "wheat boom" generated linkages to industrialization in central Canada, thanks to the wisely conceived National Policy, and created an independent and largely self-sustaining national economy. Laurier confidently predicted that the 20th century would be Canada's century.

The staple thesis has not dominated the economic historiography of the United States as it has in Canada, but it does colour the general view of the country's development.[13] Southern export staples (mainly tobacco at this time, cotton later) and the success of the Middle and New England colonies at capturing the linkages to food and transportation from these colonies as well as from the West Indies, are dominant themes in colonial history. Pre-Civil War economic history revolves around the great cotton staple of the South. The North captured linkages to transportation and manufacturing and the West, linkages to food demand. After the Civil War a staple-oriented explanation shifts to the expansion of the grain-producing regions of the West in response to opportunities for sale in European markets. Again the East industrialized and urbanized in response to the linkage of the staple. The wheat staple generated the initial demand for the growth of an independent industrial economy, but that process occurred at least a generation earlier than it did in Canada.

This view of North American history, in which abundant resources caused per capita growth over a long period, seems deficient on both analytical and factual grounds despite its popularity. A production function containing resources and labour, and exhibiting diminishing returns to labour as the ratio of labour to resources increases, will generate higher output per worker if resources increase more rapidly than labour. However, in saying this we must be careful to define what is meant by the supply of resources and recall the sophisticated view of resources David Ricardo developed in his analysis of rent. Experience of British agriculture's response to the high prices of agricultural products during the Napoleonic War led Ricardo to realize that any analysis of resources and rent must accommodate the fact that the use of potential resources depended on the price of the resulting products. Thus, during the war wasteland was brought under the plough for the production of food. The increase in the amount of land in use was not an increase in resources but rather a manifestation of diminishing returns of the production function when resources of differing qualities were available. In many equilibrium situations some resources will be unused because their productivity is too low. They are in fact worthless. In the Malthusian situation of increasing population and stable technology, when the ratio of labour to resources rises, the productivity of resources (defined either as those currently in use or the total potential stock including that currently unused) is increased. Already used resources are used more intensively and some of the most productive of the previously worthless stock is brought into production. This increase in resources of current economic value will not, of course, increase per-capita income or real wages; the fall in real income and wages has been the cause of the increase of resources. An increase in resources that increases wages must be of a different character. This must be the discovery of new resources that would have value at the pre-existing labour-to-resources ratio.

Some North American resources were probably net additions to the currently valuable stock of resources, but most were not. The fishery resources of the Grand Banks in the 16th century, discovery of the sugar potential of the West Indies and possibly the tobacco potential of the Chesapeake region in the 18th century were valuable immediately. The rest of the resources of North America almost certainly were not. This seems particularly true of the resources in the West that accompanied the growth of the United States, the Canadian wheat boom, and the timber and land resources of eastern and central Canada in the early 19th century that depended on imperial preference for their value. The existence of these resources undoubtedly increased the elasticity of supply of resources to the European economy by augmenting the resources beyond the Ricardian extensive frontier. They were, however, beyond the frontier and consequently could not have caused increases in income.

The previous statement warrants support with some more historical detail. The Puritans who settled New England in the 17th century accepted material privation as a cost of spiritual freedom. Unlike the settlers of the tobacco colonies, they moved into extra marginal land for nonpecuniary reasons. The situation of the Middle colonies of New York and Pennsylvania was somewhat more ambiguous. The agricultural resources were superior to those of New England, and the settlers of these regions also benefitted from the food and timber demands generated by the sugar colonies of the West Indies. Nonetheless, the settlers' standard of living and their slow penetration of the interior suggest that they were soon at the extensive margin and that their land was not a major increase in the currently valuable stock of land for the broader Atlantic economy. Incomes in the colonies were not sufficiently high to attract large immigration, and settlement penetrated the interior slowly because the land in the interior was unattractive under the technology and population levels that prevailed. It was that unattractiveness that made land free.

Much the same analysis can be applied to the unsettled West at nearly every period of the 19th century.[14] For example, James Monroe returned from a trip into the Ohio Valley in 1784 and reported that the land was "miserably poor." Perhaps that was a misjudgment of the future corn belt but perhaps also it was an accurate assessment, given the technology and the level of product prices prevailing in the earliest years of the Republic. The purchase of Louisiana in 1803 for merely $11 million was not an enormous bargain by crafty Americans over a rather slow-witted French emperor. The vast and ill-defined interior of the continent included in the purchase which later became of immense value was deemed of little value to either party. Louisiana, particularly the mouth of the Mississippi, was of strategic rather than economic value. To Napoleon, Louisiana had been of value as part of a Caribbean strategy that had failed; to the Americans, New Orleans ensured that the Ohio valley maintained access to the sea and protected the country's southwestern flank.

The expansion of agriculture west of the Mississippi was a succession of movements of the extensive margin. The free land was worthless. Empirical evidence indicates that the price of wheat at the farm gate was the primary determinant of settlement. Since a world market for wheat had developed by the 1850s, the local price of wheat reflected the British price — the major importer which paid the highest price — less transportation costs. These transportation costs, until at least the last third of the century, were high. In the 1850s American spring wheat that sold at $1.70 in Liverpool was worth $1.57 in New York and only $0.85 in Chicago. The Chicago price was not far above the costs of production under western conditions (probably about $0.75 or $0.80 per bushel) and transportation cost by rail was some $0.20 per hundred miles and three or four times as high by wagon. Not surprisingly the frontier had advanced little beyond Chicago. The settlement of the West proceeded as a combination of rising world population and falling transportation costs led to higher prices in the West. Thus, immediately prior to World War I, although the price of American wheat in Liverpool had fallen to $1.07 a bushel and to $1.05 in New York, it had actually increased to $0.98 in Chicago and by even more in the wheat-producing regions farther west. (In the early 1880s, for example, when the Chicago price had been $1.07, the price at the CPR track in Regina was $0.62; in the prewar years the Regina price was $0.77).[15]

The settlement of the West was not the gradual discovery of valuable resources that supported growing population and prosperity in the Atlantic economy. Rather it was the process of utilizing resources, physically productive but previously worthless because of their location, as technological change made them valuable. The development of horse-powered mechanical agriculture which became important in the West in the late 19th century was part of that change, but by far the most important was transportation by rail and sea that dramatically decreased the cost of distance and made it economically sensible to farm the interiors of vast continents. None of the technological change seems to have rested heavily on the vastness of the potential resources of the West. To be sure the specific form of farm machinery suited the specific conditions of its use. But the technology emerged from improvements in mechanical engineering that were being widely adopted throughout the economy. Transportation improvement depended on the general advance of technology, although its greatest impact was on the distant areas producing bulk commodities where transportation costs were highest relative to prices paid by final consumers. Both ships and railways improved as metallurgical science led to cheap steel and mechanical engineering permitted the construction of more efficient steam engines, neither of which depended on the expanding frontier.[16] All of this is not to deny that expansion into the West was an important factor in the economic history of the 19th century. The course of history was undoubtedly heavily influenced by the fact that technological improvements of the period made these agricultural resources valuable and induced a vast movement of population and capital. This expansion was not, however, an independent cause of growth in the North American economy but the consequence of technological change.

The Canadian situations are even clearer. The timber industry of Eastern British North America in the early 19th century depended completely on preference in the British market. The differential duty on Baltic timber in the British market approximately equalled the value of colonial timber at its point of shipment; removal of protection would have deprived timber of almost its entire value in the colonies.[17] A generation later the wheat staple of Upper Canada depended on similar but smaller protection from competition under the Corn Laws. In both these cases the value of the North American resource was created by British policy that clearly lowered the real income of British consumers. The Canadian Prairies lay, at mid-century, an unimaginable distance beyond vast wildernesses. A generation later a highly subsidized railroad, major technological change in transportation, and a vastly increased world demand for grain were insufficient to induce settlement of any but the easternmost fringe of the great grain area of the 20th century.

A more sophisticated version of the staple theory of North American growth acknowledges the predominance of technological change as the prime source of growth but sees this technological change affecting North American development through staples, which still drive the economy through their linkages. This view too has not held up well to rigorous examination. Scholarship on the ante-bellum economy of the United States, for example, has demonstrated that the South had no important linkages to the West. The plantation economy was self-sufficient in food. Furthermore, detailed study of urban development in the East shows that long distance linkages had very moderate effects. In much of the traditional view, one of the key linkages from the West to Eastern industrialization was through the railways and their demand for coal, iron and other industrial products. Here too, careful study has found the hypothesis wanting. The railroads' demands were of only minor importance to the various industries.[18]

Study of Canada's wheat boom leads to the same conclusion. Nearly twenty years ago Edward Chambers and Donald Gordon[19] considered the way in which the expansion of Prairie agriculture would have influenced Canadian per capita income and argued that the impact would be concentrated in the often implicit gain in rent on Prairie farms. They calculated this gain to be only 1.6 percent of national income. This results was so at odds with most accepted wisdom that it was subjected to extensive criticism. Various other possible influences on per capita income, such as induced increases in capital formation, rising real wages generally in the economy, and economies of scale were considered by other writers. Even at the most generous accounting these factors raised the contribution of the wheat boom to per capita income to under 10 percent over the first two decades of the century.[20] This surely is an overestimate since some of the estimated contributions have a weak empirical basis. Furthermore, these calculations fail to consider some obvious examples of productive capacity wasted during the wheat boom. The most obvious of these is the excessive railroad building stimulated by government subsidy, particularly in the two new transcontinental lines. Somewhat less obvious was the waste of resources created by the homestead method of granting Prairie land. In a growing economy Prairie land had value before it paid to cultivate it since ownership of the land conferred the ownership of its future income. However, the homestead process required that the land be farmed in order to be claimed. As a result labour and capital that would have created output of higher value elsewhere in the economy was drawn prematurely to the West.[21]

Certainly the wheat boom drew immigration to Canada; the railroad building stimulated the greatest investment boom in the country's history, and generally created buoyant economic conditions in the decade before World War I, but its impact on per capita income was very modest.[22] Real output per worker in Canada grew slowly during the first two decades of this century as the Prairie provinces were being settled. By contrast, output per worker grew rapidly in the supposedly depressed last decades of the 19th century (see Figure 1-3). Similarly the growth of industrialization in Canada does not seem closely tied to the linkages to the West.

It is hardly surprising that detailed investigation has generally led to the conclusion that the resource sectors did not dominate the growth experience in Canada. These sectors were just too small and the type of growth in incomes and industry that were occurring in Canada had their counterparts in other advanced economies with which Canada shared

FIGURE 1-3 Canadian Income per Worker 1869-1970

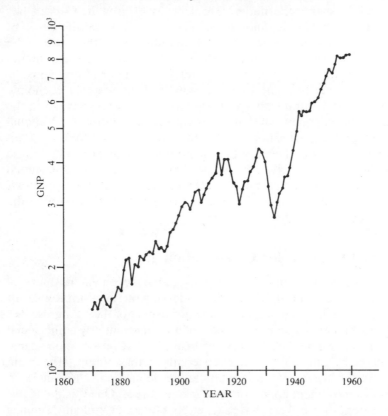

both cultural background and technological information. Those who see the development of Prairie agriculture in the early 20th century as an important factor in the long-term growth of per capita income, as opposed to having a short-run impact through the investment boom associated with railroad construction, need to explain how so small a sector using an already generally applicable technology could have such an impact. After all, in 1926 near the height of the relative importance of Prairie agriculture and the first year for which official national income estimates exist, Prairie farmers contributed less than 10 percent of national income.

There can be little doubt that the rising incomes of Canadians over the last century and a half have been generated by worldwide improvements in technology to which Canadians have contributed and from which they have reaped the benefits of higher incomes. It is, therefore, much more realistic to see the growth of incomes and the industrialization of central Canada, where the majority of Canadians have lived and worked, as a part of the same economic process that led to increasing incomes and industrialization in Britain, the United States and the other advanced economies. Within the wider world economy of which it is a part and with which it shares the underlying sources of growth, Canada has contained areas where technological change has induced the development of new and important resource-based industries. Other parts of the Canadian economy have been influenced by these developments because of geographical proximity and government restrictions. It seems appropriate to argue that the growth of income and economic development of Central Canada would have been little changed in the absence of the emergence of Prairie agriculture. To be sure, the National Policy probably deflected some of the industrial demand from the Prairies to central Canada. This would have produced higher costs on Prairie development limiting its extent somewhat, and increased the industrialization of the centre but its effects must have been modest. Remember that Prairie agriculture remained less than 10 percent of the country's economic activity.

Organized Concern for Conservation

Concern for conservation became a major social movement in American life in the late 19th century. Under the leadership of Theodore Roosevelt and Gifford Pinchot, it emerged as a major aspect of the "Progressive" reform movement. As an integral part of an important crusading social and political movement it is hardly surprising that "Conservation" came to mean many and, at times, even contradictory things. The main features of the arguments, however, can be delineated. The American Progressive movement grew from two main sources. One was the Populist movement of the West that reached its climax in William Jennings Bryan's 1896 "Cross of Gold" presidential campaign. The other was a revulsion, often led by members of old wealthy families, from the machine politics of the Eastern industrial cities. These two strands shared at least two ideas that were important in the Progressives' and the Conservationists' programs.[23]

The first was a distrust of the changes that industrialization and urbanization were bringing to American society and of the agents of that change. Both farmers and urban reformers saw capitalism, in the form of the market and large firms, destroying an older, morally superior and preferred way of life. For them, capitalist organizations were dominating markets and destroying the democratic, independent life of the farmer and the stable social arrangements of the Eastern cities. Capitalism and the market were mechanisms causing changes for the worse. It is hardly surprising that the market was seen not as an efficient mechanism of social organization but rather as an agency perverting social goals. Large capitalist firms were a social evil while small firms, particularly the independent yeoman farmer of the frontier, were seen as embodying social conscience and the ideals of America.

The second shared belief of the Progressives was that the collective will, when mobilized, could act effectively through government to achieve desired ends. Populists had actively agitated for regulation of the railroads, which they believed had been exploiting farmers. They called for silver coinage to alleviate the economic problems of the West. The Eastern urban reformers sought to capture urban political power and to replace patronage appointments with professional civil servants chosen on the basis of merit. Both believed in the efficacy of an interventionist government staffed by a professional civil service. Those who propose interventionist programs today usually share these beliefs.

The Conservation Movement also originated the practice of considering resources within an entire environmental system. Initially, this environmental approach manifested itself in an argument that large areas should be maintained in a natural state to support a full natural ecology. From this view emerged the National Park Systems of both the United States and Canada, which preserved some exceptional areas. The preservation of these areas has clearly been a wise choice; indeed their present use for recreation suggests that the areas may be too small. The current ecological approach has evolved from this beginning.

The Conservationists were also concerned with the limited nature of natural resources and stressed the need for their wise use and the elimination of waste. Here they had in mind the physical maximization of the usefulness of the resource rather than the economists' concept of maximization which involved the equation of marginal costs and benefits. Thus they advocated maximizing the yield from resources even if the costs were high in terms of non-resource inputs. Timber management received the most detailed consideration. As early as the 1870s there was concern with the rapid rate at which the virgin forests, which at the birth of the Republic had seemed limitless, were disappearing. Not only had the forest of the Ohio valley long been cleared and transformed to farmland, but also the vast pine woods of the Great Lakes and Eastern Canada were rapidly disappearing. The 1877 annual report of the Secretary of the Interior contained one of the first of many forecasts that the country's supply of timber would soon be gone because the rate of cutting of the virgin forests far exceeded the growth of standing timber. The Conservationists proposed government regulation or ownership to eliminate wasteful practices and urged the adoption of European practices of scientific silviculture.

The contemporary rapid exploitation of the timber resources of Northern Ontario caused a similar alarm and reaction in Canada. In 1893 Algonquin Park was created in response to the recommendation of the Royal Commission on Forest Reservation and National Parks. One of the Commissioners envisaged the park as an area where European methods of forest management could be introduced into Ontario. The overall aims of the park's creation were summarized in the master plan: "Maintenance of water supply in half a dozen major water systems, preservation of a primeval forest, protection of birds and animals, a field for experiments in forestry, a place of health resort, and beneficial effects on climate."[24]

The depletion of American timber has more recently been the subject of an intensive study by Sherry Olson.[25] The railways provided a useful focus for the study, since in the last quarter of the 19th century they consumed between a fifth and a quarter of American timber production. Moreover, they experimented in timber production and left extensive records of their actions. Obviously the cutting of timber resources has not required the drastic adjustment the Conservationists predicted, nor have the expensive European methods of silviculture they urged been adopted to maintain timber output. The railroads discovered from several late 19th century attempts at silviculture that it did not pay. Even today it remains too expensive to be attractive at prevailing and expected prices of timber. The implication is that increasing the stock of timber requires the use of resources whose value exceeds that of the timber produced, and thus perhaps "depletion" is appropriate. Certainly it would have been foolish to preserve the entire primeval forests of North America. The time to stop depletion will be when it pays to cultivate timber in plantations. If selfishly motivated individuals or firms can count on retaining property rights in the timber they plant, they will undertake the kind of conserving forestry that private European owners have long practiced.

In timber, the adjustment of supply and demand occurred in several ways. Technological change increased the effective supply by lowering transportation costs and making processing in remote locations economical. More importantly, the final users of timber reduced their use of timber at little cost. In part this involved the substitutions of other costs as timber prices rose. For example, in the early 20th century it became cost effective to extend the life of cross-ties and bridge members with preservatives. In part this practice was a response to higher wood prices, but the railroads' primary motive was to save the rising labour cost involved in frequent tie replacements. Various technological changes reduced wood requirements as well. In recent years, falling real price seems to have been as much a problem for the timber industry as impending depletion.

Environmental concerns continued in the inter-war period, particularly with reference to soil erosion in the Dust Bowl of the Great Plains during the 1930s drought. However, the Depression dominated social thought. Attempts to formulate policy to overcome the Depression drew heavily on Progressive ideas of the failure of the market, the failure to make wise use of resources, and the role of government as the source of solutions. Conservationist ideas led to such New Deal programs as the Civilian Conservation Corps (CCC) and to much of the farm policy of the 1930s. The period did not, however, produce much productive discussion of increasing resource scarcity.

Resource Use Projections over a Century of Experience

Projections of resource use relative to known availability is an uncertain but seemingly irresistible exercise. Predictions that the limited availability of resources will constrain growth are as old as modern economic growth itself. Malthus saw land as the constraint. By the middle of the 19th century land seemed less of a problem, primarily because of the opening up of the great land masses of North America and southern Russia to the European food market. The Industrial Revolution, however, seemed to rest firmly on steam power and in turn on coal. Between 1855 and 1865 the output from British coal mines increased by a half, and many became alarmed at this rapid exploitation of a non-renewable resource. Among these W.S. Jevons was the most prominent; he predicted that the demand for coal would limit the growth of income by the end of the century.[26] In fact, his projection was widely out of line and failed completely to anticipate the effects of technological change in decreasing the energy required for continued growth. To some extent late 19th century growth allayed concerns. In the early 20th century discussion amalgamated around the Conservation Movement's various proposals. The strategic needs of World War II and the rising prices of strategic resources during the Korean War stimulated official interest in conservation of resources. Under President Truman the Paley Commission was established to inquire "into all major aspects of the problem of assuring an adequate supply of production materials for our long-range needs." The commission found few grounds for immediate concern but did express the view that within about 20 years problems might arise in many areas. At about the same time, concern about Western water resources and about environmental pollution were attracting increasing attention. Certainly resource depletion has become a salient issue, and the energy crisis and poor economic performance of the 1970s greatly increased public awareness of its importance.

The optimal use of resources over time is clearly a desired social objective. It is possible to develop criteria for such an optimal path, but in light of the impossibility of knowing the future it is probably impossible to identify such a path empirically. The basic problem lies in the uncertainty of the future of technology. If technology continues to improve at the rate it has over the last several generations, optimal use of resources will involve more current use than if the growth of income attributable to technological change slows.

Even the optimality of past use depends on future prospects and thus seems impossible to determine. It is possible, however, to consider whether resources have been overused in the past. Overuse implies that a resource has become inappropriately scarce over time. This in turn implies that its price rose relative to the productive capacity of the average individual, that is to say, relative to the average wage, and that more effort would now be required to obtain the resource than formerly. Finally, it might imply that the commodity has become more expensive relative to other goods.

In 1962, Barnett and Morse published *Scarcity and Growth*, a classic assessment of the long-term trends in resource scarcity in the United States.[27] This book summarized the history of economic thought on resource scarcity and presented two sets of calculations that measured resource scarcity from the 1870s to the 1950s. The first, which they referred to as the strong form of the resource depletion hypothesis, related the quantity of output of various resource industries to the inputs of labour, and of labour plus capital. The results of the first are summarized in the following table:

TABLE 1-1 **Real Unit Cost, U.S. Resource Industries, 1870–1957**
(1929 = 100)

	1870–1900	1919	1957
Total Extractive Industries	134	122	60
Agriculture	132	114	61
Minerals	210	164	47
Forestry	59	106	90

The second measure, which the authors referred to as the weak scarcity hypothesis, related the price of resource products to the general price level. Neither suggested that resources are becoming increasingly scarce. More recently, Harold Barnett has extended these calculations into the 1970s and also examined information for other countries.[28] The results fully supported earlier findings. The test of the weaker hypothesis, that resources are increasing in price relative to other products, generally indicates that resource prices have not moved significantly relative to other goods. To the extent that trends can be identified they suggest a falling real price for resources. Neither of Barnett and Morse's empirical measures is immune to criticism but both suggest quite strongly the absence of increasing shortage. Barnett recently summed up the conclusions of the study as follows:

> For the United States in the period from the Civil War to 1957, the evidence denies the doctrine of increasing economic scarcity in agriculture, minerals, and the aggregate of extractive industries. The principal reasons for this were: (1) substitutions of economically more plentiful resources for less plentiful ones; (2) increased discoveries and availability of domestic mineral resources; (3) increased imports of selected metallic minerals; and (4) a marked increase in the acquisition of knowledge and sociotechnical improvements relevant to the economics of resource discovery, develop-

ment, conversion, transportation, and production. These factors have made it possible for the economy to produce larger and larger volumes of extractive goods at declining real marginal costs.

While these observations were among the major findings of *Scarcity and Growth*, we also discussed problems associated with use of natural resources and the attendant implications for intergenerational equity. We found that, in U.S. history, each generation has passed to the next improved conditions of natural resource availability and economic productivity. Moreover, the phenomena of accumulated knowledge, scientific advances, and self-generating technological change have more than overcome tendencies of increasing costs for utilization and exhaustion of specific resources. It is not by chance that advances in knowledge, market processes, and government policies provide solutions to actual and prospective natural resource cost problems. The motivations, mechanisms, and choice of solutions appear to be endogenous in modern efficiency-seeking economies.[29]

Property Rights and Resources

Many concerned with resource scarcity today share the Conservationists' view that laissez-faire capitalism manifests selfish greed. Under capitalism individuals are seen to be driven to look after their own short-run interests, disregarding the common good and the future. In fact much of the driving force of the Progressive Movement was an ethical revulsion from a society dominated by this kind of behaviour. This position did not analyze the operation of markets and formally consider the effectiveness of Adam Smith's "invisible hand." Rather the argument was based on what seemed to be obvious cases of waste, avarice, shady and illegal dealing, and general disregard for public good and future generations. Examination of some examples sheds light not only on the Conservationists' thinking but also on issues of importance in resource economics. In particular these examples highlight the role of property rights in efficient markets — an issue that the Conservationists clearly failed to understand.

One frequent misconception is that when individuals act on their selfish interests in markets, resources are inevitably overused, causing premature depletion and reducing long-run value. The example of a farmer with a limited life-span using farming methods that increase yield in the short run while depriving the soil of its long-run fertility is often used.[30] This view is not only surprising to trained economists; it would astonish medieval landlords or farmers who were well aware that certain activities could deplete the soil and reduce its long-run value. Although it seems at times to get overlooked, the value of land depends on the present value of its long-run yield. Of course no buyers of land expect to enjoy its yield forever. Rather, they regard its title with a right to sell that title as an asset that can be sold from buyer to buyer and from generation to generation. The value at every sale depends on the future fertility of the land, so that every owner has an incentive to maintain fertility. If overuse of the land creates a short-run gain that is less than the discounted value of the loss of future productivity, the value of the land falls more than the increase in short-run output and the owner loses. The pecuniary incentives are to maintain an appropriately long time horizon. Tenants in medieval times, whose interest in the land was of limited duration, had no such natural incentive to take a long view. Landlords quickly appreciated this fact and medieval tenurial arrangements in northwestern Europe were designed accordingly. First, lease tenures were generally made for long periods. Second, clauses in the leases constrained the tenant to conservation practices; for example, removal of manure from the tenanted farm was prohibited.

It is ironic that problems of overuse of a resource arising from the absence of a clear and salable property right, which would provide an incentive for someone to consider the long-run value of the resource, have come to be referred to as the "tragedy of the commons." The phrase has its origin in the alleged problems of the medieval village where animals were grazed collectively on commonly owned pasture and waste. This practice is seen to lead to deterioration in the quality of the grazing land and of the animals. With commonly held pasture where everyone was free to graze a herd, all farmers had an incentive to increase their animal holdings above the social optimum. Yet, the addition of one animal to a village herd will result not only in that animal's growth but in competition for scarce feed that will reduce the average growth of the rest of the village herd. Collectively the village should not increase its herd when the addition of one more animal fails to increase the productivity of the herd as a whole by as much as the extra costs incurred as a result of the additional animal. Individuals, however, do not have to bear the "cost" of reduced growth of their neighbours' cattle and so they will profit from the addition of an animal of their own even when the village as a whole is hurt. Since every farmer faces these incentives, the village herd will increase beyond the optimal size and the total output of the village will be reduced. If land were owned privately and all ' owners confined their animals to land they owned, the total output would rise substantially.

This is an argument that was widely used by the proponents of enclosure of the open fields in England in the late 18th and early 19th century. The same argument is used to explain overuse and failure of individual action in the market to make optimal intertemporal decisions in resources not under private ownership (ocean fish for example). It is an important argument that we will return to in our discussion but nevertheless it seems to have had only modest relevance to the open field agriculture of northwestern Europe with its common pasture. In fact, European peasants were sensitive to the conditions under which they lived. We have evidence of numerous cases where potential overgrazing of the commons with its adverse results was not allowed to harm the productivity of village agriculture. The village instead adopted "stinting" rules that limited the number of cattle that could be kept by each farmer, usually in proportion to his landholdings in the arable fields.

Many of the cases of environmental abuse that the Conservationists pointed to as evidence of the destructive nature of capitalist greed are better understood when the specific property rights involved are considered. Often perverse results were generated by inappropriate restrictions and subsidies established primarily in an attempt to aid the small farmer who formed the basis of the Conservationists' ideal society. Specifically, for example, the public land policies adopted in the United States after the Civil War were designed primarily to grant property to small farmers. Legislation limited the legal disposition of the land to 160 acres per claimant, and this land was only to be granted to bona fide settlers. Such restrictions were compatible with technological efficiency on lands suitable to grain and mixed farming in the non-arid regions of the West, but their application to situations where the 160-acre limitation was in conflict with technological efficiency created problems. Four such cases are discussed below. Each led to a situation that Conservationists pointed to as evidence of the failure and immorality of the market.

The arid range land of the high plains is the first case in point.[31] Here, as John Wesley Powell had recognized in his survey of the region in the 1870s, extensive grazing was the only viable form of agriculture. Powell estimated the minimum efficient size of operation of 2,560 acres of land and possession of a reliable source of water. Units of this size and larger that would have been attractive for private ownership were not, however, available from the government. Instead, cattle were raised on the open range in the manner made familiar in the fiction of the West. There were no legally enforceable property rights, nor was any other method used to control use of the arid grasslands. As a consequence the horrors attributed to the medieval commons occurred in the Great Plains of the American West. Initially the lands were occupied by well-financed operations of the "cattle barons" who were able to reach informal agreement regarding land use. They could not, however, prevent the entry of smaller operations despite efforts at intimidation. As a result the resource was overused, the grass destroyed and the holding capacity of the land reduced. The culmination of the tragedy was the disastrous winter of 1887 when tens of thousands of cattle perished in the high plains. A traditional view blames this result on the greed of the cattle barons. It seems preferable to see it as the consequence of government action that created property rights that were inappropriate for raising cattle on the arid plains.

The accumulation of public lands for logging operations in the Pacific Northwest is a second example.[32] The technology of the industry gave considerable advantage to large operations, primarily because of the investment in temporary railroads needed to move timber from the woods. The 160-acre lots available under the public land law were too small to be attractive. Additionally, the claimant was required to swear that he "did not apply to purchase the same on speculation, but in good faith to appropriate it to his own exclusive use and benefit; and that he had not directly or indirectly, made any agreement or contract, with any person or persons whomsoever, by which title he might acquire from the Government should inure the others."[33]

From 1880 to 1909, the law notwithstanding, vast amounts of timberland were acquired under the federal land laws and transferred to large investors and corporations. The General Land Office estimated that fully 10 million of the 12 million acres of timberland alienated under the Timber and Stone Act had been fraudulently obtained through the use of entrymen. Certainly the process appeared immoral but the alternative would seem to have been to leave the forest in the public domain, for the land was not attractive to bone fide settlers in 160-acre lots. In the public domain, at least until the creation of an efficient National Forest system, the woodlands were not properly managed but subject to timber theft and the problems of the commons. Thus underlying the issue was a conflict of goals that was unrecognized by the Conservationists, for generally the preference for the small unit overrode concern for efficiency. Eventually the Conservationists argued, without understanding the influence of property rights on behaviour, that this sort of action demonstrated the immorality and inefficiency of private interests. Their solution was administrative control and they lobbied successfully for the creation of the National Forests managed by a professional forest service.

The early history of petroleum extraction provides a third example of inadequate property rights leading to inappropriate over-exploitation of a resource under capitalist incentives.[34] Here too the Conservationists and government regulation favoured small units that created problems for efficient management. The major common property problem arises from the migratory character of oil. As it is pumped from an underground pool, what is left will migrate toward the area of low pressure created by extraction. Prior to 1909, on federal oil lands such as predominated in California, individuals could obtain title to 20 acres of land on which oil had been discovered. Since the major oil-bearing formations were thousands of acres in extent, and property rights to oil itself could only be obtained by extraction, title holders drilled and drained the reserve as rapidly as possible. Not only did this practice result in excessively rapid depletion of the reserve but also, by rapidly lowering the underground pressure, it limited the total oil recoverable from the field. One contemporary estimate suggested that competitive policies of "drill and drain" recovered between 20 and 25 percent of the oil in the formation while more orderly controlled extraction could have recovered up to 90 percent. On federal land, oil holdings were kept small by legislation until 1930, when concern regarding the rapid competitive extraction in the North Dome Kettleman Hills field in California led to the passage of an amendment to the Mineral Leasing Act that permitted lease consolidation for unitized field production. The unified control of the production of the field internalized the effects of rapid drilling and led the private producer to undertake optimal extraction. Oil pools underlying privately owned lands, such as occurred in Texas and Oklahoma, presented similar problems. Individual owners were motivated to encourage drilling on their land to obtain royalties and so a "drill and drain" exploitation pattern developed because property rights to subterranean oil were deficient. Eventually private bargaining in these fields reduced, but seldom completely eliminated, the wasteful extraction procedures. By 1947 only 12 of some 3,000 oil fields in the United States were fully unitized to completely internalize the costs of extraction. The benefits of internalizing the potential common property problems of the oil fields, presumably, is a major explanation of the concentration of the oil industry into the hands of large companies.

Historical property right developments seem prone to ironic incidents, and American oil extraction is no exception. The Teapot Dome scandal of the Harding administration is perhaps the most famous example of private company greed and political corruption combining to thwart wise resource policy. The basic facts are fairly straightforward. In 1922, the U.S. Secretary of the Interior granted leases on the Elk Hills and Teapot Dome naval oil reserves, in each case to a single oil company. This created the first situation in which the externalities of an oil field were internalized by an appropriate property right. A considerable political furor arose immediately, with opposition not only from those who had been excluded from the fields but also from Conservationists. The Conservationists' concern arose out of apparent favouritism to big business and opposition to any exploitation of the reserves. They seem to have paid little or no attention to the problems of competitive extraction that were present before the granting of the leases. In 1927, before any significant experience could be gained regarding the operation of leases, the Secretary was convicted of bribery for receipt of $100,000 in connection with the granting of the leases, and the leases were cancelled.

Libecap has recently summarized the effect of the Teapot Dome Scandal on the oil industry:

> The federal lands literature almost unanimously views the original leases as examples of corruption and as evidence of the need for greater government intervention in oil markets. This view, however, obscures the conservation potential of the large leases, the contracting problems of combining small leases, and the political rivalries over federal land that underlay the criticism of conservation groups. The Teapot Dome controversy illustrates the friction involved in political allocation of federal land at a time when institu-

tional arrangements were being established. The record reveals that for the parties involved, control of federal land and federal land policies, rather than conservation was the primary concern. The Teapot Dome controversy also had a longer term impact on oil production. It provided justification for the establishment of institutions for broad regulation of output.[35]

The final example that deserves brief consideration here is the issue of the water needs of the arid regions of the western United States,[36] which is often cited as a coming resource crisis. It, too, is a tangle of externalities, legal property rights, equity and government subsidization. In the space available I can do little more than outline the problem. A basic premise of efficient use is that a scarce good should be provided only to the point at which its marginal social cost equals its marginal social benefit. In situations where costs and benefits are internalized and exchange rights are well specified legally, a private market is an excellent way to approximate this condition. For Western water the conditions for efficient use are violated. Water is even more migratory than oil, and natural externalities exist in the use of ground water, river water and irrigation water. Common law property rights to scarce water require "beneficial use," which discourages both conservation and the sale of water rights. Federal irrigation projects, furthermore, have contained substantial subsidies so that the actual cost of water greatly exceeds the costs users pay. Moreover, federal regulations contain the familiar bias in favour of small users that has led to further subsidization and fraudulent behaviour to make the cheap water available to larger operators. The result of all these distortions seems to be that water is currently overused in the West; the marginal cost of its provision considerably exceeds its marginal benefit. So long as demand is considered independent of costs — as it often seems to be in the neo-Malthusian literature — a shortage may be perceived. This seems likely to be the product of a combination of inappropriate analysis and inappropriate property rights, which have often arisen from that analysis.

Conclusion: Resource Shortage and the Market in Historical Perspective

There has long been concern over the approaching scarcity of raw materials of various sorts but no such shortage has had an important impact in the West for well over a century and a half. The combination of technological change and the market have adjusted to changing conditions of scarcity. Many historians, for example, see the Industrial Revolution as being in large measure the process of substituting relatively abundant mineral resources for less abundant animal and vegetable products. The substitution was a response to prices.

Markets are not perfect instruments of control; not only do externalities often lead to distorted outcomes, but commodities may not pass through markets and thus may be poorly allocated. Moreover, it is possible, and some argue it is likely, that since market economies have incentives to use free resources, the improvement in measured productivity has been bought at the price of environmental degradation of a sort that cannot, because of its technical characteristics, be brought into the market. Certainly this issue cannot be ignored, but the historian is perhaps entitled to a bit of skepticism. The pollution and environmental degradation caused by current activities, despite legitimate areas of concern, do not seem obviously worse than the fatal industrial hazards and urban pollution of a century or more ago. Another important reservation regarding market processes arises from concern over the destruction of the unique and irreplaceable, from creatures like the blue whale to, ultimately, many of the world's mineral resources. There is strong appeal in arguments that suggest that these should be preserved for the future of mankind and that market decisions based on a positive rate of interest that discounts future values are inappropriate. Thus, large payments can be justified to avoid possible catastrophic outcomes. Such an argument must have its limits, however. Would it have been appropriate to have had those living a century and a half ago limit their use of coal and iron in our interest?

Despite their imperfections, markets have performed well over the last century and more. In many cases externalities can be internalized by appropriate property rights to remove distortions, just as inappropriate property rights will introduce distortions of their own. The great advantage of markets lies in their ability to use the information acquired by individuals whose direct pecuniary interests are engaged and to provide incentives that reinforce appropriate action. This is not to deny a place for the professional civil servants from whom the Progressives hoped so much, but they have their own incentives which are unlikely to be directly tied to efficient use of scarce resources. In politics, power and interest dominate. Thus, society's choice is between imperfect instruments — the market and the political process. It seems appropriate to rely on the political process for resource allocation only when the market is clearly inappropriate because of the technological characteristics of the product.

Some of the statements of the neo-Malthusians notwithstanding, it is clear that markets respond to increasing shortage and higher prices. For example in 19th century Britain, steam engines on the coal fields burned three times as much coal per horsepower as steam engines in the Cornish mines or on ocean vessels where coal was scarce and thus expensive. More recent energy use shows a similar clear relationship to the cost consumers pay. In 1978, the rate of energy consumption in industrial countries was related closely to the price of energy to users. Observations lay fairly closely along a line connecting Canada, where average energy costs US$170 per oil-equivalent ton and consumption was

0.7 tons per US$1,000 of GDP, and Switzerland, where costs were $340 and consumption was 0.2 tons respectively.[37] These figures suggest quite an elastic response to energy prices. We have also examined in some detail the case of American timber. Here the market did well in equating supply and demand over time.

Historians normally hesitate to draw policy conclusions from their work because one of history's surest lessons is the unreliability of projection. Nonetheless, policy will be made and the study of resource scarcity and economic growth strongly suggests two conclusions. First, to focus on the availability of resources as either a constraint or a cause of growth is to fail to understand the essence of growth in modern economies. The rising standards of living of the past two centuries have rested on the twin supports of the fruitfulness of man's imagination in the generation of technology and the flexibility of economies organized through markets adopting that technology and adjusting to changing conditions of resource supply. The constant process of adjustment and change has been as much a part of the growth process as the increasing standard of living. The policy implication is obvious. Interference in the economy risks distorting or dissipating the creative forces that have generated growth, just as the inappropriate property rights in the range and timber lands in the American West distorted activities there. This is not to say that there is no role for policy, since property rights themselves are the creation of government policy. Rather, policy must be carefully considered not only with respect to its goals but also with reference to how it influences the dynamics of technological change and markets.

The second conclusion that may be safely drawn from this study is that there is little or no evidence that increasing resource scarcity will justify substantial policy initiatives in the near future. Careful consideration of property rights and their limitations in certain resources, however, requires continuing attention. The problems of pollution, both currently realized and potential, may usefully be seen as the consequence of imperfect rights to air and water — probably made inevitable by the nature of the resources. In other cases, property rights may be created by policy that leads to inappropriate action — as in Western American water — and policy reform may be in order. Finally, society collectively has a legitimate concern for the future and should take account of possible unforeseen and irreversible consequences of current actions. State policy directed at reducing the risk of such outcomes may be appropriate. Nonetheless, the evidence suggests it is best to proceed slowly and with care rather than launch major policy initiatives which inevitably contain unforeseen side effects.

Notes

This study was completed in November 1984.

1. See, for two prominent examples, Meadows et al. (1972) and U.S. Department of State (1980).
2. See Phelps-Brown and Hopkins (1955), and Phelps-Brown and Hopkins (1956). Any such long-time series is inevitably open to some questions of interpretation. How comparable are skills, the method of payment, the commodities used to construct the cost of living index; can conditions at Oxford colleges be used to indicate conditions generally in a largely agricultural and noticeably regionalized, if not localized economy? Nonetheless, research by other scholars has generally confirmed the broad outlines of Phelps-Brown and Hopkins' work. Modifications have occurred but the broad thrust of their conclusions remain. In Figure 1, the Phelps-Brown and Hopkins data are used until the early seventeenth century and then I have replaced this data with the results that represent my reading of the best current research.
3. See Schofield (1981).
4. The demographic historians have found, however, that the mechanics of European demography relied more on conscious decisions to limit family size through the age of marriage and childbearing behaviour, what Malthus (1798) called "moral restraint" in the later editions of the Essay and less on elevated death rates brought on by poverty, the "misery and vice" of the first edition — see the discussion below.
5. This conclusion must be interpreted with care, however, since the observations at the end of the eighteenth century are influenced by the great war with France at least as much as they are by the demographic trends.
6. See Deane and Cole (1967), chap. 9.
7. See Kuznets (1954), pp. 82–83.
8. The income data are from Heston (1983), and the population data from Visaria and Visaria (1983). There are significant questions yet to be settled regarding the income data for this period so these results must be somewhat tentative in detail if not in general outline. Data for industrial real wages show impressive increases during these years. Furthermore, the national income estimates have been constructed on an assumption of constant agricultural yields which implies a declining availability of food per capita during the period. The real price of food declined during these decades. This suggests that perhaps the growth of income is understated in the estimates.
9. For a brief introduction to European demographic history see Wrigley(1969).
10. Turner's seminal article was "The Significance of the Frontier in American History," read before the American Historical Association in 1893. For an excellent consideration of Turner and his influence see Hofstadter (1968), part 2.
11. The idea of the staple thesis pervades Innis' writing. It was put forward in a particularly influential way in Mackintosh (1939). An extremely influential statement of the thesis is Watkins (1963), pp. 141–58. A useful collection of articles, many of which develop the staple thesis, is Easterbrook and Watkins (1967).
12. The most prominent example is Easterbrook and Aitken (1958), *Canadian Economic History*, which was until very recently universally used as a text in courses on Canadian economic history. This view has not been all pervasive, however, see particularly Buckley (1958). Marr and Paterson (1980), a recent text, has placed much greater emphasis on non-staple-related issues than did earlier texts.
13. See particularly North (1966 and 1967).
14. For a very interesting discussion of both contemporary perceptions of the West and the settlement process see Boorstin (1965), part five, "The Vagueness of the Land."
15. See Harley (1978, pp. 865–78), and Harley (1980, pp. 218–50). See also Norrie (1975) and Lewis (1981).
16. See Fishlow (1966) and Harley (1974).
17. See Lower (1973) and McClelland (1966).
18. On the linkages to the South see Fishlow (1964) and Gallman (1970). On the railroads see Fishlow (1965), and Fogel (1964).

19. See Chambers and Gordon (1966, pp. 315–22).
20. See Caves (1971).
21. See Dennen (1977) and Southey (1978).
22. This statement and the data underlying Figure 3 come from Urquhart (1984).
23. See Barnett and Morse (1962, chap. 4), and Hofstadter (1968, part 1).
24. See Ontario Ministry of Natural Resources (1974).
25. See Olson (1971).
26. See Jevons (1865).
27. *Ibid.*
28. See Barnett (1979).
29. *Ibid.*, pp. 164–65.
30. For example, Nicholas Georgescu-Roegen seems to take this view. See Georgescu-Roegen (1979). More explicitly see Okay (1982, pp. 87–88).
31. A fascinating discussion of aspects of this problem appear in Boorstin (1965), chaps. 2 and 3 which include, among other things the "Johnson County (Wyoming) War" which forms the basis of the novel and motion picture *Shane*.
32. See Libecap and Johnson (1979, pp. 129–42).
33. *Ibid.*, p. 131.
34. See Libecap (1984, pp. 381–93), and Wiggins (1984, pp. 87–98).
35. Libecap (1984, p. 391).
36. The classic source on California water issues is Bain et al. (1966).
37. "World Business Gains Pounds on a Low Oil Diet," *Economist*, December 26, 1981, p. 66.

Bibliography

Bain, Joseph S., Richard E. Caves, and Julius Margolis. 1966. *Northern California's Water Industry: The Comparative Efficiency of Public Enterprise in Developing a Scarce Natural Resource*. Baltimore: Johns Hopkins University Press for Resources for the Future, Inc.

Barnett, Harold J. 1979. "Scarcity and Growth Revisited." In *Scarcity and Growth Reconsidered*, edited by V. Kerry Smith. Baltimore: Johns Hopkins University Press for Resources for the Future, Inc.

Barnett, Harold J., and Chandler Morse. 1962. *Scarcity and Growth: The Economics of Natural Resource Availability*. Baltimore: Johns Hopkins University Press for Resources for the Future, Inc.

Boorstin, Daniel J. 1965. *The Americans: The National Experience*. New York: Random House.

————. 1973. *The Americans: The Democratic Experience*. New York: Random House.

Brown, E.H. Phelps, and Sheila Hopkins. 1955. "Seven Centuries of Building Wages." *Economica* 22: 195–206.

————. 1956. "Seven Centuries of the Prices of Consumables, Compared with Builders Wage Rates." *Economica* 23: 296–314.

Buckley, K.A.H. 1958. "The Role of Staple Industries in Canadian Economic Development." *Journal of Economic History* 18.

Caves, R.E. 1971. "Export Led Growth and the New Economic History." In *Trade, Balance of Payments, and Growth*, edited by J. Bhagwati, R. Jones, R. Mundell, and J. Vanek. Amsterdam: North-Holland.

Chambers, Edward J., and Donald F. Gordon. 1966. "Primary Products and Economic Growth: An Empirical Measurement." *Journal of Political Economy* 74 (August): 315–22.

Deane, Phyllis, and W.A. Cole. 1967. *British Economic Growth, 1688–1950*. Cambridge: Cambridge University Press. 2d ed.

Dennen, R.T. 1977. "Some Efficiency Effects of the Nineteenth Century Federal Land Policy." *Agricultural History* (October).

Easterbrook, W.T., and H.G.J. Aitken. 1958. *Canadian Economic History*. Toronto: Macmillan.

Easterbrook, W.T., and M.H. Watkins. 1967. *Approaches to Canadian Economic History*. Toronto: McClelland and Stewart.

Fishlow, Albert. 1964. "Antebellum Interregional Trade Reconsidered." *American Economic Review* (May).

_____. 1965. *American Railroads and the Transformation of the Ante-Bellum Economy*. Cambridge, Mass: Harvard University Press.

_____. 1966. "Productivity and Technological Change in the Railroad Sector, 1840–1910." In *Output, Employment and Productivity in the United States after 1800*. New York: National Bureau of Economic Research.

Fogel, Robert W. 1964. *Railroads and American Economic Growth*. Baltimore: Johns Hopkins University Press.

Gallman, Robert. 1970. "Self-Sufficiency in the Cotton Economy of the Antebellum South." *Agricultural History* (January).

Georgescu-Roegen, Nicholas. 1979. "Comments on the Papers by Daly and Stiglitz." In *Scarcity and Growth Reconsidered*, edited by V. Kerry Smith. Baltimore: Johns Hopkins University Press for Resources for the Future, Inc.

Harley, C. Knick. 1974. "The Shift from Sailing Ships to Steamships, 1850–1890: A Study in Technological Change and Its Diffusion." In *Essays on a Mature Economy: Britain After 1840*, edited by D.N. McCloskey. London: Methuen.

_____. 1978. "Western Settlement and the Price of Wheat." *Journal of Economic History* 38 (December): 865–78.

_____. 1980. "Transportation, the World Wheat Trade and the Kuznets Cycle." *Explorations in Economic History* 17 (July): 218–50.

Heston, Alan. 1983. "National Income." In *The Cambridge Economic History of India, Vol. 2: c. 1757 – c. 1970*, edited by Dhama Kumar. Cambridge: Cambridge University Press.

Hofstadter, Richard. 1968. *The Progressive Historians*. New York: Alfred A. Knopf.

Jevons, William S. 1865. *On the Coal Question*. London, 1865.

Keynes, John Maynard. 1936. *The General Theory of Employment, Interest and Money*. London: Macmillan.

Kuznets, Simon S. 1954. *National Income and Its Composition, 1919–1938*. New York: National Bureau of Economic Research.

Lewis, Frank D. 1981. "Farm Settlement on the Canadian Prairies, 1898 to 1911." *Journal of Economic History* 41 (September): 517–35.

Libecap, Gary D. 1984. "The Political Allocation of Mineral Rights: A Re-evaluation of Teapot Dome." *Journal of Economic History* 44:381–93.

Libecap, Gary D., and Ronald N. Johnson. 1979. "Property Rights, Nineteenth Century Federal Timber Policy and the Conservation Movement." *Journal of Economic History* 39 (March): 129–42.

Libecap, Gary D., and Steven N. Wiggins. 1984. "Contractual Responses to the Common Pool: Prorationing of Crude Oil Production." *American Economic Review* 74 (March): 87–98.

Lower, Arthur R.M. 1973. *Great Britain's Woodyard*. Montreal: McGill-Queens University Press.

McClelland, Peter D. 1966. "The New Brunswick Economy in the Nineteenth Century." Ph.D. dissertation, Harvard University.

Mackintosh, W.A. 1939. *The Economic Background of Dominion-Provincial Relations*. Appendix 3 of the Royal Commission Report on Dominion-Provincial Relations. Ottawa: King's Printer.

Malthus, Thomas R. 1798. *Essay on the Principles of Population*. London: Dent.

Marr, William L., and Donald G. Paterson. 1980. *Canada: An Economic History*. Toronto: Macmillan.

Marx, Karl. 1867. *Capital: A Critique of Political Economy*. Vol. 1. *The Process of Capitalist Production*. London: Lawrence.

Meadows, Donella H., Dennis L. Meadows, Jorgen Randers, and William W. Behrens III. 1972. *The Limits to Growth: A Report for the Club of Rome's Project on the Predicament of Mankind*. Washington D.C.: Potomac Associates.

Norrie, Ken. 1975. "The Rate of Settlement of the Canadian Prairies." *Journal of Economic History* 35 (June).

North, Douglass C. 1966. *The Economic Growth of the United States, 1790–1860*. New York: Norton.

——. 1976. *Growth and Welfare in the American Past: A New Economic History*. 2d ed. Englewood Cliffs, N.J.: Prentice-Hall.

Okay, John. 1982. "Economic Forces." In *Renewable Natural Resources: A Management Handbook for the 1980s*, edited by Dennis L. Little, Robert E. Dils, and John Gray. Boulder, Col.: Westview Press.

Olson, Sherry H. 1971. *The Depletion Myth: A History of Railroad Use of Timber*. Cambridge, Mass.: Harvard University Press.

Ontario Ministry of Natural Resources. 1974. *Algonquin Provincial Park Master Plan*. Toronto: Queen's Printer.

Ricardo, David. 1817. *The Principles of Political Economy and Taxation*. London: Dent.

Schofield, R.S., and E.A. Wrigley. 1981. *The Population History of England, 1541–1871: A Reconstruction*. Cambridge, Mass.: Harvard University Press.

Southey, Clive. 1978. "The Staple Thesis, Common Property and Homesteading." *Canadian Journal of Economics* (August).

Turner, Frederick Jackson. 1893. "The Significance of the Frontier in American History." *American Historical Review*.

Urquhart, M.C. 1984. "New Estimates of Gross National Product, Canada 1879 to 1926: Some Implications for Canadian Development." Discussion Paper. Kingston: Queen's University, Department of Economics.

U.S. Department of State. 1980. *The Global 2000 Report to the President: Entering the Twenty-First Century*. 3 vols. A report prepared by the Council of Environmental Quality and the Department of State. Gerald O. Barney, Study Director. Washington D.C.: Government Publishing Office.

Visaria, Leela, and Pravin Visaria. 1983. "Population, 1757–1947." In *The Cambridge Economic History of India, Vol. 2: c. 1757 – c. 1970*, edited by Dhama Kumar. Cambridge: Cambridge University Press.

Watkins, M.H. 1963. "A Staple Theory of Economic Growth." *Canadian Journal of Economics and Political Science* 29 (May): 141–58.

Wrigley, E.A. 1969. *Population and History*. New York: McGraw Hill.

2

Entrepreneurship, Innovation and Economic Change

DAVID W. CONKLIN

Some Aspects of Entrepreneurship

People use the word "entrepreneurship" to convey a variety of meanings. This paper looks at the role of entrepreneurship as part of the process of innovation, considering it both as a cause of economic change and as a response to economic change.

The paper examines four aspects of entrepreneurship. First, entrepreneurship involves both the perception of an opportunity to innovate and the creativity entailed in responding to that opportunity. Some individuals, understanding the potential to alter previous production methods, may implement new techniques or organizational arrangements based upon that understanding, while others may confront the same situation but not share the same insight or creativity. Second, entrepreneurship entails decisions based upon an analysis of uncertainty and risk. An error may occur; an attempt to innovate may fail. There is no guarantee that a new production method will succeed. Third, prices, profit and competition are an implicit and essential part of much of the literature on entrepreneurship. Prices and profit provide a set of guidelines for decision-making criteria for evaluating success. The desire to acquire profit forms a powerful incentive to innovate; furthermore, competitors will strive to imitate a successful innovator, thereby reducing that innovator's profit. Finally, entrepreneurship may have significant effects on people not directly involved in the process. Such third-party effects may reach beyond the realm of competitors and customers and lead to changes in society as a whole. This examination of 'perception and creativity,' 'uncertainty and risk,' 'prices, profit and competition,' and 'third-party effects' will help us in considering the prospects of a society's development. For any society, the pace of economic growth and job creation may be strongly influenced by the extent of entrepreneurship and innovation. The appropriate role of government in this process is examined at the conclusion of the paper.

Because of constraints on the length of the paper, however, a substantial body of literature on entrepreneurship will not be dealt with here.

There are differences of opinion about whether one should discuss entrepreneurship as an exogenous force that disrupts an economy's equilibrium, or rather as the market mechanism whereby this equilibrium is attained (Kirzner, 1973, 1979). In the former view, one can develop an economic theory about the determination of prices by analyzing equilibrium situations; meanwhile, entrepreneurship can be set aside for separate examination. Much modern neoclassical microeconomic theory does just this. In the opposing view, entrepreneurship is the process through which price changes occur, so that entrepreneurship must be at the centre of any discussion of prices and markets. Many scholars of the 'Austrian school,' following Hayek, emphasize the real world's disequilibrium and the role of entrepreneurship in taking advantage of disequilibrium opportunities. The present paper will not be concerned with this debate, although insights from both schools of thought will contribute to our discussion.

Furthermore, the paper does not address a wide range of business attributes which are generally considered to be good management practices and which entrepreneurs must share in order to conduct their daily work successfully. Examples of such characteristics include the ability to sell products, to direct and encourage personnel, to understand accounting techniques, and to negotiate contracts. Rather, this study will focus on aspects that the author considers most significant for the process of innovation and economic change. Likewise, when considering the role of government, only selected aspects are examined, as the number and variety of government programs and regulations is immense. The paper comments on a few of the more important implications that a discussion of entrepreneurship and innovation can have for government activities.

Perception and Creativity

Entrepreneurship is not simply the luck of being in the right place at the right time. Many people and institutions may possess the knowledge necessary for innovation, but they may lack the perception of how this knowledge can be used in business, or they may lack creativity and originality. Over the years, economists have written about perception and creativity in a variety of ways, leading to a number of interpretations of the word "entrepreneurship."

In a presidential address to the 1946 annual meeting of the U.S.

Economic History Association, Arthur H. Cole (1953, p. 183) emphasized that the entrepreneur "must have special personal qualities." To illustrate these qualities, Cole quoted Jean-Baptiste Say, who wrote at the beginning of the nineteenth century that the entrepreneur must possess "judgment, perseverance, and a knowledge of the world as well as of business. He is called upon to estimate . . . the importance of the specific product, the probable amount of the demand, and the means of its production. . . . In the course of such complex operations, there are abundance of obstacles to be surmounted, of anxieties to be repressed, of misfortunes to be repaired and of expedients to be devised." (Ibid., p. 183).

Joseph Schumpeter (1961, p. 129) referred to entrepreneurs as "the leaders of modern economic life" and described the "characteristic entrepreneurial function" as "the carrying out of new combinations." (Ibid., p. 137). These new combinations may include technical inventions, but the entrepreneur need not be a scientific inventor. In Schumpeter's view, the entrepreneur is an innovator who creatively brings together the various elements necessary for a new business process. This process is not restricted to changes in production techniques. It may include new products, new services, or new ways of organizing economic activities, and the improvements may be made in sales, distribution, or management systems, as well as in production facilities.

By emphasizing "special personal qualities," one may focus on major undertakings and on innovators like John D. Rockefeller, Andrew Carnegie and Henry Ford. On the other hand, some economists, including Israel Kirzner, have viewed perception and creativity as a frequent response to the myriad opportunities that exist in a world of disequilibrium. "Because the participants in this market are less than omniscient, there are likely to exist, at any given time, a multitude of opportunities that have not yet been taken advantage of" (Kirzner, 1973, p. 41). From this perspective, "in an important sense, each human decision is an entrepreneurial decision" (Kirzner, 1979, p. 158). This draws attention to entrepreneurship as a part of each individual's economic activities, rather than solely within the large-scale innovations of well-known business leaders. An example of such entrepreneurship that will be considered later occurs when individuals make decisions about the development of their own education and abilities, as well as decisions about their choice of job.

Uncertainty and Risk

"The earliest use of the term entrepreneur did not include risk bearing and capital provision among his duties. Cantillon, however, originated the theory of entrepreneurship as risk taker and in so doing, set the theory of entrepreneurship on a new course" (Hebert and Link, 1983,

p. 17). In his discussion of the early history of entrepreneurial theory, Hoselitz (1960, p. 250) states succinctly, "Cantillon's theory of entrepreneurship is very simple. The function of the entrepreneur is to bear uncertainty." It should be emphasized, however, that economists have seen this taking of risks not as the purchase of a lottery ticket, when the outcome is dependent on chance, but rather as the conscious calculation of "risk-return outcomes" and the rational choice of a particular decision within a world where uncertainty exists and where errors can occur.

Several economists have looked at the individual decision to pursue a specific course of action that carries with it a particular set of risk-return outcomes. This analysis has often been conducted within mathematical models based on assumptions concerning the structure of risk-return outcomes and the nature of the human decision process (Shackle, 1968, 1970; Carter and Ford, 1972). Sometimes, one particular aspect of the entrepreneurial decision is examined. For example, Green and Shoven have focussed on the contractual relationships through which the entrepreneur borrows capital under conditions where a risk of bankruptcy exists. They "show how the risk of bankruptcy shapes the financial contract, and how the contract can be used to regulate the subsequent choices of the entrepreneur" (Green and Shoven, 1982, p. 49).

In recent years, a different approach to this subject has also been pursued with the examination of new small businesses and, in particular, "venture capital" firms that have both an original production process and the risk of capital loss. These studies have included empirical analyses of many different sets of data in order to learn something about methods of financing, profitability, and survival rates (Wetzel, 1982; Brophy, 1982; Cooper, 1982). Knight (1982, p. 35) has pointed out that, "For the most part, these are limited to the study of highly successful entrepreneurs," and has urged that more research should examine unsuccessful entrepreneurs, as well as those whose daily work is "unsophisticated."

Two methods of reducing uncertainty and risk deserve particular mention: investment in knowledge and information, and purchase of insurance. Economists have recently devoted special attention to the former, attempting to analyze the optimal degree of ignorance under a variety of conditions. In a seminal article Stigler emphasized "the problem of determining which technologies will be used by each firm (and, for that matter, each person). The choice is fundamentally a matter of investment in knowledge: the costs and returns of acquiring various kinds and amounts of technological information vary systematically with various characteristics of a firm: its size, the age of its present capital assets, the experience of its managers, the prospects of the trade" (Stigler, 1976, p. 215). Before each entrepreneurial action, a decision must be made about how much should be spent on acquiring knowledge and information. In some cases, this decision itself could be considered entrepreneurial.

In many instances, insurance can be purchased to reduce or eliminate particular risks. Writers like Knight have examined the differences between risks that can be insured against and those that cannot. As Hebert and Link say: "The essential point for profit theory is that insofar as it is possible to insure by any method against risk, the cost of carrying it is converted into a constant element of expense, and it ceases to be a cause of profit and loss. The uncertainties which persist as causes of profit are those which are uninsurable because there is no objective measure of the probability of gain or loss" (Hebert and Link, 1982, p. 69). Entrepreneurship involves judgment in the face of risks that are uninsurable and that, consequently, expose one to loss. However, it should be noted that this decision about how much insurance to purchase for each aspect of the business process could also, in itself, be considered entrepreneurial. Both methods for reducing uncertainty and risk will enter our later discussion of the appropriate role of government.

"One of the perpetual points of contention in competing theories of entrepreneurship is to what extent the roles of entrepreneur and capitalist can be separated" (ibid, p. 19). Should the word entrepreneur be reserved for that individual who manages the innovating firm, bringing together the means of production in an original way? Or are the financial institutions and individuals that invest their capital also to be considered as entrepreneurs? Are perception and creativity the characteristics that make someone an entrepreneur? Or are entrepreneurial decisions only those that deal with uncertainty and risk? This paper argues that since both characteristics are essential components of innovation and economic change, both must be considered when a society's development prospects and the appropriate role of government are analyzed.

Prices, Profit and Competition

Implicit in the above discussion is the assumption of the existence of a set of guidelines and success criteria. The potential entrepreneur is able to make calculations about costs and sales and therefore is able to develop expectations about his own rewards. In the literature of Western economists, the set of guidelines and success criteria are formed by prices and profit. The various aspects of an opportunity can be denominated in terms of a currency so that the potential entrepreneur can judge whether or not a proposed innovation will be an improvement over existing practices. Competitors will watch the entrepreneur to determine whether the innovation is successful — that is, profitable; if so, they will probably copy the process. Such competitive imitation will tend to reduce the initial profitability. In writing about entrepreneurs,

Taussig has concluded that "by taking the lead in utilizing inventions or improving organization they make extra gains, which last so long as they succeed in holding the lead. Business profits, so considered, are ever vanishing, ever reappearing. They are the stimulus to improvement and the reward for improvement, tending to cease once the improvement is fully applied" (Hebert and Link, 1982, p. 68).

This perspective emphasizes the importance of a society's price system in determining the extent of entrepreneurship and the impact it will have on a society's welfare. If the relationship among prices reflects relative scarcities and demands, then decisions on production and investment will be guided in the interests of society, given a particular income distribution. A great deal of microeconomic theory has regarded the establishment of these relationships as automatic in a free enterprise economy. However, a considerable body of literature looks at situations in which a free market will not provide guidelines that are in the society's best interests, (Boadway, 1979, chap. 2) and it is important to recognize that this literature about market failure is meaningful in a discussion of entrepreneurship.

In certain societies, some or all prices are not determined by the market but rather are set by government. This section underlines the significance of government price setting not only for current decisions about production and consumption — that is, static efficiency — but also for entrepreneurial decisions whose effects may not be felt immediately. In this sense, profit can be seen not only as the personal material reward — a powerful incentive for entrepreneurship — but also as an important criterion for success from society's perspective.

Kirzner has asserted that "entrepreneurship and competitiveness are two sides of the same coin: that entrepreneurial activity is always competitive and that competitive activity is always entrepreneurial" (Kirzner, 1973, p. 94). The potential entrepreneur reaches a decision after contemplating market opportunities and assessing the degree to which these have been met, or are likely to be met, by competitors. How the entrepreneur acts will affect the economic prospects of the competitors, and the existence of competition stimulates entrepreneurship. Profitability depends upon an individual's position vis-à-vis one's competitors; achievement of success is affected by how an individual's economic behaviour compares with that of others.

Competition forms a significant aspect of entrepreneurship for more specific reasons than these. Many governments provide patent protection, so that an inventor may work and invest without the fear that his competitors will appropriate the benefits of new production methods. Economists have analyzed possible patent conditions, such as time limits, to determine how much they affect the benefits received by society (Kotowitz and Berkowitz, 1982, pp. 1–17). Even with patent protection for inventions, competition may reduce entrepreneurial innovation below socially optimal levels. Pakes and Schankermann emphasize "two fundamental characteristics of knowledge as an economic commodity, its low or zero cost of reproduction and the difficulty of excluding others from its use. These features give knowledge the character of a public good and suggest that the structure of market incentives may not elicit the socially desirable level (or pattern) of research and development expenditures" (Pakes and Schankerman, 1984). This argument leads readily to the following discussion of "third-party effects" and will reappear in the conclusion, which examines the appropriate role of government.

Third-Party Effects

Entrepreneurship can give rise to significant third-party effects since it influences people and firms other than the entrepreneur. Innovation may reduce the profits of competitors and may even drive them out of business; on the other hand, it may cause other businesses, which sell materials and equipment to the innovator, to expand. Furthermore, innovation may reduce the prices that consumers have to pay for goods and services. Some employees may be hurt if technological change makes their skills obsolete. Yet other employees may enjoy an increased demand for their services. Such third-party effects may warrant government intervention for several reasons. First, a government may attempt to alter the pace and extent of an entrepreneurial activity in accordance with its assessment of likely third-party effects and the social rate of return (as distinct from the private rate of return). A second reason why third-party effects of entrepreneurship may lead to government intervention is that people who expect to be affected by an entrepreneurial activity may lobby the government, and so bring political pressure for such intervention. People likely to be thrown out of work, for example, may lobby for adjustment assistance or even for the pace of change to be retarded.

Quite apart from these third-party effects on an individual or one sector of the economy, there are aspects that affect society as a whole. Entrepreneurial activity is a means of raising a society's rate of growth. Overall, it appears that entrepreneurial activity has improved certain societies. In particular, productivity growth — which may be linked with such activity — seems to be a major component of economic growth. These relationship and economists' analyses of them were surveyed by Griliches (1979). Five years later, Griliches (1984, p. 1) again examined "the most important themes of research in this field," including the "belief that invention and technical change are the major driving forces of economic growth." Recently, many countries have experienced what Denny and Fuss have referred to as "The Great Productivity Slowdown." In their words, "Productivity growth has been very slow in the early 1980s, and there is growing concern that the government must undertake some action" (Denny and Fuss, 1982). Many commentators suggest that governments should provide special stimulus for entrepreneurial activities. In 1983, Baumol stated, "The great productivity crisis of the past fifteen years has brought with it renewed concern over entrepreneurship. . . . The shadow that hangs over all this is the fear that, for some reason, the American entrepreneurial spirit has gone into decline, and that the pre-eminence of the U.S. economy is threatened by a newly emerging army of entrepreneurs marching forth from the societies of Japan, Taiwan, Hong Kong, South Korea, and Singapore" (Baumol, 1983, p. ix). A closely related broad third-party effect that impinges on society as a whole is that government revenues and expenditures are affected by the rate of economic expansion. In a time of large deficits, the argument for special stimulus for entrepreneurial activities to provide jobs and growth and to reduce social security payments for the unemployed may receive strong support for this particular fiscal reason.

An entrepreneur invests capital, hires employees, buys materials from other firms, and sells new products to customers. It appears that the entrepreneurship that creates innovation and economic change can increase a society's growth and development, raise its productivity, and create jobs for its citizens. These linkages deserve attention. But entrepreneurship may result in losers as well as winners, and may bring undesired or negative third-party effects as well. It is to these linkages that we now turn.

Innovation and Economic Change

The Impetus for Change

In the 1920s, Kondratiev perceived and analyzed long-term trends in economic activities. He (Rothwell and Zegveld, 1981, pp. 36–43) suggested that an economic upturn contained forces that strengthened each other in a cumulative advance that could go on for several decades. One such force could be the application of inventions that had never been implemented because of depressed economic conditions. With an economic upturn and expanding customer demand, entrepreneurs would have the confidence to introduce such inventions as innovations. Joseph Schumpeter refined Kondratiev's insights and interpreted economic history largely in terms of the strength of entrepreneurial activity.

Schumpeter (1939) focussed on a few pathbreaking innovations, each of which had cleared the way for many related innovations. The application of steam power to the manufacturing process provided an important 19th-century example. Once steam technology had been applied in one process, the equipment could be modified quickly and easily for many other kinds of manufacturing. This soon reduced manufacturing costs. The need for new facilities and equipment created a demand for capital goods, which caused job opportunities. Growth, development, productivity, and jobs — all were enhanced.

The development of railroads greatly reduced transportation costs. Since transportation forms a component of most product costs, these became cheaper; new agricultural areas could be cultivated; competition increased as the scope of each market widened; and railroads needed substantial quantities of capital goods. The railroad revolution affected all businesses. The lower costs and new marketing opportunities opened up a wide range of possible innovations for all businesses. That is, the railroad innovation made possible a long series of other innovations. Furthermore, the railroad innovation meant that new capital investments had to be made to produce specific commodities like trains, tracks and steel.

In the first fifty years of this century, the development of electric power, together with its application in both production and consumption, provided unlimited opportunities for manufacturers to reduce costs. These opportunities were also found throughout the agricultural sector as rural electrification expanded, and as innovations in the processing and storage of food altered traditional marketing procedures. Domestic electrification spawned myriad new products. In this way electric power was an important innovation not only in itself but also by leading the way to countless other innovations as well. During the same period, automobiles and trucks became a major force in most economies. Like railroads, they reduced transportation costs and expanded the scope of most markets. More than the other key innovations, motor vehicles came to form a large component of many nations' economic activities, directly employing millions of people. The expansion plans of the motor vehicle producers could affect a society's growth rate; their location decisions could alter the relative prosperity of entire regions; and their purchases of raw materials and components could determine the success and scale of hundreds of other businesses.

Schumpeter explained the trends and cycles of many aggregate economic variables by relating them to these major entrepreneurial activities. The latter reduced production and distribution costs throughout the economy, permitted the development of innovations in many other types of businesses, and caused a greatly increased demand for new capital goods facilities to produce machinery, equipment and construction materials. Economic expansion was cumulative.

The basic insight of this Kondratiev-Schumpeter analysis is still relevant: innovations may affect the existing processes and relationships beyond the immediate business activities of the originating entrepreneurs. Relative prices can shift rapidly and can influence other sectors of the economy. As a consequence of these changes, some people will become financially successful; others will be hard hit. This view of history suggests that attempts to check economic change will probably ultimately fail. Rather, a forthright recognition and understanding of the entrepreneurial process may help the public to accept the inevitability of adjustment, and its long-term advantages.

A major impetus for economic change has been the growth of new trade relationships — a growth based on several significant trends. Within the past two decades certain developing countries have become newly industrialized and have created a manufacturing sector capable of exporting goods to Europe and North America. By paying extremely low wages, these countries are now able to compete within the markets of the developed nations in a wide range of manufactured goods. For generations, Britain and the United States were technologically ahead of other industrialized nations, but for the past few decades, this lead has been challenged. Most dramatically, Japan has been able to develop new manufacturing techniques and new forms of business organization that have created products for consumers in North America and Europe. Technological advance can have a sudden and substantial effect on existing markets, abruptly reducing the sales volumes, prices and profits of traditional manufacturers. Since World War II, political leaders have recognized that lower tariff barriers can increase international trade and so raise average incomes for all trading partners. New trade agreements that will expand trade are being sought. Often such arrangements expose traditional manufacturers to an unaccustomed competition for which they are unprepared (Department of External Affairs, 1983a, 1983b).

European and North American manufacturers have been exposed to new competition because of these developments. Rapid shifts in foreign exchange rates have added to the surprising alterations in competitive positions. For all these reasons, business adjustment has become a daily requirement rather than a periodic search for improvement. A nation whose businesses rely on the growth of existing facilities and the expansion of current practices may find that its firms are losing sales, profits and jobs. The importance of entrepreneurship — and the preparedness to innovate and to experiment with new methods — has been increased by all these developments.

The Impact of Economic Change on Jobs

Looking ahead a decade or more, it seems likely that a society's jobs will depend on its entrepreneurial capacity — its ability to take advantage of economic opportunities and to adjust to changes in international competition. This capacity will affect the number and nature of jobs to be done, including the level of knowledge and skill that they require and the rate of remuneration. Being a leader in entrepreneurial activity will provide a society with substantial economic rewards; being a laggard will mean a lower growth rate and higher unemployment. The presence or absence of natural resources will not in itself shape a society's destiny to the degree that it has in the past. Rather, the society's technology and human capabilities may be the key determinant in its relative costs and its comparative prosperity.

Bird (1984, p. 23) has warned that for Canada "it is most unlikely that enough new high tech industrial jobs can be created to stem the long-standing relative decline of manufacturing employment," and has suggested that government policy should encourage "the transformation of existing industries" and "the upgrading of the skills and education of the labour force for better jobs — which will not, however, usually be in the manufacturing sector." Benson Wilson has also predicted that "job access for the great majority of people entering the labour market, including university graduates, is going to mean access to relatively conventional jobs with the ability to respond to, utilize, and move with the application of these new technologies as they are applied to these conventional jobs" (Wilson, 1985). Technological change will affect job prospects not so much by creating large numbers of new high-tech firms offering new high-tech jobs, but rather by enabling traditional industries to adopt new production techniques. Technological change will alter the content of many people's jobs, requiring continual re-education and the acquisition of new skills.

Any one particular innovation may hurt specific employees by reducing their relative wages or by eliminating their jobs. For the workers who are hurt, technological change may be undesirable. At best, they may have to move to another corporation; at worst, they may have to retire early or spend a long time searching for work or being involved in retraining; they may even have to sell their home and move to a different city, paying relocation costs and possibly losing equity in their home as well as their company pension rights. If their community is small or offers few other employment opportunities, or if it is particularly hard hit by job losses, then the suffering may be severe and the unemployed may form a noticeable and politically powerful group. Hence, a society experiencing rapid and substantial technological change will inevitably contain workers who are hurt by the loss of their jobs and who may consequently seek government assistance, both to retard change and to help them with relocation, retraining, or early retirement (Green, 1984).

What may be true for a society as a whole — that technological change enhances growth, productivity, income levels and jobs — may not be so for those members of society whose jobs have been adversely affected. This phenomenon — more and better jobs for most, yet fewer and worse jobs for some — may become more common as the pace of technological change quickens. It may give rise to political conflict over the optimal pace of technological change, over specific policies that could stem that change, and over programs for assisting those who are hurt by the change. The proponents of change usually cannot point to specific new jobs that can immediately make up for the lost jobs brought about by change. They may point to expected cost reductions, quality enhancement, or new products, but these improvements cannot easily be quantified and balanced against lost jobs. Often the beneficiaries of change cannot be identified ex ante. This is particularly troublesome when the jobs being lost are obvious and when the employees who face severe adjustment problems plead for government obstacles to change.

In the new international trade relationships discussed above, government policies will have a clear and dramatic impact on specific Canadian jobs. The current and prospective reductions of Canadian tariff barriers in accordance with existing General Agreement on Tariffs and Trade (GATT) arrangements and the negotiations over freer trade with the United States will probably result in job losses and reduced incomes for certain Canadian workers. Benefits from these government policies cannot be guaranteed, nor can they even be predicted precisely. Furthermore, the advantages of reduced import prices will be spread over the entire consuming population and, consequently, will be of rather minor significance for each individual, even though they may be substantial for society as a whole. The losers know who they are and can foresee their losses; the prospective winners do not know the degree of their potential gain. Similarly, the developments abroad — technological leadership in non-North American nations, and competitiveness from newly industrialized countries — are having a strong effect on specific Canadians whose jobs and incomes are being eliminated or cut back. The reduction of import prices often does not create an obvious group of beneficiaries. Consequently, government erection of non-tariff barriers, such as import quotas, government procurement policies that favour Canadians, and special financial assistance to domestic firms, will create social conflict (Quinn and Slayton, 1982). By retarding change, such policies will maintain existing jobs and incomes at the cost of reductions in long-term gains that depend upon that change.

Government programs to assist private corporate R&D expenditures appear not to have become the focus for conflict over the pace of technological change. Government assistance for university research and the current trend toward corporate-university cooperation in research have also not elicited political opposition from interests opposed to change. Nor have recently constructed government facilities that disseminate new production techniques. Yet it is clear that some industrial policies, such as government grants and tax concessions for R&D, will hasten change, leading to job and income losses for some producers as well as gains for entrepreneurs and possibly for all Canadians as consumers. Perhaps the conflict is minimal simply because the losses created by such changes were not clear when these programs were being debated. The employees and firms who will be hurt have not realized the extent of their future losses. Perhaps they have felt that they too could obtain special government assistance if they became victims of such losses.

It is also significant that regional and provincial conflicts have not focussed on such government programs, whose objective is to stimulate technological change. It appears that modern entrepreneurship brings with it special economic advantages of regional agglomeration, in which geographical proximity facilitates the innovation process. Consequently, these government programs will eventually assist certain specific regions and cities — perhaps Ontario more than other provinces, and Metropolitan Toronto more than other cities. The unfortunate regions may simply not yet understand the extent of their probable losses, or perhaps they expect to be compensated for such losses through the federal system of income redistribution.

Most individuals may face entrepreneurial opportunities and have the capability of substantially altering their income. One common example is deciding about a career, which today requires great investment in one's own skills and knowledge as well as the risks involved in one's choice of employer. Today job obsolescence and employer bankruptcy are apt to reduce or even eliminate one's income, while alterations in circumstances can provide new demands for one's talents and, consequently, possibly higher income. The extent to which most citizens have become entrepreneurs and as a consequence face uninsurable risks in their daily economic activities may have implications for the appropriate role that government can play.

In sum, technological change will hurt some jobs and benefit others. Changes in international trade may provide entrepreneurial opportunities, but at the same time may be opposed by the particular firms and employees who will be hurt. These firms and employees may lobby Canadian governments to introduce policies that can protect their interests and that can retard change and reduce concomitant benefits. Meanwhile, government industrial policies that stimulate technological change through grants, tax concessions and public research facilities appear to have not yet elicited a similar opposition from the interests that will be hurt. What is clear is that entrepreneurship and technological change interact with the social and political structure, creating conflict within that structure and, in turn, being affected by government policies that are formulated by that structure. It is to this broad issue that we now turn our attention.

The Social and Political Structure

In capitalist nations, the desire to attain material success and advanced social status has served as a major incentive for entrepreneurial activities; entrepreneurship has been intimately linked with social change. It has been able to alter existing social relationships, and some people have seen it as their best means of advancement. Yet social rigidities and attempts to maintain the status quo can act as strong barriers to entrepreneurship.

Many studies of pre-World War II entrepreneurship have examined particular success stories. They have emphasized the fluidity and openness of social and political structures that permitted the speedy introduction of new techniques, the rapid growth of new corporations, and the swift acquisition of wealth, power and prestige by successful entrepreneurs. In the 19th century, the United States stood out as a nation whose social and political structure permitted economic change to a degree not found in other nations. Many writers have commented positively on the lack of government intervention and the general laissez-faire environment in United States history. Post-World War II studies of entrepreneurship and growth look at the same subject from a more negative perspective, discussing the obstacles to change that a government can establish in its efforts to protect vested interests. Olson, in particular, has investigated this theme, concluding that the governmental protection of vested interests almost inevitably ossifies a society. He identifies the lobbying by special interest groups that leads a government to create barriers to change. In his opinion, a society that does this slows down its own progress. Only a dramatic and pervasive shock, like military loss in a major war, can smash the rigidity of such arrangements and open a society once more to economic change and progress.

Both historical and modern analyses emphasize how dependent entrepreneurship is on the absence of government impediments. These studies conclude that the pace of change is largely determined by the extent of government interference. Criticism of mercantilism, arguments for free trade, and insistence on the rights of individuals vis-à-vis the state have all touched upon the relationships between economic change and the rigidity of the social and political structure. In this sense, the writings of Olson and his followers are not entirely original. What is new and significant is that the latter have concentrated on the process of current government decision making within democracies, making use of the recent literature on public choice. They examine the impact of vested interests on that process and the ability of established groups to maintain their income, wealth and social status by preventing change. Several of Olson's central tenets bear on this issue:

- "On balance, special-interest organizations and collusions reduce efficiency and aggregate income in the societies in which they operate and make political life more divisive."
- "Distributional coalitions slow down a society's capacity to adopt new technologies and to allocate resources in response to changing conditions, and thereby reduce the rate of economic growth."

- "The accumulation of distributional coalitions increases the complexity of regulation, the role of government, and the complexity of understandings, and changes the direction of social evolution" (Olson, 1982, p. 74).

Olson explains the "economic miracles" of nations defeated in World War II, particularly Japan and West Germany. Military defeat shattered the protective privileges that government had established in response to traditional vested interests, and it enabled new groups and individuals to advance unhampered by restrictions. "At least in the first two decades after the war," Olson writes, "the Japanese and West Germans had not developed the degree of regulatory complexity and scale of government that characterized more stable societies" (Ibid., p. 76).

At the other extreme, Olson describes the calcification of relationships and practices in Britain, detailing the way in which it has retarded economic change. He points out that this is the nation with the longest period of time since suffering from any major national disaster such as revolution, invasion, or dictatorship. He links this political stability with the fact that the economic growth of other large democracies has surpassed Britain's. Olson discusses Britain's calcifying special interest groups, particularly the trade unions, professional associations such as lawyers, and producers' organizations such as farmers' groups. "In short, with age, British society has acquired so many strong organizations and collusions that it suffers from an institutional sclerosis that slows its adaptation to changing circumstances and technologies" (Ibid., pp. 77–78).

Olson's argument should be kept in mind when Canada's development prospects are examined. Courchene has drawn attention to the tendency of Canadian governments to create what he has termed "a protected society," and he has warned that "this new wave of government intervention is likely to be particularly inimical to the viability and flexibility of the market economy" (Courchene, 1980, p. 557). It should be emphasized that government policies can act in this manner and, consequently, that the evaluation of policies should devote attention to their long-term retardation of change. Considerable support can be found in this argument for the minimization of government intervention, for sunset laws that require periodic future evaluation of current policies, and for political processes that minimize the political power of special interests. Olson himself has placed great stress on the ability of free trade, together with the free movement of labour, capital and firms, to disrupt established procedures and to break the protective policies created by and for domestic interests. Canadians should give special attention to Olson's advice about the importance of ensuring that international economic relations are free from government intervention and so are able to stimulate innovation and economic change.

A separate literature has argued that entrepreneurship alters social and political relationships, destroying established patterns and replacing them with new arrangements. The editors of *Entrepreneurs in Cultural Context* summarize this argument:

> Cultures are ultimately transformed by the actions and decisions of individuals. Perhaps in no area of social science research is this process more dramatically illustrated than in the study of the entrepreneur. . . . The entrepreneur is also able to work within the cultural system while consciously upsetting its state of equilibrium to his advantage. . . . In many ways then, the entrepreneurs are the movers and shakers of any society (Greenfield, Strickon and Aubey, 1979, p. vii).

Schumpeter was a prominent proponent of this view. He explained the economic development of capitalist societies as a "process of creative destruction" in which the "fundamental impulse that sets and keeps the capitalist engine in motion comes from the new consumers' goods, the new methods of production or transportation, the new markets, the new forms of industrial organization that capitalist enterprise creates." Schumpeter (1962, p. 83) described the "process of industrial mutation. . . that incessantly revolutionizes the industrial structure from within, incessantly destroying the old one, incessantly creating a new one. This process of Creative Destruction is the essential fact about capitalism."

Landes (1969, p. 545) has linked these two perspectives, noting that "economic theory has traditionally been interested in one half of the problem — the determinants of economic change — rather than its non-economic effects; and it has long vitiated that half by holding non-economic variables constant." Landes stresses the fact that economic development is a process that "affects all aspects of social life and is affected in turn by them." Referring to specific economic achievements, he has concluded that these "material advances in turn have provoked and promoted a large complex of economic, social, political, and cultural changes, which have reciprocally influenced the rate and course of technological development" (Ibid., p. 544).

This combination of the two perspectives suggests the self-reinforcing nature of change and the self-reinforcing nature of ossification. Rapid entrepreneurial advances alter relationships, thereby preventing the codification and regulation of conduct that could hinder future advances. But a society that falters in its economic development will automatically lose the fluidity of structure upon which a revival of development depends. The second perspective, which sees social and political structures as being changed by entrepreneurial advances in a cumulative process, strengthens Olson's warning that governmental protection of vested interests can lead a nation into decline.

The careers of individual entrepreneurs add another dimension to the relationships between social structure and entrepreneurship. A disproportionate number of entrepreneurs have come from minority groups who are outside the mainstream of society. Wilken (1979, p. 11) refers to many authors who have concluded "that entrepreneurship very often is promoted by social marginality. . . . Individuals or groups on the perimeter of a given social system or between two social systems are believed to provide the personnel to fill entrepreneurial roles. They may be drawn from religious, cultural, ethnic, or migrant minority groups, and their marginal social position is generally believed to have psychological effects which make entrepreneurship a particularly attractive alternative for them." Hagen has carried this an additional step by focussing not simply on minorities but on minorities who have suffered "withdrawal of status respect." He looks at various situations that lead to such "withdrawal of status respect" and, in particular, has noted the importance of self-selection immigration and non-acceptance in a new society.

Immigration entails self-selection in that immigrants generally are aggressive and optimistic risk takers. Furthermore, they may find that avenues to success in their new country are blocked: they are not part of the established culture and their professional qualifications may not be honoured. Their only available route for advancement may be to go into business. Exposure to different production methods in their homeland may spur certain immigrants to take risks and pursue an entrepreneurial career (Hagen, 1962, p. 190).

Wilken has noted the importance of cohesion within the immigrant community and "the presence of positive attitudes toward entrepreneurship within the group . . . a high degree of group solidarity or cohesion . . . is necessary to counteract whatever opposition may be forthcoming from mainstream groups within the larger social situation" (Wilken, 1979, p. 12).

Of course, a society does have the ability to modify its entrepreneurial climate. Many modifications involve trade-offs with other social objectives, and these trade-offs will be examined in a later section. Although much of the modification occurs as a result of government intervention, some comes about through changes in social values. If citizens are concerned about their prospects for economic development, then they should be aware of how their country's social and political structure affects the entrepreneurial climate on which those prospects depend. There is an essential relationship between the extent of fluidity, openness and adaptability in a society and the degree of entrepreneurship that is found there.

Some commentators have suggested that the individual decision making upon which Western progress was based has been supplemented by group decision making within the private corporation that is contemplating innovation. Within each firm, creative and conscientious initiative has become necessary at many different stages of the production process. Entrepreneurial characteristics must be cultivated throughout economic organizations. Some authors argue that this requires a radically new approach to management-labour relations and group versus individual success criteria within each firm. For corporate employees to work together in joint problem solving will require new decision-making procedures and structures, as well as new social attitudes toward consensus building. Reich, whose views have been shaped by Japan's experience, is a proponent of this theory:

> The success of modern Japan, in particular, seems to contradict Max Weber, the German sociologist, who attributed the West's economic progress to the demise of traditional relations like guilds, parishes, and clans and to the simultaneous rise of individualism. Japan's emphasis on community, consensus, and long-term security for its workers — based squarely on traditional communal relationships — appears to have spurred its citizens to greater feats of production than has the rugged individualism of modern America. . . (Reich, 1983, p. 16).
>
> A social organization premised on equity, security, and participation will generate greater productivity than one premised on greed and fear. Collaboration and collective adaptation are coming to be more important to an industrialized nation's well-being than are personal daring and ambition (Reich, 1983, p. 20).

Reich places great emphasis on what he terms "flexible-system production." The era of standardized mass production is disappearing in the Western world, largely because the newly industrialized countries are able to manufacture at much lower costs. In its place has come a demand for commodities that are unique or that have small production runs. In Reich's opinion, such commodities require innovation as well as special skills. All workers must be involved in the development of the product. The traditional corporate command structure cannot respond quickly or appropriately enough to the customers' specialized needs. New patterns of corporate organization are necessary, Reich argues — patterns that foster entrepreneurial attitudes among all workers.

In his book, *How American Business Can Meet the Japanese Challenge*, Ouchi (1981, p. 50) has gone so far as to claim that in Japan "nothing of consequence occurs as a result of individual effort." Similarly, Athos and Pascale state in their book, *The Art of Japanese Management: Application for American Executives*, that "for the Japanese, independence in an organizational context has negative connotations; it implies disregard for others and self-centredness. . . . The work group is the basic building block of Japanese organizations. Owing to the central importance of group efforts in their thinking the Japanese are extremely sensitive to and concerned about group interactions and relationships" (Athos and Pascale, 1981, p. 125). The participative approach to decision making requires the exploration of alternative solutions by managers and production workers until a consensus is reached. This process minimizes the role of middle management by bringing senior management into direct contact with the workers.

Currently, many Western corporations are attempting to introduce some elements of the Japanese approach and to imbue production workers with more feeling for their company's objectives and success. The concept of "quality circles," for example, requires groups of employees to develop new techniques to improve the quality of the product they are manufacturing. The expansion of profit sharing is based on a hope that production workers will be more conscientious and creative so that their firm will benefit.

Some authors, like Reich, believe that a basic change in social attitudes and in government intervention will be necessary to attain Japan's pervasive entrepreneurial initiative. Rugged individualism must be replaced with group decision making and consensus; laissez-faire capitalism must be replaced with a much greater commitment to education, retraining and adjustment assistance.

Yet such opinions are not universally accepted. Many observers focus on the achievements of individual entrepreneurs, even within Japan; others note that the Japanese have had more success in imitating the innovations of other nations than in innovating themselves.

Urban and Regional Concentration

Urban and regional studies have emphasized "agglomeration economies," which are the special benefits that accrue to individuals and firms simply because of an increase in the size of the community within which they live and work. A wide variety of goods and services provides the consumer with more choice and the prices of some things may be reduced. This may be true of government goods and services as well as those privately produced. Individuals know that if they lose their jobs, they have a better chance of finding new jobs, and they have more opportunities to move upwards by changing their jobs. Firms may save on transportation and communication costs by locating in a densely populated region. Inventories can be smaller; production schedules may well be smoother. Firms have access to a larger work force with a wider variety of skills. Advertising may be more effective, and firms may operate on a larger scale with lower unit costs.

Quite apart from such traditional urban and regional economies, there are particular reasons why entrepreneurial activities will be more geographically concentrated. To the extent that innovation is an inter-firm process with one company's entrepreneurial activity being linked with that of others, it may be essential for some firms to locate near one another. To the extent that innovation depends upon university research facilities, firms will locate near the leading universities and, consequently, near each other. To the extent that innovation requires highly sophisticated and specialized scientific skill, it may be necessary for an entrepreneurial firm to locate near similar firms, from which it may entice employees.

Earlier, we examined the relationships between entrepreneurship and the social and political structure. A federal nation may contain cities and regions with widely varying social and political regimes and entrepreneurial activity may find a more welcome environment in some locations than in others. One criticism of Olson's writings, for example, is that he treats nations as homogeneous units. For a federal nation like Canada, Olson's argument should be modified so that differences in the entrepreneurial environment among provinces, regions and cities are made clear. These differences in entrepreneurial environment cumulate on top of the reasons cited above for regional concentration, particularly since entrepreneurial success will, of itself, alter the social and political structure in ways favourable to further entrepreneurship.

A survey of 250 high technology firms in California's Silicon Valley sought to determine where and how new companies were started, who started them and why. Of the firms examined, 85.5 percent were begun by former employees of existing firms. Researchers concluded that "A tremendous amount of work is involved in starting up a new business. New employees must be recruited, facilities and supplies must be lined up. Founders of new enterprises are less likely to find these in unfamiliar areas than in locations where their own companies were" (Shapiro, 1983, p. 60).

The significance of these tendencies can be seen in the postwar growth of microelectronic firms, which have concentrated in a few urban regions — highway 128 in Boston, the Silicon Valley near Stanford, and, in Canada, the Ottawa valley and Metropolitan Toronto. To the extent that the ready availability of natural resources loses its importance as the determinant of investment location, and to the extent that urban and regional concentration is intensified by the special agglomeration economies of entrepreneurial activities, we may expect an increase in disparities based on city, region and province in Canada. In the process of entrepreneurial adjustment, we may expect some cities to forge ahead quickly while other cities and regions will suffer as their growth prospects diminish. It is therefore likely that social and political conflict over the optimal pace of adjustment and over the appropriate role of government will increasingly follow regional and provincial lines.

The Role of Government

Stimulating Perception and Creativity in an International Context

Historians usually examine entrepreneurs and their innovations from an international perspective, describing each individual's accomplishments in the context of world progress. Much current discussion of entrepreneurship and innovation similarly ignores a society's boundaries. This can be an error when evaluating public policy issues, such as the appropriateness of using government funds to stimulate entrepreneurship. Should a government assist creativity and originality or should it assist in the diffusion of innovations developed in other nations? Daly and Globerman (1976) have examined the Canadian self-interest by scrutinizing "existing and proposed policies." They believe that at present "Particular encouragement is given to the indigenous development of new technology of a 'break-through' nature, rather than to the rapid diffusion of existing new products and techniques that could have a quicker and more predictable impact on output and performance." The Canadian government seeks to encourage "significant technical advances," while "Much of the recently emerging evidence belies this notion and suggests that achieving increased efficiency and greater international competitiveness in Canadian industry requires that higher priority be given to encouraging more rapid *diffusion* of new technology" (Daly and Globerman, 1976, p. 7).

A small country will capture a relatively small proportion of the gains from an original innovation since many of the firms that can exploit it operate in other jurisdictions. For a small country, the current state of international patent protection — which may offer inadequate legal power to capture all these foreign benefits — is an additional incentive for governments and private interests to invest in diffusion. This situation demonstrates a weakness in the common reference to research and development. Basic research, even when it leads to specific innovations, may yield gains that cannot easily be captured by the innovating firm or by others within the country of origin. Development funds that enable an innovating firm to adopt and adapt practices that have already been discovered may provide benefits, of which a much higher proportion can be captured by that firm or by others within the same country. In public policy discussions, then, it may be useful to draw a distinction between programs that assist truly original innovation and programs that assist the diffusion of new technologies.

In the first section, it was suggested that private interests may rationally reject certain types of research and development because they correctly recognize their inability to capture an adequate portion of the favourable results. To the extent that such private rejection is based upon the probable capture of favourable results by other firms in the same nation, a government may intervene to stimulate research and development, knowing that its citizens, as a group, will capture and benefit from all the favourable results. Government provision of public funds to cover part of the costs of innovation may be the only means whereby a society can achieve an advance that is financially worthwhile for that society as a whole. A really difficult element enters when one attempts to calculate the degree to which the favourable results will be captured by other nations rather than by one's fellow citizens. How can one predict the ability of other nations to copy the advance, the price at which they will market the products that result from it, and the timescale of such responses? These are particularly serious questions in a world where industry is being rapidly restructured and where trade relationships are changing. International agreements to protect patents could be important, but many nations refuse to sign such agreements and their enforceability is severely limited. The recent case in which IBM claimed that certain Japanese had illegally obtained scientific secrets presents an interesting example of these difficulties (Eells and Nehemkis, 1984, p. 46).

In theory, one might hope for international funding to stimulate innovations from which all nations may benefit. A small step has been taken with international cooperation in space research, and discussions about nuclear fusion research have dealt seriously with the possibility of joint funding. But so far governments have been reluctant to share the costs of innovation.

International agreements to protect patents, together with international flows of trade and investment, tend to counteract these free rider problems. A substantial literature has examined "technology transfer" within the private sector, and particularly within multinational corporations. Hymer (1976, p. 25) has shown how foreign direct investment is used "to appropriate fully the returns on certain skills and abilities." Noting that a firm can sell or rent its special expertise, Hymer suggests that "which method it chooses depends largely on the degree of imperfection in the market for the skill. If the market is imperfect, the owner may not be able to appropriate fully the returns to the ability unless he controls its use" (Hymer, 1976, p. 26).

In a review of "Harry Johnson's Contributions to International Trade Theory," Corden (1984, p. 581) has stated that "the much-cited 'International Corporations' paper is built around the idea that the primary function of the multinational enterprise is the generation and international transfer of productive knowledge. . . ." However, Corden quotes Johnson's warning that "it does not necessarily follow that recompense through monopoly profits on the use of knowledge is the ideal arrangement for the host country" (Corden, 1984, p. 581). In his recent article on international trade, foreign investment, and the formation of the entrepreneurial class, Grossman (1984, pp. 605–14), has examined, by means of a theoretical model, how both trade and investment can have negative long-term effects on the development prospects of certain societies. In Canada, there has been considerable debate about the disadvantages of relying on foreign direct investment as the vehicle for technology transfer. Many Canadians consider the entrepreneurial achievements of domestically located, foreign-owned companies to be different from the technological advances of Canadian-owned firms. Because of these differences, it is argued that Canada will receive greater economic benefits from the latter than it will from the former. Canadians who share this view advocate public policies to stimulate the entrepreneurship of Canadian-owned firms, rather than foreign multinationals (Britton and Gilmour, 1978).

Economists have no definitive answers to these questions, and one can expect that debate over the optimal mechanism for international technology transfer will continue to remain near the centre of public policy controversy. What is left is the practical need to examine proposals for stimulating entrepreneurship in the context of national boundaries, trade competition and "free rider" problems. In many instances, this narrower perspective may lead to public policies that help firms to adapt foreign innovations rather than policies directed at more original, creative objectives — that is, policies aimed at development and diffusion rather than at research.

International trade patterns, and the trade agreements on which they are based, inevitably are affected by entrepreneurial activities since they bring down costs and provide new and better consumer products. A nation's entrepreneurial success may create advantages for its trading partners by reducing the price they pay for their imports. Yet disadvantages may accrue as well, since competitors may have to make adjustments or fall by the wayside. The losses and adjustment difficulties in the non-innovating society lead to even more frustration if the foreign innovation has been helped by a foreign government's financial assistance. With government programs to stimulate entrepreneurship, the total production costs of economic activities diverge from the individual firm's costs. In such cases, export prices may be much less than total costs would be if public funds were included as part of the real production costs. Consequently, the trading partner whose businesses are being compelled to adjust may justifiably regard the entrepreneurial achievements as unfair competition. A government's programs to stimulate entrepreneurship may prompt foreign governments to respond as their domestic producers realize how they are being hurt. Governments must take into consideration the foreign retaliation that may ensue before they undertake such programs.

Sharing Uncertainty and Risk

A distinction is sometimes drawn between government aid that is directed to those people who happen to have low incomes and to those corporations that require "bail-outs" to survive, and government aid that represents an ex ante social sharing of entrepreneurial risk. The former may result in some reduction of entrepreneurship, while the latter may actually stimulate entrepreneurship. On the one hand, rational analysis of risk-return outcomes, and the incentives promised by successful innovations, will be different if decision makers know that they may receive government aid regardless of their success or failure. A substantial and pertinent body of economic literature has examined this problem, referred to as "moral hazard" (Shavell, 1979, pp. 541–62). Furthermore, entrepreneurial efforts may be sidetracked to try to maximize the aid that can be obtained through government lobbying and public appeals. The economic literature known as "public choice" has dealt with this danger, inherent in government programs that offer financial assistance to particular individuals, groups or businesses (Trebilcock et al., 1982). On the other hand, a society may recognize that some of its members could be hurt by economic change occasioned by circumstances beyond their control; and the government may develop programs that form both a safety net to limit the extent of such individual losses and also an adjustment process to assist individuals and firms who wish to move away from obsolete economic activities. Canada's recent Industry and Labour Adjustment Program (ILAP) grants illustrate this, since they fund equipment for new production processes and retraining for workers within firms that have been severely hurt by recent competition attributable to changes in international trade relationships. But the distinction is not always clear-cut; observers may disagree about whether a particular program is of the former type or of the latter. Let us examine this issue in more detail.

Reference was made in the first section to the fact that nearly everyone in a changing society must make judgments in the face of uninsurable risks. Personal decisions concerning education, career, employer and private investments all involve such risks. Since modern life has automatically subjected everyone to important risk bearing, an argument is sometimes made for a new kind of government intervention that pools specific risks and rewards so that individuals are less exposed to economic misfortune. That is, government may be able to insure against risks in a situation where citizens want such insurance and where no institution other than government can provide it. The enormity of the risk sharing may be so great and its nature so complex that private institutions may not be able to administer it effectively. Present-day economic activities now involve such new and severe risks for all citizens that the optimal social contract may entail a sharing of many of these risks, as well as a sharing of the concomitant rewards and losses. Arguments for such risk sharing may recommend provision of public funds for many specific purposes: the personal acquisition of knowledge and skills; employment relocation costs, retraining, and the sale of homes; or guarantees of certain investments, such as deposits in financial institutions.

Of particular importance is the view which sees the development of human capital as the result of individual entrepreneurial decisions and which sees risk sharing as an appropriate insurance purpose of government policies. This view has received special attention in a recent article on "Market Adjustment and Government Policy." The three authors suggest that a "well-known failure in the market for human capital stems from the inability of workers to diversify their portfolios across alternative skills or professions. As a result, workers are said to be too risk averse from society's perspective. Numerous schemes have been proposed to offset this risk aversion, including the financing of job retraining and other subsidies to promote human capital formation" (Harris, Lewis and Purvis, 1984, p. 112). In a "Comment" on the paper, Proulx has discussed a number of specific Canadian government programs that act in this way (Proulx, 1984, pp. 124–30).

Some observers have applied a similar argument to the Canadian government programs that provide loans to corporations and guarantees for loans that corporations have borrowed privately. The Economic Council of Canada (1982, 1983) has analyzed these activities in several of its recent publications. One rationale for a public sharing of uninsurable risk of capital loss is illustrated by the following example, taken from one of these publications:

> Suppose that there were 100 R&D projects that could be undertaken in totally unrelated fields, each costing $1 million and each with a 50 percent chance of success. Suppose further that for each successful project, the revenue would be $4 million, thus generating a profit of $3 million; for each unsuccessful project, the $1 million would be lost. If all the projects were undertaken, one would expect about 50 of them to succeed, generating a total profit of $150 million (50 x $3 million). When the $50 million spent on the 50 projects that are expected to fail is subtracted from that amount, there is a net profit of $100 million for all the projects combined. Yet it is quite conceivable that a firm would hesitate to invest $1 million if the 50 percent chance of a $3 million profit were offset by an equivalent chance of losing its investment. If such risk aversion were widespread, most of the 100 projects could remain untackled, and most of the $100 million gain could remain unrealized. This example illustrates all at once that risk-spreading can be a reason for government to assist the R&D process and that it need not be a reason if firms are not especially reluctant to face risks or if the odds are not good enough, even from society's point of view (Economic Council of Canada, 1983, p. 32).

The application of the government risk-sharing argument to corporations seems to involve the concept of an acceptable size of downside risk based on the size of the decision-making entity. In the above example, a large enough corporation would conduct all the projects, but a corporation of adequate size may simply not exist. This type of market failure, based on the inability of the private market to create a sufficiently large corporation to conduct the necessary number of high-risk projects, may vary in significance over time and among countries. For example, it may be that the United States has venture capital investment firms of greater number and size than does Canada. So this government risk-sharing argument may be appropriate in Canada but not in its larger neighbour.

Other aspects of government risk sharing also deserve mention. In a modern democracy, some special interest groups will actively try to retard those aspects of economic growth that will inflict hardship on them. Special payments may be a necessary compensation in a democracy to purchase the acquiescence of those who will be hurt by economic growth. In this sense, a social consensus may involve an acceptance by society of change and growth because a safety net exists for those who will be hurt. The safety net of government assistance programs may be seen as a sharing of the risks of economic change. In this view, such programs may enable more rapid economic change than could otherwise occur. Public pensions, for example, could be seen as the only politically acceptable way of forcing older workers to retire, thereby giving way to younger workers who may be more capable of implementing new production methods.

A substantial theoretical literature assesses the effects on society's well-being of changes that improve the welfare of some while reducing the welfare of others, and (Asimakopulos, 1978, pp. 418–40) the concept of compensation payments is a central element. Government may be the most appropriate mechanism to make such payments. In any case, the literature dealing with compensation criteria forms a useful framework for evaluating certain government programs of financial redistribution. From this perspective, one may appreciate that these programs facilitate entrepreneurship and innovation by compensating those who are harmed and by thus reducing their potential opposition. Much government planning and regulation seeks to reduce risk, not in the manner described above — through the social acceptance of risk as a form of insurance — but rather by eliminating spontaneous or unanticipated change. This general desire for planning can lead to greater certainty, but, at the same time, can reduce the opportunity for entrepreneurial initiative. Some regulations can be seen as a form of government planning, by which the scope for private decisions is sharply restricted, often to the advantage of vested interests. Other regulations seek to enforce social accountability and social obligations on private firms. Acceptable behaviour is described by government and required by government. The post-World War II expansion of planning and regulation has no doubt diminished entrepreneurial activity below the level it would otherwise have attained. In demanding government intervention, citizens should be aware of these long-term costs of forgone innovations, which exist apart from the current increases in production costs. The view is often expressed that "a more permissive public policy and attitude — that is, a reduced regulatory environment — would foster both organizational and technological innovation" (Ronen, 1982, p. 3). In its paper on reforming regulation, the Economic Council of Canada concluded, "Our research suggests that Canada's comprehensive system of direct economic controls has resulted in a substantial waste of economic resources and reduced the degree of dynamism and innovation in several important sectors of the Canadian economy" (Economic Council of Canada, 1981, p. 136). The long-term implications of many kinds of planning and regulation are relatively uncertain. Society should be prepared to recognize the experimental nature of these regulations and should try to modify those government interventions which are later seen to have had deleterious effects; society should know, too, that reduction of uncertainty and risk through planning and regulation may have particularly serious effects in reducing entrepreneurship and innovation.

Assessing Government Employees as Entrepreneurs

Governments have often chosen to own and operate economic activities. A central message of this paper is that, as in the past, so in the foreseeable future, all economic activities will be buffeted by change. Ours is an era of rapid change and adjustment. Established practices and procedures will inevitably be replaced by new methodologies and new products, frequently because of competition from foreign enterprises, but often simply because of the overwhelming pace of technological advances. Entrepreneurial adjustment will be essential for all economic activities, including those owned and operated by governments.

Quite apart from the need for entrepreneurship within its own economic activities, is the need for entrepreneurship in its decisions that affect the private sector. When a government decides to give grants or loans to individuals or firms in the private sector, then the public service becomes a part of the entrepreneurial process: the public service must possess enough perception and creativity to recognize and support perception and creativity; it must evaluate risk-return outcomes and decide which possibilities it will support. Deciding which funding requests should be accepted and which should be rejected are entrepreneurial decisions. Government employees may even attempt to negotiate changes in the applications for funding. To the degree that government employees lack entrepreneurial characteristics, a society may wish to avoid these kinds of government intervention, and it may wish to adopt practices that are aimed specifically at stimulating entrepreneurship within the public sector.

The historical, classical analyses of entrepreneurship are helpful in investigating this issue. Examples of successful entrepreneurs and bureaucrats are believed by some to be at opposite ends of any spectrum of entrepreneurial behaviour. The creativity and spontaneity, the individual initiative and personal risk taking of the entrepreneur contrast sharply with the obedience to bureaucratic rules, concern for proper process, and reference to chains of authority that mark the government employee. Individuals who seek the financial rewards that accompany successful risk taking and originality probably will not apply for public service positions, while those citizens who fear risk taking and appreciate an occupation that has clear guidelines, may be more inclined to apply for government positions. In describing entrepreneurs, Ronen states simply, "Rarely does this individual reside in the large, bureaucratic organization. . . . The entrepreneur and the small firm seek each other out. The managerial-type individuals, preferring the executive suites of large organizations, hardly encourage alert entrepreneurs to cast permanent anchor anywhere near them" (Ronen, 1982, pp. x and 5). As was indicated earlier, marginal individuals who have been raised outside the established social order — for example, members of minority groups and immigrants — may see private entrepreneurship as their only route to wealth and prestige. Such backgrounds and personalities may not be accepted readily into the elite ranks of civil service leadership.

Bureaucracies are endemically resistant to change. Thompson has emphasized that "in the case of the bureaucratic organization, however, there is special need for caution with regard to change" (Thompson, 1965, p. 19). Specialization is part of the bureaucratic structure, and those who have become proficient at one particular activity have a strong vested interest in opposing change. Furthermore, the employees become "specialized in working with one another. . . . Consequently, any suggestion for change must be measured against its effect on the cooperative system as a whole. Bureaucratic organizations must plan and control change" (Thompson, 1965, p. 19). Perception and creativity are not encouraged — and may even be discouraged. Elsewhere, Thompson carries this view further: "Many studies attest to the fact that groups, over a period of time, exert powerful conformist pressures on their members. . . . Consequently, there is nothing about groups as such that can be guaranteed to increase individual creativity; they could, in fact, have just the opposite effect" (Thompson, 1969, p. 14).

Thompson's basic theme is that "the literature on problem-solving suggests that for some kinds of tasks, groups are more effective than individuals, while for other tasks the reverse is true" (Thompson, 1969, p. 11). This theme is pursued by Arrow in an article on innovation in large and small firms. Arrow bases his analysis on the belief that "entrepreneurial activity, however defined, operates in different ways in large firms than in small ones" (Arrow, 1983, p. 16). Decisions about capital allocation differ because they are based on different decision-making procedures; the internal accounting prices of large firms may not reflect relative costs; and information may not be conveyed as readily within large firms as it is through changes in market prices. In some ways, large firms are in the same position as government bureaucracies in fostering entrepreneurship, but in several very important respects government bureaucracies face much greater barriers. The large firm does respond to market prices; it pursues profit as a clear success criterion, and it is shaped by and interacts with its competitors. By contrast, government bureaucracies may not respond to market prices, they may not pursue profit as a criterion of success, and they may lack competitors. Let us consider how these combine to determine the pace of investment and disinvestment; then let us examine prices, profit and competition separately.

Stories are recounted of entrepreneurs selling their prized personal possessions to gain the final small funding necessary to attain success. Certainly, many entrepreneurs sign personal guarantees by which their personal wealth is loaned to the capital funds of their companies. In undertaking new and original activities, such individuals recognize the importance of being persistent and the likelihood of initial losses before ultimate victory. It is easy to look toward government support as simply an extension of this type of persistence. Public funds can enable an enterprise to continue beyond the point at which private owners would have to capitulate. Occasionally, such persistence leads to an otherwise unattainable achievement.

Government financial support for entrepreneurial activity can alter the natural pace of expansion as well as the natural disinvestment process. Initial smallness and growth based on success in the marketplace, minimize the probability of large-scale losses when new projects fail. Many entrepreneurial activities will fail regardless of the amount of capital that is poured into them. Knowing this, the private sector will demand results before providing additional funding. Governments seem much more reluctant to cut their losses and end attempts to innovate. Consequently, the persistence that governments alone can support will often be an unwise extension that simply loses more capital than is necessary. This danger of government participation in the entrepreneurial process deserves special mention, together with the need for governments to formulate better rules governing the pace of expansion and the timing of disinvestment, as well as the desirability of better public awareness of the inevitability of failures and losses in entrepreneurial activities.

The earlier discussion of entrepreneurship may lead one to doubt the ability of a government administration to attract potential entrepreneurs, and thereby may lead one to argue for a minimization of government ownership, operation and control of particular firms. Apart from this issue, the earlier discussion may also cast some light on how best to foster entrepreneurship in those areas that a society chooses to leave in the hands of government. Particularly relevant, perhaps, are the comments on prices, profit and competition.

In order to reach an entrepreneurial decision that involves new production methods, the decision maker must be able to measure, compile and compare the many changing aspects of these methods in some common scale, so as to ascertain whether the new combination of costs and outputs will be more or less favourable than those yielded by the existing production methods. The price structure is absolutely decisive; it is through price comparisons and combinations that the decision maker can anticipate probable results. The price structure sets the guidelines for entrepreneurial decisions. Simple repetition of traditional production processes need not rely on these guidelines nearly as much as do the deliberations over the advisability of adopting particular innovations.

In the past, non-communist governments have probably not paid sufficient attention to the implications of the price structure for entrepreneurial activity. To some degree, this need has not been as pressing as it is today, because decision makers within non-communist governments have been able to refer to free market prices as the basis for their calculations. Now, however, governments themselves are playing a major role in determining the price structure, with the result that prices may be influenced significantly by administrators, rather than by market forces of relative scarcity and demand. Observers who have examined economic practices in communist nations have devoted considerable attention to the implications of government price intervention for entrepreneurial decisions. The concerns about communist price-setting expressed in that literature have a growing relevance for non-communist nations, since the latter have extended their governments' influences over prices.

An example of such concerns is the literature dealing with a firm's decision to alter a product's quality, and increase profits, when confronting prices set by government rather than by the marketplace. Competition among firms may take the form of quality competition rather than price competition. Faced with such a possibility, a government may be tempted to establish quality standards as well as to set prices. "For central planners to respond to quality debasement by lowering the market price is not a reasonable solution if central planners desire production of a better quality product" (Conklin, 1970, p. 143). The possibility of altering quality severely complicates government price-setting. In a market where prices are set by government, the quality issue is intimately linked with possibilities for innovation. "Central planners may find it particularly difficult to obtain detailed information concerning the cost and quality changes that potential innovations would entail if implemented; and so the implications of time lags in the price adjustment process are especially important in the realm of technological change" (Conklin, 1970, p. 119). Decisions to innovate will be affected by the existing price structure, and the resulting pattern of innovations may not be the most socially desirable. Central planners may not be able to respond as quickly or as well as could the continual process of price adjustments in a free market. A recent body of literature within Western economics has begun to address these issues. General programs of wage and price controls, implemented to restrain inflation, have been reviewed from this perspective. Studies have also been made of specific programs that deal with individual economic activities, where a government has decided to interfere with market price-setting (Walker, 1976; Levin, 1981, pp. 1–26; Viton, 1981, pp. 362–79; Heinkel, 1981, pp. 625–36).

A major concern is that price relationships determined by government that may have once been appropriate may no longer be so, and may be sending the wrong signals to agents in both the government and the private sectors. The need to change such government regulations as circumstances change is illustrated by the following quotation from the Economic Council of Canada's report *Reforming Regulation:*

> Eventually, however, many regulations tend to outlive their usefulness. The conditions that led to their introduction may no longer exist or, even if they do, there may be new and more pressing demands for the employment of the economy's scarce resources. Technological change has substantially altered the structural and competitive conditions in some industries; overall growth and change within the economy have, furthermore, altered the income position of various groups in society. Government regulatory policies, especially those that seem to inhibit the natural dynamics of markets, have very different consequences and meaning in the halting economic environment of the 1980s than they had in the high-growth climate of the 1950s and 1960s.
>
> The question that then arises is: how can we offset the tendency in the policy-making process to adopt new regulations uncritically and to maintain existing ones long after they have outlived their usefulness? (Economic Council of Canada, 1981, p. 5).

Entrepreneurial decisions within government activities can be sensitive to profit both as a success criterion and as a personal financial incentive. Once again, reference to the experiences of communist nations is useful. Decision makers must be given some success criterion, and communist countries have experimented with a wide variety of yardsticks, including minimization of average production costs, maximization of output denominated in some physical attribute such as weight or number of units, and several aspects of profit: profit per unit of capital, profit per unit of labour, and the ratio of profits to total production costs. A substantial literature has developed on the distortions fostered by such criteria; this literature may now be relevant in non-communist nations that have extensive government enterprises (Wood, 1958, pp. 566–89; Domar, 1966, pp. 734–57; and Conklin, 1969, pp. 452–55). Communist nations have learned that even within government-owned enterprises, people do respond to personal financial incentives to a degree that cannot be achieved solely on the basis of exhortation or appeals to comradeship and patriotism. Bergson has drawn together a variety of data that reveal that even the U.S.S.R. has continued to rely upon substantial income differentials (Bergson, 1984, pp. 1052–99).

Entrepreneurship and competition are regarded as being intimately linked, with the latter acting as a constant stimulus to the technological advance of all participants. This literature indicates the importance of creating government structures within which separate units can compete. This competition should enable the more successful units to expand and to receive financial rewards as well as social recognition. At the same time, the competition among public institutions should compel the contraction, or at least prevent the expansion, of those units that are less successful. The array of possible competitive modes deserves more detailed analysis and experimentation so that entrepreneurship can be fostered within government.

Rivlin (1970, p. 120) has emphasized the need to learn more about different ways of providing government services. She has analyzed "three strategies for finding more effective methods of producing education, health, and other social services: (1) analysis of the 'natural experiment,' (2) random innovation, and (3) systematic experimentation. The major conclusion was that all three strategies should be pursued with increased energy and greater methodological sophistication." Rivlin has recommended that governments should actively experiment with new, alternative approaches as a permanent entrepreneurial search for improved programs and procedures. The present paper suggests the value of conducting this search within a competitive environment. It is through competition that firms that deliver goods and services will display their most creative and diligent efforts, and it is through competitive comparisons that choices among alternative modes can best be made. In this regard, special mention should be made of an advantage that may accrue to nations with federal political structures. Within broad nationally established objectives, it may be possible for the subnational governments to pursue different methods for delivering goods and services. A federal state may thereby provide a natural laboratory for the kinds of experimentation advocated by Rivlin.

Many government programs have been designed specifically to foster productivity improvements in particular sectors of the economy. For example, Ontario's recently established six high technology centres seek to encourage the adoption by private corporations of innovations in the production of automobiles and farm machinery, and in the use of robotics, microelectronics, and computer-assisted design, computer-assisted manufacturing (CAD-CAM). Other programs have been designed to improve productivity throughout the economy. Assistance for investment, such as accelerated depreciation, is seen as one means of increasing the use of the newest machinery and equipment, which will, it is hoped, make use of the latest and most efficient technology. Special tax concessions for research and development are regarded as one means of advancing the frontier of that technology. As Denny and Fuss (1982, p. x) have emphasized, it is not possible to predict accurately what the actual impact will be of changes that, in theory, promise improved productivity. In referring to "a menu of possible policies," they warn that "With our current knowledge, we cannot be certain of the size of net benefits of any policy to enhance productivity growth. Any steps taken to improve our productivity performance should be monitored carefully to ensure that the net benefits are positive." No doubt this is true for all the government programs and policies discussed above. This paper suggests that experimentation and evaluation should be pursued, as much as possible, within a price structure, where prices do reflect relative scarcities and production costs; within a framework of clear success criteria, including profits based on those prices; and within an environment of competition, where successful units will expand while unsuccessful units will contract.

Dealing with Third-Party Effects: Social Rate of Return Versus Private Rate of Return

Quite apart from the risk-bearing argument for government capital assistance are possible shortfalls of the private rate of return realized by innovation from the social rate of return it generates. Such shortfalls may arise, for example, from the ease with which knowledge is diffused beyond the firm that is undertaking an innovation, and the difficulty that the firm in question has in capturing any payments for the returns that such knowledge generates for others. The Economic Council of Canada (1983, p. 28) has argued that:

> Estimates of the social and private rates of return for 17 product and process innovations introduced by U.S. firms of different sizes in several manufacturing industries from the early 1950s to the early 1970s show that the average social rate for these innovations was 56 percent. The private rates were much lower, the average being 25 percent before taxes.

Government intervention to assist R&D is often justified on the basis of such calculations. Over the past few decades, some economists have devoted considerable attention to determining which benefits and costs outside the individual or firm should be included in ascertaining the true social effect of private decisions by these individuals or firms. Furthermore, they have developed an extensive literature on the technical calculations one may use in this type of analysis. It should be pointed out that disagreements do still exist as to the most appropriate methodology (Misham, 1976). Consequently, one cannot accept the precision of such calculations as those of the Economic Council of Canada, quoted above. It is also important to note that these difficulties of calculating third-party effects are relevant for much of the discussion throughout this paper. In the preceding section, Rivlin was quoted as emphasizing the importance of experimentation in the provision of government services. In the present context, we can stress the practical difficulties of evaluating the results of such experimentation because of the near impossibility of calculating third-party effects. In fact, theoretical disagreements can arise about whether particular third-party effects should even be included in a government's calculations (Gunderson, Halpern, and Quinn, forthcoming).

Certain activities have a set of third-party effects that warrant special mention. Sometimes, once an innovation has been made by one individual or firm, the use of that innovation by others involves no additional cost. Difficulties of excluding others from its use may mean that benefits from the innovation accrue to society in general. In the first section, authors were quoted who emphasized this "public good" nature of knowledge and the research and development that can produce knowledge. It is to this subject that we now turn.

In our modern age, knowledge and skills are regarded by many as new types of social overhead capital, essential for society's progress and yet not adequately developed if they are left entirely to private concerns. Consequently, many see the government's participation as decisive. Knowledge and skills form the framework for today's entrepreneurial activities. Reich has termed our age "the era of human capital." He emphasizes the need for government adjustment assistance to enable those workers displaced by economic change to develop new skills for new jobs. The above discussion of public risk sharing suggests that individual investment in one's education and skills entails a large risk of obsolescence, and that this alone could justify public funding as the only means for insuring the otherwise uninsurable risks involved. Third-party effects of educational and research facilities provide a strong additional argument for public funding.

Public research facilities deserve special mention, as a modern form of social overhead capital, necessary for today's entrepreneurship. A precursor of this was the creation of agricultural research institutes and the development of linkages between university agricultural science departments and the implementation of new farming techniques, together with the use of new seeds and new fertilizers. This agricultural revolution, with its pervasive entrepreneurial innovation, depended very much on public research facilities. Individual farmers and the corporations supplying those farmers were able to experiment with new production methods based on the research conducted in the publicly funded institutions. Left to themselves, farmers and corporations could not have afforded this level of institutional development, largely because they could not capture all the benefits of the research and because their organizational problems would have been immense. Schultz has emphasized the importance of externalities in this type of research: "under competition, the reductions in real costs of producing agricultural products realized as a consequence of agricultural research are transferred in large measure to consumers" (Schultz, 1981, p. 11). Such externalities occur through price reductions and cause the social rate of return in research investment to exceed the private rate of return.

A recent book by MacAulay and Dufour examines the increasing devotion of university research to industrial technology. Their concern is that "Perhaps the major barrier to the adoption of industrial research by universities is the idea that academic science must somehow be pure and above strictly utilitarian considerations." The authors argue that "the machine (i.e., industrial research and technology) has long ago made its appearance in the quiet gardens of academe, without the devastating effects that have been feared" (MacAulay and Dufour, 1984, p. 12). It now seems clear that university research facilities are increasingly being linked with the practical innovation difficulties that Canadian firms are facing.

These linkages are not necessarily obvious or easy. The public good nature of knowledge can prevent a university-corporate activity from capturing even a major portion of the benefits from a joint investment in R&D. To the degree that universities themselves are regarded as being publicly owned, it is not clear how much of the knowledge that can be derived from the activity should automatically enter the public domain and become generally available. On the other hand, to the extent that a university and a corporation have a right to preclude others, how should the financial costs and benefits be apportioned between the two parties? These issues have gained prominence as joint university and corporate R&D activities have increased greatly in recent years. Maxwell and Currie, in a study of this issue, conclude that "The bottom line of this analysis is that there are clear benefits to the participants and to the country as a whole from increased collaboration" (Maxwell and Currie, 1984).

Choosing a Socially Optimal Rate of Economic Change

A society that makes its economic environment more favourable for entrepreneurship may also reduce the degree to which it can achieve other objectives. Conversely, the implementation of new social programs and the adoption of new social values may impair entrepreneurial activity. Within society, particular groups may advocate the pursuit of objectives that are in their own interest, and so the trade-off process may spark social and political conflict. Since many of the direct beneficiaries of an entrepreneurial environment do not possess established social, economic, or political power, the proponents of an entrepreneurial environment must wage an uneven struggle against vested interests. Olson, of course, feels that the unevenness of this struggle dooms a nation's progress. Conceivably, a better understanding of the entrepreneurial process and of the trade-offs with other social objectives may lead a nation to a wiser set of decisions that will prevent Olson's gloomy prognostications.

Some nations view inequality of income and wealth as socially undesirable. A basic purpose of some political parties is to reduce such inequality. A myriad of government programs seek to provide financial assistance to less fortunate individuals. To finance such programs, government taxation systems are designed to take funds disproportionately from the wealthy, who are often those to whom market mechanisms allocate high rewards for their activities. To what extent does such redistribution alter economic incentives? The answer to this question is not clear, and yet it is obvious that some substantial after-tax incentives must be left if entrepreneurship is to be a pervasive and strong source of progress. Furthermore, it is in the interests of society to design expenditure and tax programs so as to impair such incentives as little as possible. Many such programs are relatively new, and their effects on incentives are relatively unknown. The experimental nature of these programs should be recognized, and society should be prepared to modify programs that appear to have the most deleterious effects.

Canada is a nation with significant regional inequalities of income and wealth. Many government expenditure and taxation programs have sought to reduce these regional inequalities. Some critics believe that these efforts have significantly reduced the adjustment process within Canada. Individuals and firms have rejected the greater risks of migration and the development of new skills and new production processes because of the security offered by government programs, which enable them to continue with their old, established economic activities in the same geographical locations.

A society may feel that some regulations over private sector activity can enhance important aspects of living. Environmental regulations may improve the quality of life. Other regulations may protect people as consumers. Truth-in-advertising and anti-combines legislation are examples of such protection. A society may believe that some business circumstances require government to set prices directly. This paper argues that, in making decisions such as these, a society may often face a trade-off between government intervention and future innovations. This trade-off deserves attention because it is usually not explicitly seen — future innovations form an ephemeral concept that cannot be quantified. It is difficult to make a trade-off when only one-half of the ledger is clearly visible. This paper emphasizes the importance of the hidden part of the trade-off, and the value in each such circumstance of attempting to understand the long-term impact on innovation.

In general, the process for deciding upon public policies should try to clarify the trade-offs that society will face. As we have seen, those government policies that aim to protect the economic prosperity of vested interests stand in opposition to entrepreneurship. Policy makers must recognize that future beneficiaries of change are not able to plead their case as effectively as vested interests. Gains to consumers will be spread across the population. Furthermore, many future beneficiaries of change are unaware of their potential gains. This inability of beneficiaries to plead their case should be recognized by policy makers when they weigh the advantages and disadvantages of policies that attempt to limit change. A society's leaders have a role to play in drawing attention to long-term implications for society's economic development and in representing future beneficiaries, in spite of the fact that these beneficiaries may not be heard in the political process.

A society's leaders must improve the public understanding of entrepreneurship, so that people may accept a wiser set of decisions concerning policies that affect the pace of change. Income differentials among individuals, firms and regions can be seen as incentives for change and as rewards for entrepreneurship, rather than simply as an injustice to be corrected by government programs that redistribute income and wealth. With the probable concentration of entrepreneurial success in particular cities and regions, social discord over the substantial differences in opportunities and incomes can only be alleviated if the public understands the process.

Underlying this view of the responsibility of a society's leaders is the fact that entrepreneurship is an act of faith, hope and courage in which the ultimate results are uncertain and imprecise (and which may in many cases even be of negative value) and in which the ultimate results may not be achieved for many years. An entrepreneurial society requires a cohesive social purpose in which individuals realize and accept two essential elements: first, that entrepreneurial change and adjustment, overall, may help social progress, even though they as particular individuals may not gain and may in fact lose; and, second, that the future success and prosperity of their society may be worth the current pain caused by change and adjustment. The first requires that individuals see themselves and their success as part of a society and of that society's success; the second requires that individuals see themselves and their children as part of the future society for whose general well-being current sacrifice is desirable. These objectives and values now seem not to be universally recognized. For people to adopt them requires a social cohesiveness and a personal understanding that a society's leaders should seek to develop in its citizens.

To the extent that innovation has become a chain-like process requiring the involvement of many people, including production workers as well as managers, this need for public understanding acquires an even greater importance. If citizens are to play an entrepreneurial role in their private economic activities, they must appreciate the nature of entrepreneurship. To the extent that citizens influence their government's intervention in the entrepreneurial process, they must learn to make reasoned judgments about the ability of government employees to act as entrepreneurs within different organizational structures, as well as judgments about the success and failure of particular government policies. The public must accept the experimental nature of many programs since these are relatively new and their full implications will become apparent only with the passage of time. Special mention should be made of the need to accept disinvestment and the cutting of society's losses within government's entrepreneurial activities. A major issue must be the degree to which a society will wish to share entrepreneurial risks through government programs that provide a safety net and adjustment assistance. All of this requires that the public gain a better understanding of entrepreneurship and its relevance for public policies.

The role of minority groups in the entrepreneurial process may be particularly important in Canada. Some authors have stressed the tendency for minority groups to be entrepreneurial leaders, and Canada may find that it is particularly blessed in this regard because of its large immigrant population. Special attention should be directed to the obstacles that may block their business success, including their ability to borrow from a financial system that has been criticized by some for being controlled by an established elite. As Olson has said, a society may gain from immigration, not only because of the arrival of potential entrepreneurs, but also because immigrants help to shatter the protective policies that lead inevitably to a society's decline.

Entrepreneurship has attained a new significance in the modern world. Its nature has changed and become more complex. The discussion of entrepreneurship may involve many different perspectives and distinctions, yet the basic elements of entrepreneurship have retained their significance, and will continue to play a major role in a society's innovation and economic change. Clearly, entrepreneurship is central to Canada's development prospects. Canadian governments must inevitably deal with the many aspects of entrepreneurship, and citizens as individuals and as members of society cannot ignore this subject. Entrepreneurship will impinge on our lives, will mould our choice of public policies, and will play a major role in determining our economic future.

Notes

This paper was completed in November 1984. The author wishes to thank the many people who have contributed to the development of this paper, in particular, David Laidler and members of his research advisory group, and the referees.

Bibliography

Arrow, Kenneth J. 1983. "Innovation in Large and Small Firms." In *Entrepreneurship*, edited by Joshua Ronen. Lexington, Mass.: D.C. Heath.

Asimakopulos, A. 1978. *An Introduction to Economic Theory: Microeconomics*. Toronto: Oxford University Press.

Athos, G. Anthony, and Richard T. Pascale. 1981. *The Art of Japanese Management: Applications for American Executives*. New York: Simon and Schuster.

Baumol, William J. 1983. "Preface." In *Entrepreneurship*, edited by Joshua Ronen. Lexington, Mass.: D.C. Heath.

Bergson, Abram. 1984. "Income Inequality Under Soviet Socialism." *Journal of Economic Literature* (September).

Bird, Richard. "Few Jobs in High Tech: There May Be Good Reasons for Developing High Tech Manufacturing But It Is Not What We Can Look To for Future Jobs in Canada." *Policy Options* 5 (September, 1984).

Boadway, Robin W. 1979. *Public Sector Economics*. Boston: Little, Brown.

Britton, John N.H., and James M. Gilmour. 1978. *The Weakest Link: A Technological Perspective on Canadian Industrial Underdevelopment*. Science Council of Canada Background Studies, no. 43. Ottawa: Science Council of Canada.

Brophy, David J. 1982. "Venture Capital Research." In *Encyclopedia of Entrepreneurship*, edited by Calvin A. Kent, Donald L. Sexton, and Karl H. Vesper. Englewood Cliffs, N.J.: Prentice-Hall.

Canada. Department of External Affairs. 1983a. *Canadian Trade Policy for the 1980s*. Discussion Paper. Ottawa: Minister of Supply and Services Canada.

———. 1983b. *A Review of Canadian Trade Policy: A Background Document to Canadian Trade Policy for the 1980s*. Ottawa: Minister of Supply and Services Canada.

Carter, C.F., and J.L. Ford, eds. 1972. *Uncertainty and Expectations in Economics: Essays in Honour of G.L.S. Shackle*. Oxford: Basil Blackwell.

Cole, Arthur H. 1953. "An Approach to the Study of Entrepreneurship." *Journal of Economic History* 1946: 1–15; reprinted in *Enterprise and Secular Change*, edited by Frederic Lane and Jelle Riemersma. Homewood, Ill.: Richard Irwin.

Conklin, David W. 1970. *An Evaluation of the Soviet Profit Reforms*. New York: Praeger.

———. 1969. "A Note on Soviet Profit Maximization." *Canadian Journal of Economics* (August).

Cooper, Arnold C. 1982. "The Entrepreneurship — Small Business Interface." In *Encyclopedia of Entrepreneurship*, edited by Calvin A. Kent, Donald L. Sexton, and Karl H. Vesper. Englewood Cliffs, N.J.: Prentice-Hall.

Corden, W.M. 1984. "Harry Johnson's Contributions to International Trade Theory." *Journal of Political Economy* 92 (August).

Courchene, Thomas J. 1980. "Towards a Protected Society: The Politicization of Economic Life." *Canadian Journal of Economics* (November 1980).

Daly, Donald, and Steven Globerman. 1976. *Tariff and Science Policies: Applications of a Model of Nationalism*. Toronto: Ontario Economic Council.

Denny, Michael, and Melvin Fuss. 1982. *Productivity: A Selective Survey of Recent Developments and the Canadian Experience*. Toronto: Ontario Economic Council.

Domar, E.A. 1966. "The Soviet Collective Farm." *American Economic Review* (September 1966): 734–57.

Economic Council of Canada. 1981. *Reforming Regulation*. Ottawa: Minister of Supply and Services Canada.

_____. 1982. *Intervention and Efficiency: A Study of Government Credit and Credit Guarantees to the Private Sector*. Ottawa: Minister of Supply and Services Canada.

_____. 1983. *The Bottom Line: Technology, Trade, and Income Growth*. Ottawa: Minister of Supply and Services Canada.

Eells, Richard, and Peter Nehemkis. 1984. *Corporate Intelligence and Espionage: A Blueprint for Executive Decision Making*. New York: Macmillan.

Gagnon, Jean-Marie, and Benoit Papillon. 1984. *Financial Risk, Rate of Return of Canadian Firms and Implications for Government Intervention*. Study prepared for the Economic Council of Canada. Ottawa: Minister of Supply and Services, Canada.

Green, Christopher. 1984. *Industrial Policy: The Fixities Hypothesis*. Toronto: Ontario Economic Council.

Green, Jerry R., and John B. Shoven. 1982. "The Effects of Financing Opportunities and Bankruptcy on Entrepreneurial Risk Bearing." In *Entrepreneurship*, edited by Joshua Ronen. Lexington, Mass.: D.C. Heath.

Greenfield, Sidney M., Arnold Strickon, and Robert T. Aubey, eds. *Entrepreneurs in Cultural Context*. Albuquerque: University of New Mexico Press.

Griliches, Zvi. 1979. "Issues in Assessing the Contribution of Research and Development to Productivity Growth." *Bell Journal of Economics* 10 (1) (Spring).

Griliches, Zvi, ed. 1984. *R&D Patents and Productivity*. Chicago: University of Chicago Press.

Grossman, Gene. 1984. "International Trade, Foreign Investment, and the Formation of the Entrepreneurial Class." *American Economic Review* 74 (September): 605–14.

Gunderson, M., P. Halpern, and J. Quinn. 1985. *The Political Economy of Corporate Bailouts*. Toronto: Ontario Economic Council, forthcoming.

Hagen, Everett E. 1962. *On the Theory of Social Change*. Homewood, Ill.: Dorsey Press.

Harris, Richard G., Frank D. Lewis, and Douglas D. Purvis, eds. 1984. "Market Adjustment and Government Policy." In *Economic Adjustment and Public Policy in Canada*, Kingston, Ont.: Queen's University Press.

Hebert, Robert F., and Albert N. Link. 1982. *The Entrepreneur: Mainstream Views and Radical Critiques*. New York: Praeger.

Heinkel, Robert. 1981. "Uncertain Product Quality: The Market for Lemons with an Imperfect Testing Technology." *Bell Journal of Economics* 12 (Autumn): 625–36.

Hoselitz, Bert F. 1960. "The Early History of Entrepreneurial Theory." *Explorations in Entrepreneurial History* 3 (April 1951): 193–220, reprinted in Joseph J. Spengler and William R. Allen. *Essays in Economic Thought: Aristotle to Marshall*. Chicago: Rand McNally.

Hymer, Stephen H. 1976. The International Operations of National Firms: A Study of Direct Foreign Investment. Cambridge, Mass.: MIT Press.

Kent, Calvin A., Donald L. Sexton, and Karl Vesper. 1982. *Encyclopedia of Entrepreneurship*. Englewood Cliffs, N.J.: Prentice-Hall.

Kirzner, Israel M. 1973. *Competition and Entrepreneurship*. Chicago: University of Chicago Press.

_____. 1979. *Perception, Opportunity and Profit: Studies in the Theory of Entrepreneurship*. Chicago: University of Chicago Press.

Knight, Russell. 1982. "Additional Considerations of Research About Living Entrepreneurs." In *Encyclopedia of Entrepreneurship*, edited by Calvin A. Kent, Donald L. Sexton and Karl H. Vesper. Englewood Cliffs, N.J.: Prentice-Hall.

Kotowitz, Yehuda, and M.D. Berkowitz. 1982. "Patent Policy in an Open Economy." *Canadian Journal of Economics* 15 (1) (February).

Landes, David. 1969. *The Unbound Prometheus: Technological Change and Industrial Development in Western Europe from 1750 to the Present*. Cambridge: Cambridge University Press.

Lane, Frederic, and Jelle Riemersma. eds. 1953. *Enterprise and Secular Change*. Homewood, Ill.: Richard Irwin.

Levin, Richard C. 1981. "Railroad Rates, Profitability, and Welfare Under Deregulation." *Bell Journal of Economics* 12 (1) (Spring): 1–26.

Litvak, I.A., and C.J. Maule. 1971. *Canadian Entrepreneurship: A Study of Small Newly Established Firms*. Technological Innovation Studies Program Research Reports. Ottawa: Department of Regional Industrial Expansion, Office of Industrial Innovation.

———. 1972. *A Study of Successful Entrepreneurs in Canada*. Technological Innovation Studies Program Research Reports. Ottawa: Department of Regional Industrial Expansion, Office of Industrial Innovation.

———. 1980. *Entrepreneurial Success or Failure Ten Years Later: A Study of 47 Technologically Oriented Enterprises*. Technological Innovation Studies Program Research Reports. Ottawa: Department of Regional Industrial Expansion, Office of Industrial Innovation.

MacAuley, James B., and Paul Dufour. 1984. *The Machine in the Garden: The Advent of Industrial Research Infrastructure in the Academic Milieu*. Ottawa: Science Council of Canada.

Maxwell, Judith, and Stephanie Currie. 1984. *Partnership for Growth: Corporate-University Cooperation in Canada*. Montreal: The Corporate-Higher Education Forum.

Mishan, E.J. 1976. *Cost-Benefit Analysis*. New York: Praeger.

Olson, Mancur. 1982. *The Rise and Decline of Nations: Economic Growth, Stagflation, and Social Rigidities*. New Haven: Yale University Press.

Ouchi, William G. 1981. *Theory Z: How American Business Can Meet the Japanese Challenge*. Reading, Mass.: Addison-Wesley.

Pakes, Ariel, and Mark Schankerman. 1984. "The Rate of Obsolescence of Patents, Research Gestation Lags, and the Private Rate of Return to Research Resources." In *R&D, Patents, and Productivity*, edited by Zvi Griliches. Chicago: University of Chicago Press.

Proulx, Pierre-Paul. 1984. "Comment." In *Economic Adjustment and Public Policy in Canada*, edited by Douglas D. Purvis. Kingston, Ont.: Queen's University Press.

Quinn, John, and Philip Slayton, eds. 1982. *Non-Tariff Barriers after the Tokyo Round*. Montréal: The Institute for Research on Public Policy.

Reich, Robert B. 1983. *The Next American Frontier*. New York: Times Books.

Rivlin, Alice. 1970. *Systematic Thinking for Social Action*. Washington, D.C.: Brookings Institution.

Ronen, Joshua, ed. 1982. *Entrepreneurship*. Lexington, Mass.: D.C. Heath.

Rothwell, Roy, and Walter Zegveld. 1981. *Industrial Innovation and Public Policy: Preparing for the 1980s and 1990s*. Westport, Conn.: Greenwood Press.

Schultz, Theodore W. 1981. "Knowledge is Power in Agriculture." *Challenge* (September/October).

Schumpeter, Joseph A. 1961. *The Theory of Economic Development*. New York: Oxford University Press.

———. 1939. *Business Cycles: A Theoretical, Historical and Statistical Analysis of the Capitalist Process*. New York: McGraw-Hill.

———. 1962. *Capitalism, Socialism and Democracy*. 3d ed. New York: Harper and Row.

———. 1968. *Uncertainty in Economics and Other Reflections*. Cambridge: Cambridge University Press.

Shackle, George Lennox Sharman. 1970. *Expectation, Enterprise and Profit: The Theory of the Firm*. London: Allen and Unwin.

Shapiro, Moses. 1983. "The Entrepreneurial Individual in the Large Organization." In *Entrepreneurship and the Outlook for America*, edited by Jules Backman. New York: Free Press.

Shavell, Steven. 1979. "On Moral Hazard and Insurance." *Quarterly Journal of Economics* (November): 541–62.

Spengler, Joseph J. and William R. Allen. 1960. *Essays in Economic Thought: Aristotle to Marshall*. Chicago: Rand McNally.

Stigler, George. 1976. "The Xistence of X-Efficiency." *American Economic Review* 4 (March 1976), p. 215.

———. 1965. *Modern Organization*. 1965. New York: Alfred A. Knopf.

Thompson, Victor A. 1969. *Bureaucracy and Innovation*. Alabama: University of Alabama Press.

Trebilcock, M.J., D.G. Hartle, R.S.J. Prichard, and D.N. Dewees. *The Choice of Governing Instrument*. Ottawa: Economic Council of Canada.

Viton, Paul A. 1981. "On Competition and Product Differentitation in Urban Transportation: The San Francisco Bay Area." *Bell Journal of Economics* 12 (2) (Autumn): 362–79.

Walker, Michael. 1976. *The Illusion of Wage and Price Controls*. Vancouver: Fraser Institute.

Ward, B.W. 1958. "The Firm in Illyria: Market Syndicalism." *American Economic Review* (September): 566–89.

Wetzel, William E., Jr. 1982. "Risk Capital Research." In *Encyclopedia of Entrepreneurship*, edited by Calvin Kent, Donald H. Sexton, and Karl H. Vesper. Englewood Cliffs, N.J.: Prentice-Hall.

Wilken, Paul H. 1979. *Entrepreneurship: A Comparative and Historical Study*. Norwood, N.J.: ABLEX Publishing.

Wilson, Benson A. 1985. "Access to Ontario Universities in the 1990s: Comments." In *Ontario Universities: Access, Operations and Funding*, edited by David W. Conklin and Thomas J. Courchene. Toronto: Ontario Economic Council.

3

Rules versus Discretion in Constitutional Design

CHARLES K. ROWLEY

Introduction

The balance between rules and discretion in the political management of any economy involves complex and often controversial issues in constitutional design. This paper outlines the most important of these issues in the light of recent literature that applies economic analysis to the working of the political system, but makes no attempt to present a blueprint for Canada. Readers must weigh for themselves the pros and cons of the various alternatives under review.

In the section titled "The Reason of Rules" I consider various justifications that have been advanced for the adoption of rules designed to constrain governments in their economic interventions. These justifications range, for example, from recognition of the importance of protecting minorities from the possible tyranny of majorities, to concern that powerful competing groups might destroy wealth if allowed an unconstrained environment in which to test their relative strengths. Of course, no society can function in a complete regulatory vacuum, for most economic decisions involve the investment of economic resources and, inevitably, are taken with an eye to a somewhat distant future. Property rights established and supported by an effective legal system are a minimum requirement for effective economic exchange.

Because by its very nature a more generalized system of rules than this limits the authority of elected governments, any decision to invoke such rules constitutes a criticism, however implicit, of unfettered parliamentary democracy. Therefore, the subsequent two sections are devoted to an outline of the principal forces of supply and demand that interact within the political marketplace to determine public policy. In particular, attention is directed to such important issues as the effectiveness of voter majorities in controlling the behaviour of their political representatives in a largely ruleless system, the role and likely impact of special interest groups, and the relevance of bureaucracy itself as an independent agent in public policy determination. Throughout, possible implications for constitutional rules are outlined and evaluated. The approach adopted is that of public choice (an application of economics in the analysis of political behaviour) and the objectives of all agents in the political process are assumed to be self-seeking.

A general discussion of the reason of rules[1] without reference to the particular institutions and constitutional design of Canada, however useful in offering broad insights, must fail to confront important specific problems. Therefore, the paper concludes by looking at the problem of designing a constitution that strikes an appropriate balance between rules and discretion in the Canadian federal context, given Canada's historical tradition.

The Reason of Rules

All societies are founded on rules designed to regulate individual behaviour and to facilitate economic exchange, rules that protect individuals in society from the Hobbesian jungle and the war of each against all. Property rights themselves, in the absence of which society itself does not exist, are dependent upon the rule of law which, if effective, provides a framework within which long-term contracts may be struck and honoured.

Rules usually are intended to endure across successive governments, thus providing protection from the day-to-day pressures of the political marketplace. To the extent that they are sheltered from repeal by supramajority vote requirements, however, they must be viewed as negating the democratic political process as customarily conceived. The contractual explanation of the factors leading to the establishment of rules and of the equilibrium between rules and discretion in particular political markets, therefore, requires a close and critical evaluation.

In this section, the reason of rules is evaluated from a variety of perspectives, but always within a framework of democratic representative government. Dictatorships, monarchies and juntas may or may not prefer to govern via rules rather than via discretion, but the rationale of their political calculus has no direct relevance to the Canadian democratic tradition and is not considered here.

The Veil of Ignorance

The debate over the appropriate balance within society between rules and discretion is rendered controversial by the knowledge of individuals and of groups of their approximate relative positions in society ex ante and by their views of how constitutional change, or otherwise, is likely to affect their life chances ex post. Conflict, in such circumstances, is almost inevitable and has posed a serious problem for economists concerned to promote the unanimity concepts of Wicksell (1896) and of Pareto (1909) into the arena of constitutional design. This problem may well be most acute in the case of economic rules, given the diversity of individual and group economic interests compared with the relative agreement on human and political rights.

To overcome such serious problems, the philosopher John Rawls (1972) attempts to abstract from the process of political bargaining and the conflicting calculus of competing collective interests which he sees to be incompatible with a "just" society. In an important contribution to moral philosophy, Rawls sets out the principles of justice that free and rational persons would accept — and in his view would accept unanimously — if they were able to deliberate in a hypothetical situation corresponding to the state of nature in traditional social contract theory.

In this initial position, individuals do not know their places in society, their class position or social status, their fortunes in the distribution of natural assets and abilities, nor even their conception of the good. Thus, deliberating behind a veil of ignorance, individuals determine their rights and duties. Within this framework, Rawls seeks to derive a theory of justice that generalizes and carries to a higher level of abstraction the theories of the social contract as found in Locke (1955), Rousseau (1913) and Kant (1965).

The original contract, for Rawls, is not a contract of entry into a particular society or a contract to set up a particular form of government. Rather, the principles of justice derived are those governing the basic structure of society. These principles are to regulate all further agreements; they specify the kinds of social cooperation that can be entered into and the forms of government that can be established. 'Justice as fairness' therefore may be viewed as the fundamental rule according to which all other issues of rules versus discretion are decided. Individuals are to choose a constitution, a legislature to enact laws, and so on, in accordance with the conception of justice initially agreed upon.

Rawls makes it clear that a system of justice as fairness derived from deliberations under conditions as outlined above is morally superior to systems otherwise derived; this is the value judgment underlying his analysis. By ascertaining which principles it would be rational to adopt, given the contractual situation, he attempts to connect the theory of justice with the theory of rational choice. Indeed, he views the theory of justice as part of the theory of rational choice — more precisely, as part of a reflective equilibrium of rational choice. It is indeed a theory of moral sentiments.

Rawls suggests that the conditions of the original position are such as to induce all deliberators to use the extremely risk-averse strategy of maxi-min when selecting the principles of justice that are to govern the basic structure of society; thus individuals are supposed to take positions that maximize their minimum possible gain. On this centrally important pivot, he derives two principles of justice and asserts that they would be chosen universally by self-seeking deliberators acting under the conditions of his model, both to govern the assignment of rights and duties and to regulate the distribution of social and economic advantages.

The first principle so derived is that each person is to have an equal right to the most extensive basic liberty compatible with a similar liberty for others. The basic liberties are political liberty (the right to vote and to be eligible for public office) together with freedom of speech and assembly, liberty of conscience and freedom of thought, freedom of the person along with the right to hold personal property, and freedom from arbitrary arrest and seizure as defined by the concept of the rule of law.

These liberties are required to be equal by the first principle, because citizens of a just society are to have the same basic rights. The first principle is viewed to be so fundamental to the just society that it takes full precedence over the second principle. Thus, a departure from the institutions of equal liberty cannot be justified in terms of any other perceived gain. It is worth reflecting that some such notion as this presumably guided those American founding fathers like George Mason who refused to sign the U.S. Constitution because it failed to provide a bill of rights.

The second principle derived behind the veil of ignorance is that social and economic inequalities are to be arranged so that they are both (a) reasonably expected to be to everyone's advantage, and (b) attached to positions and offices open to all. This principle leads to the concept of a just distribution of wealth and income, and the notion that individuals should share equality of opportunity and be unfettered by discrimination in their pursuit of authority and offices of command.

Rawls, in fact, takes the second principle yet further by associating it with his now-famous "difference principle." The difference principle determines the particular position from which the social and economic inequalities of the basic structure are to be judged given the institutional framework established by equal liberty and equality of opportunity. Specifically, it suggests that the higher expectations of those better situated are just if and only if they work as part of a scheme that improves the expectations of the least advantaged members of society.

The difference principle proved controversial among philosophers and economists.[2] Such controversy was inevitable, given its somewhat egalitarian implications for the distribution of income and wealth. It should be emphasized that the message is not necessarily total equality. That would be incompatible with equality of opportunity, probably with the superior first principle, and possibly even with the difference principle itself, if a degree of inequality is necessary to the process of wealth creation. Nevertheless, if accepted, it provides for a degree of ongoing redistribution as part of the basic structure of society.

Rawls' theory of justice provides food for thought for those in Canada who are concerned about the basic structure of their society. Not everyone will find plausible Rawls' assumption of an extremely risk-averse attitude by all those deliberating behind the veil; yet without it the Rawlsian world disintegrates. Those who are prepared to go along with the experiment may not accept the principles of justice that Rawls derives. Those who are prepared to accept the principles may see insuperable difficulties in organizing any society to satisfy them. I am doubtful about Rawls' solution precisely on these grounds.

Yet all those who recognize the constitutional conflict that can arise in society because of the conflicting expectations of individuals must respect the Rawlsian experiment. Each Canadian, after all, can conduct his or her own experiment behind a suitably devised veil to search out the fairness of existing viewpoints concerning the basic structure of society. Such reflection may lead to a significant reduction in tension and social conflict.

Rules Protect Society from Anarchy

The Rawlsian experiment attempts to release individuals from the chains of their own condition in a search to devise basic rules. Once the basic structure is established, the more detailed decisions concerning the constitution (and the precise balance between rules and discretion) will be made by free individuals deliberating in accordance with the principles of justice. Everything is to be subject to these principles.

The real world, however, does not conform to the original condition. The real position typically is closer to the Hobbesian jungle (Hobbes, 1943) than to the Rawlsian constitutional conference. The Hobbesian jungle is characterized by the absence of any rules including those governing property rights. It is a war of each against all in which Rawls' principles of justice exert no influence at all. It is an environment in which life typically is brutish and short — the rulers have the greatest possible discretion.

Even in such an environment, as Buchanan (1975) and Tullock (1974) note, a natural distribution of resources will emerge. This distribution will reflect the tastes, capacities, strengths, cunning and ingenuity of the various rivalrous individuals. It will not be based upon consent nor will it provide a basis for contractual exchange. Potential wealth will be destroyed as individuals divert from production into predation and defence given the absence of rights and any rule of law. In the recognition of such imposed losses, be they political or economic, lies the opportunity for constitutional settlement.

An agreement on rights in such circumstances may be viewed as laying the foundations for liberty, exchange efficiency and, possibly, justice. The extent to which agreement would be free of coercion depends on the balance of the natural distribution, and on the willingness of the weak to accept an unfair distribution of rights. History informs us that most societies emerge from the jungle, not always via dictatorship, but never via universal consent.

The Hobbesian jungle is far removed from the condition of contemporary Canada, which is one of the most stable democracies, with an enviable reputation for liberty and equality of opportunity; nevertheless, the extreme example offers some insights into the debate about rules versus discretion even in the Canadian example.

How important, for instance, is a written constitution, or a bill of rights, for protecting citizens from political pressures that may tend to erode their rights even under conditions of democracy? How important is legislation concerning taxation powers or the nature of government fiscal policy as a protection from majority tyranny within the life of a specific government? How important is the precise balance of power between the various layers of a federal government to protect the lower layers from wrongdoing by the higher layers; or, even, the higher layers from civil disobedience by the lower?

These questions and their answers may prove central to the maintenance of rights and the rule of law during troubled times. Anarchy always awaits those who are profligate with rights even in the best ordered of societies. In the Canadian perspective, the threatened split of Quebec from the rest of the union is a recent example of concern over the existing structure of rights.

Rules Protect against Political Myopia

Most democracies, whether or not they have a written constitution or a bill or charter of rights, operate with rules enforceable via the legal process to protect citizens from "aberrant" political behaviour. Such rules are viewed as basic in the sense of Rawls: governments seeking to overthrow them would be disciplined by judicial review. Such clearly now is the case of Canada, with its repatriated Constitution and its Charter of Rights and Freedoms. Parliamentary sovereignty is constrained by the existence of such rules. Even the United Kingdom parliament, which operates without any written constitution or bill of rights, would find its legislation overturned by the courts on grounds of natural justice if it sought to repeal habeas corpus or otherwise seriously to erode established individual rights.

Once less basic rules are under consideration, however, the case for impeding Parliament in its day-to-day administrations becomes less self-evident. For example, rules concerning the power to tax, the money supply and the budget, enshrined in supramajority vote constraints, clearly restrict the scope of elected governments. Some might see such rules as the dictatorship of a transient majority. Good reasons obviously are required in defence of rules of this kind.

Buchanan and Lee (1982) suggest, as one explanation for the strength of feeling evidenced in favour of such rules, a fear that the political process otherwise tends toward excessive myopia. Two reasons for such myopia have been advanced: the first concerns the vote motive and the second concerns elected governments.

Myopia in the vote motive is predicted as the consequence of significant differences in the nature of individual choice in the private and in the political spheres. Privately, individuals' choices are unconstrained; if they are sufficiently far-sighted, their decisions may reflect lifetime consequences, or even implications long after death. Publicly, however, individuals exercise only a severely attenuated control over the options available. In particular, the discrete nature of politics makes it difficult to take account of the full temporal implications of vote decisions. Governments may change; policies may be disrupted. Almost inevitably, in such circumstances, voters become myopic in their vote behaviour. To the extent that such reactions are seen to be undesirable, constitutional constraints may emerge as voters protect themselves against the political system.

Governments are agents and voters are principals.[3] Herein lies a further reason for myopia in public choice. For the principal-agent relationship is seriously flawed in comparison with the equity shareholder-management relationship in corporate enterprise. First, there is no capital market in politics and thus no means, such as stock-option schemes, of enabling individual politicians to share in the present value of future wealth generation. Second, during their terms of office elected governments are sheltered from competition, save that of opposition voice and citizen exit. Future generations simply do not vote. Third, political output is a nebulous concept, susceptible to distortion by the media. In consequence, the political labour market is less open to effective upward and downward monitoring than the private sector managerial market. In combination, these weaknesses offer powerful incentives for politicians to pursue short-term gains.

The real danger for Canada from myopic politics lies with its natural resources; the environmental problem (Rowley, 1974). Natural resources in transition from non-scarcity to scarcity are extremely vulnerable to myopic politics. The price mechanism, which operates extremely effectively in allocating scarce commodities to wealth-maximizing ends (with market failure exceptions outlined elsewhere in this text) itself stumbles when property rights are not established. Natural resources within the public domain often do not have the protection of property rights.

In the absence of long-term rules clearly defining resource rights in the private domain and firmly controlling the rate of depletion in the public domain, Canada's natural resources (its major heritage) are seriously at risk from vote-seeking politicians operating myopically within their chosen environment. Nor should this problem be conceived of as marginal, responsive to nudges and shifts of political perspective.

For, as Boulding (1971) emphasizes, whereas crises are unusual over minor changes in resource allocation, major social problems arise as a consequence of threshold adjustments: the road that jams as one more car appears, the river that refuses to clean itself under a single addition of sewage, the forest that dies under an increment of acid rain, and the animal species that disappears following one season of overkill. Faced with the prospect of irreversible damage to the environment, Canadian voters well may wish to rein in their political representatives, for the latter usually impose the tyranny of small decisions.

Rules Protect Voters from Self-Seeking Politicians

The classical economists clearly warned against treating politicians as if they were public-spirited. For some 20 years public choice economists have suggested that politicians are wealth-maximizing vote seekers. Recent history, not least the Watergate scandal, has confirmed such impressions. Yet many economists persist in a search for market failure, with recommendations for intervention by governments evidently assumed to be the impartial and omniscient servants of the public good. Voters, more perspicacious than many economists, tend to accept the self-seeking notion and to be concerned about excessive discretion in the political marketplace.

John Stuart Mill (1977) exemplifies the fear of classical economists of the coercive potential of all representative governments. He claims that the very principle of constitutional government requires an assumption that political power would be abused to promote the purposes of the holder; not because that would always be the case but because such was the natural tendency of things. To guard against such tendencies was the especial purpose of free institutions. In this sense, Mill presages Rawls in attaching prime importance to the basic structure of society.

David Hume (1963), more bluntly than Mill, stresses the self-seeking nature of politicians as a reason for constitutional constraints. He argues that those engaged in fixing the several checks and controls of the constitution should suppose that every politician is a knave; that politicians have no other end in all their actions than private interest.

Of course, self-seeking behaviour does not necessarily lead to social harm: Adam Smith's (1937) "invisible hand" theorem is testament enough to that. Much depends upon the institutional framework within which public choice proceeds. Literature central to such issues is surveyed in the two following sections of this paper, which look at the roles played by voters, the opposition, special interest groups and bureaucracy. Insofar as political discretion does exist, however, it is dangerous to ignore the classical warning. Power corrupts and almost always results in coercive behaviour.

An interesting application of this theorem is presented by Brennan and Buchanan (1980) in their analysis of the power to tax. Predicating their analysis on the proposition that politicians indeed do possess the discretionary power to coerce, not least with respect to the taxation instrument, Brennan and Buchanan engage in Rawlsian constitutional analytics. Behind the veil of ignorance, voters are seen to deliberate and to define detailed rules to contain the power to tax, rules that break with recent economics on optimal taxation theory and recommend a narrow rather than a broad base, with steeply progressive rather than uniform or even declining rates imposed upon that base.

Such analysis follows closely the classical tradition of protecting against the worst possible contingencies that might arise within a fiscal constitution.[4] Not all students of public choice would endorse the taxation example. Indeed, theory suggests that vote-seeking politicians even may undertax upon occasion.[5] But the notion of worst-case avoidance surely is central to all discussion of constitutional constraints on representative government.

The problem of coercive government increases as its general area of influence expands (Rowley, 1983). The minimal state, with government merely the referee, can be constrained simply by adopting Rawls' first principle of equality of liberty, with the rules therein implied. The productive state, even if confined to the provision of public goods, potentially has greater opportunity for discretionary behaviour. The welfare state, empowered to effect transfers between citizens, potentially has yet greater powers and a much increased incentive to engage in coercion. The issue of discretionary power and how coercive abuses of such power (especially the power to transfer) should be constrainted was absolutely central to the recent Canadian constitutional debate.

Rules Protect Minorities

In an extremely important study of the principles of constitutionally limited government, Knut Wicksell (1896)[6] described institutions that might promote consensual rather than factional or majority democracy in Sweden. Recognizing the expansionist designs of the Crown and the pressures to increase taxes that the Crown placed upon Parliament, Wicksell developed an ingenious form of protection for minority groups.

Wicksell predicted that under proportionate representation Parliament would be composed of a small number of relatively homogeneous parties. To establish consensual democracy, he proposed to allow each such group to withhold the tax payments from its constituency if it considered that its supporters were receiving an inadequate return. It is this proposal that became famous as the "near-unanimity rule"; the rule offered obvious protection for homogeneous minorities.

Of course, each solution must be specific to the particular system of government under deliberation. In the United States, the separation of powers was designed to moderate majority tyranny. Congress tends to dominate the Executive, not least because the latter is dependent upon appropriations from the former. However, the president can require Congress to operate on a two-thirds voting rule through the veto power. The judiciary also is independent, with the salaries of its judges protected through their tenure, but its powers are limited to the cases that arise. Madison (Hamilton, Jay and Madison, 1937) believed that the majority power in Congress would be dispersed by the different principles of selection for the Senate and the House of Representatives. To secure a concurrent majority in both chambers usually would require a supramajority position overall.

Canada well may have something to learn from such attempts to protect minorities. Its Senate is weak and is appointed rather than elected. Its processes of judicial review under the repatriated Constitution as yet are untried. A more detailed review of relevant issues, however, is reserved until the final section, on Canadian constitutional design.

Voter Power

This section surveys recent literature on the relationship between voters and their political representatives; it also evaluates the extent to which political parties are able to deviate in their electoral manifestoes from majority vote positions and yet achieve electoral success.

Building on important contributions by Hotelling (1929), Smithies (1941) and Black (1958), Downs (1957) renders earlier mechanistic accounts of the political process behavioural by endowing candidates and political parties with vote-seeking objectives, and by assuming that they sought to maximize their constituency within specific political environments. In so doing, Downs lays the foundations for a positive economic theory of politics based on the notion that parties formulate policies to win elections and do not win elections in order to formulate policies.

The median voter theorem, which originally had been outlined by Black as relevant to certain categories of committee voting, is applied by Downs to the electoral process for representative government. The theorem is assumed to hold only in the presence of the following somewhat stringent requirements:

- election contested by two political parties (or candidates);
- election contested over policies that collapse into a single-dimension, left-right space;

- single-peaking of voters' preferences over such left-right space;
- political parties mobile in their positioning over such space;
- political parties informed as to the voter preference distribution;
- voters informed as to the positions of the competing parties; and
- no voter abstentions.

In such circumstances, if the political parties are vote maximizers (and here there is no difference between vote and plurality maximization), the political market equilibrium exists, is unique and is stable. Political parties cannot diverge from the issue preferences of the median of the voter distribution. This result holds whether the voter distribution is normal (in which case the median is the same as other measures of central tendency, the mean and the mode) or whether it is skewed (in which case the median may differ significantly from the other measures). An obvious attraction of the median voter theorem is that it provides no freedom whatsoever for political parties seeking governmental office to deviate in their election manifestoes from the wishes of the majority voters.

However, once the assumptions underpinning the theorem are relaxed to take account of the realities of political markets, the median solution is seen to be much less dominant. Even the existence of a political equilibrium is placed in doubt and, what is more serious, the uniqueness and stability of any equilibrium must be questioned. In consequence, the grip of voter majorities over the election manifestoes of competing parties is seen, for the most part, to be much looser than Downs is willing to acknowledge. Since this loosening of majority control has implications for the balance between rules and discretion, it merits a brief review.

In the absence of compulsion (as occurs for example in Australia) the Downsian assumption that all voters vote must be challenged empirically, because abstentions do occur, often involving more than 50 percent of the electorate. A priori, it is ironic that there is no convincing explanation why rational individuals vote in major political elections. The probability of an individual vote determining an election is very low (one in ten million in U.S. presidential elections). Thus, however large the net benefits an individual voter perceives from a particular party's victory, expected benefits vanish almost to zero once the probability factor is applied. Voting costs in contrast are never zero; indeed they may be high, if complex and time-consuming registration procedures are employed. Such costs almost always exceed expected benefits. In consequence, the vote motive can be explained only by reliance upon such concepts as civil duty.

Potential voters may abstain as a consequence either of indifference or of alienation (or, of course, of both). Abstentions through indifference, if evenly matched, are unlikely to disturb the median voter solution. Abstentions through alienation, however, may disturb the equilibrium, especially when the voter preference distribution is skewed and fear of vote losses in the extended tail pull competing political parties in that direction. Where alienation abstentions are especially forceful, at both ends of the distribution, equilibrium may not occur; both parties may be rendered immobile for fear of vote losses at their respective extremes. In such circumstances, majority control of the political process may well fail. The abstention factor cannot be ignored when one analyzes majority control over provincial and municipal governments, where voter participation rates tend to be especially low.

Further problems arise when Downs' assumption that competing parties are mobile over political space[7] is relaxed. Enelow and Hinich (1984) recently have argued that in the short run parties are politically immobile; that they can manoeuvre only by shifting the voter preference distribution in their direction by effective campaign expenditures. In my view, this assertion is incorrect and stems from their overemphasis on U.S. presidential elections where past reputations are more difficult to disperse, and where primary election commitments restrict political mobility during the post-primary campaign. To the extent that political parties do restrict their own political mobility, be it as a consequence of candidate preselection or of special interest commitments, the convergence characteristics of Downs' theory may be dampened and majority control over the election process may be further loosened. Of course, if only one party is immobilized away from the centre of the distribution, its rival has some discretion to move away from the centre itself while retaining a victorious electoral position: majority control once again is weakened.

Additional problems for majority control occur if the assumption is relaxed that political space is a single-dimension, left-right space. In such circumstances, the relevant issues must be identified and dealt with or the median voter theorem is an empty political box. Even if all parties are able effectively to identify commonly perceived issues, problems for equilibrium in political markets are likely to persist and, even if voters' preferences are single-peaked over each issue, instability may occur overall. The larger the number of issue dimensions, the more susceptible the election to agenda manipulation. Downs argues that high information costs induce voters to collapse issues into a single left-right dimension. Davis, Hinich and Ordeshook (1970) argue that they do not do so. Evidence as yet is ambiguous on this important controversy.

Even if elections are conducted in single-dimension space, majority equilibrium may not exist if the voters' preference distribution is multipeaked. In such circumstances, rival parties may locate themselves at separate peaks, pursuing divisive election campaigns and ensuring a political outcome well away from the centre of the voter distribution. Having so located themselves, each competing party will be tempted to utilize campaign expenditures to consolidate the voter preference peak corresponding to their chosen position. Political instability with high associated costs of policy cycling may well result from such conditions in the absence of constitutional constraints. Only where the multi-peaked distribution is symmetrical and where vote abstentions are not anticipated is it likely that competing parties will abandon their respective peaks and locate themselves at the centre of the voter distribution.

Problems for majority vote equilibrium also arise, in the absence of proportional representation vote mechanisms, where more than two political parties compete in elections. As Tullock (1967) has indicated, convergence may not occur under such conditions; third or fourth parties rationally may space themselves well away from the major parties and may even gain electoral success from such a strategy. Coalition possibilities also jeopardize majority voter control over the election process and may result in electoral instabilities involving high associated political cost. Gaullist France is one example of constitutional reform designed to control by rules the high incidence of political instability evident throughout the early postwar period.

The ability of the majority to control the election manifestoes of competing political parties depends on the specifics of the political marketplace. In the absence of rules, it is not obvious that majority control will occur systematically in most political markets.

Finally, if the perfect information assumption is abandoned in analyzing election behaviour, the scope for political parties to evade majority voter control is widened. In particular, political parties may emit ambiguous signals concerning their position on controversial issues leaving voters at best with a probabilistic evaluation of their true position. Politicians may utilize campaign expenditures to promote a false image of their position on issues where they in fact evidence a minority stance. Special interest groups equally may project incorrect information concerning the nature of the voter preference distribution in order to shift the political parties toward their own preferred positions.

Incumbent Governments

The spatial theory of political markets outlined in the preceding section deals only with the election process. In this section I refer to the new institutional economics as a basis for analyzing the behaviour in office of elected governments. The approach adopted employs the self-interest calculus as a vehicle for understanding political market behaviour.

Voters and Incumbent Governments

The relationship between voters as principals and government as agents was noted in the second section, together with the risk of myopic decision making predictable from the principal-agent problem (Wagner,

1984). Governments are owned by their individual citizens in the sense that the latter are residual claimants with respect to government behaviour.

Governments are non-profit organizations to which ownership shares are inalienable; therefore, such shares cannot acquire a capital value. The absence of a market in ownership shares also implies that it is impossible for citizens to specialize in ownership or indeed to acquire multiple ownership shares. Shares are acquired or forfeited for the most part by changes in citizen residence. In such circumstances, the principal-agent relationship differs sharply from that evident in the market for corporate enterprise. In particular, an opportunity exists for a conflict of interest between majority voter-citizens and their elected political representatives.

To the extent that governments take advantage of the limited monitoring opportunities available to majority voters once the election is over, to divert policy in favour of special interest constituencies, they run the risk of eventual electoral failure. But elections usually are infrequent, and voter memories poor. In the absence of rules, significant discretionary power may be exploited within the term of office without invoking government collapse. Even at subsequent elections, the ability of political parties to bundle policies and to force them as a package upon the electorate offers considerable defence against a vote collapse.

The Role of the Opposition

Opposition parties exert only a limited impact upon a majority government during the latter's tenure of office in the absence of carefully designed constitutional constraints (Breton, 1974). Indeed, in elections governed by "first-past-the-post" voting rules rather than by proportional representation, a government may obtain a parliamentary majority, and overall command of the political process, from a minority vote of the electorate.

Whether or not governments with clear seat majorities should be treated as monopolists is an unresolved question. Certainly, competition from oppositions is weak in such circumstances. They can and do refresh voter memories concerning broken election pledges; they can and do improve information flows concerning damaging consequences of proposed policies; they can and do offer support and guidance for special interest groups alienated from the incumbent government; they can and do engage in persuasive advertising to shift voter preferences into hostility toward the government. Usually, however, they cannot oust the government during its term of office.

Increasingly, public choice analysts have abandoned the win-all/lose-all approach to democratic politics. Theories of government now recognize that the effective mandate of the incumbent is likely to be related directly to the size of the vote plurality (Rowley, 1984). Recent evidence tentatively supports this hypothesis. Even vote losses during the term of office, whether actual as a consequence of by-elections, or hypothetical from the opinion polls, may serve to moderate the monopoly influence of the incumbent. Thus, the opposition is not to be discarded entirely as a competitive mechanism in the control of discretionary government. The mechanism falls far short, however, of that which operates in competitive commodity markets. Constitutional checks and balances, of course, can significantly increase its constraining role.

The Role of Special Interest Groups

Special interest groups may be viewed as rent seekers whose principal objective is that of transferring rights (or more narrowly wealth) from others in society to themselves. Since rents, by definition, are returns in excess of opportunity cost, special interest groups typically do not engage in directly productive activity. Indeed, rent seeking takes place in institutional settings where the pursuit of private gain generates social waste rather than social surplus. Usually, such settings involve manipulation of the political process. Rent seeking is to be distinguished sharply from profit seeking in private markets which, in the absence of market failure, is wealth enhancing for society.

The early literature on special interest groups suggested that their principal impact was to reinforce the convergence processes of an essentially benevolent political process. Freedom to enter such groups was viewed as an effective defence against exploitation. However, Olson (1965, 1982) stresses that special interest groups experience differential impacts in terms of rent-seeking success.

The returns to collective action, successfully initiated, typically take the form of a collective consumption good available to all members of the special interest group, irrespective of their own role in the rent-seeking exercise. For this reason, rent seeking by special interest groups tends to be eroded by the free rider problem in the absence of advantageous circumstances. Specifically, special interest groups will tend to perform effectively only where membership coercion is feasible, or where private membership benefits can be made available to the active membership. Even in such circumstances, Olson demonstrates that the initial organization of large special interest groups requires gifted entrepreneurial leadership, together with the inducement of significant rents available for exploitation.

Special interest groups thrive on government-imposed barriers to entry; this is the condition required for the long-run preservation of rents. For this reason, countries with stable frontiers, stable democratic governments and an absence of defeat in wars are most vulnerable to their infiltration and to their rent seeking. Olson, indeed, explains the relative decline of the United States and the United Kingdom in recent years essentially as a consequence of special interest group consolidation. More generally, rent seeking has emerged as a significant phenomenon in all advanced western economies as institutions have moved away from ordered markets toward the new chaos of direct political allocation (Buchanan et al., 1980).

Rent seeking as here defined involves social waste: resources which otherwise might have been devoted to value-producing activity are diverted into a wasteful competitive effort to determine merely distributive outcomes. In principle, if rent seeking imposes significant net losses upon society, a contractual solution should be forthcoming, with the gainers from the elimination of rent seeking compensating those who forego their rents. In essence, such a solution is equivalent to the social contract which creates society and eliminates the horrors of the Hobbesian jungle. In practice, such a social contract frequently is extremely elusive.

The likelihood of a contractual solution, whether or not reinforced by government legislation, depends upon the precise nature of the rent-seeking problem. If a number of special interest groups simultaneously recognize that they are systematically harming each other — that their losses are symmetrical — some negotiated resolution of the problem is predictable. Free rider problems may result in the use of government to effect the resolution. However, if some special interest groups are persistent winners — for example, specific professional associations and selected labour unions — the solution may not be easy. Those who lose in the rent-seeking struggle may not be willing to bribe those who gain to desist from their activities; they may not believe that a deal would be honoured, even if supported by legislation.

The possibility that gains and losses from particular kinds of rent seeking might be asymmetrical has stimulated interest in constitutional rather than discretionary solutions to the special interest group problem. Buchanan et al. (1980, pp. 359–67) argues that, by extending the overall range of the contract, asymmetries in gains and losses may balance out for all participants. Moreover, the greater stability of a constitutional settlement, it is argued, will encourage agreements from groups who otherwise might fear reneging on the part of their rent-seeking rivals. However, should the more successful special interest groups obtain special concessions written into the constitution itself, the consequent social waste undoubtedly would be exacerbated.

If the unconstrained legislature is vulnerable to rent seeking — and recent evidence in the United States suggests that it is — then federalism and the division of powers might offer greater protection to the electorate than would straightforward rules derived from an infiltrated legislature. Certainly, this is Madison's belief in the *Federalist Papers*. More recently, the idea of offering line-vetoes on budget proposals to the U.S. president reflects similar considerations. The specific implications for Canada are reviewed in the final section, on Canadian constitutional design.

The Role of Bureaucracy

Early theories of bureaucracy tended to be dominated by Weberian notions of impartial, efficient service provision. Senior bureaucrats were viewed as carefully mirroring the policy objectives of the incumbent government, without reference to their own self-interest. Economists, for the most part, took little account, in analyzing market failure and recommending efficiency-enhancing bureaucratic interventions, of the undercurrent of popular criticism of bureaucrats on grounds of laziness, insensitivity to citizen preferences and indeed of gross self-seeking behaviour. Even Khrushchev referred contemptuously to his own bureaucrats as "busy loafers."

Early challenges to this nirvana model stem from Tullock (1965) and from Downs (1966). Both analyze the internal organization of bureaucracy, subjecting bureaucrats to critical scrutiny and noting the inevitable control loss associated with this form of economic organization. However, Niskanen (1971) is the first to subject bureaucracy to a comprehensive critique with respect to both its internal organization and its external environment.

Bureaucracy is a concept that can be defined broadly or narrowly, with some, like Breton and Wintrobe (1982), extending its domain to include even private corporations that raise their revenues by selling commodities at a per unit price. In this paper, however, bureaus are defined narrowly in the sense of Niskanen as public sector organizations in which the owners and employees cannot appropriate directly any part of the difference between revenues and costs as personal income, and in which a significant part of recurring revenues derive from other than the sale of output at a per unit price.

Niskanen's theory of bureaucracy and representative goverment is predicated on the assumption that senior bureaucrats who exercise responsibility over bureau budgets are self-seeking. Of the several variables seen to influence the bureaucrat's well-being — salary, perquisites of office, public reputation, power, patronage, output of the bureau, ease of making changes and ease of managing the bureau — Niskanen suggests that all except the last two are positively associated with the total size of the bureau's budget. Thus, he employs budget maximization as a proxy for utility maximization by senior bureaucrats.

Niskanen further assumes for the most part that government bureaus are imbued with supply monopolies, and that they bargain with governments or their appropriations committees over their budgets from positions of information advantage. Given that they trade a total output for a total budget, they are able to exercise their monopoly power, in the limit, so as to extract for the bureau the total consumers' surplus associated with their commodity provisions. Typically, they are seen to dominate government in the bilateral budget bargain.

In consequence, Niskanen views oversupply (in terms of the Pareto criterion) to be a major problem with bureaucracy. Moreover, the bureau would tend to supply outputs at rates well in excess of those that would maximize net value to its government sponsor. A secondary problem, avoided only in the rare case of budget-constrained output, is the provision of output at above minimum average cost. A third problem is the tendency of bureaus to overemploy capital in order to boost the present value of the budget. In general, Niskanen-type bureaus diverge sharply from the Weberian ideal.

A significant weakness in the Niskanen approach is the absence of any clearly specified relationship between government and its bureaus other than that of bureau dominance under conditions of bilateral monopoly. Rowley and Elgin (1985) attempt to remedy this defect by treating the government/bureau relationship as a principal/agent problem. In this case, elected politicians (whether in or out of office) designated to supervise specific bureaus are treated as principals; all others are treated as agents within the bureaucratic structure.

Problems arise in the monitoring process similar to those that occur in the monitoring by voters of their elected government, for both governments (or their representatives) and bureaus are non-proprietary organizations. Government members and bureaucrats do not hold private property rights in their organizations, nor do they own alienable rights to the net assets of individuals. This poses an obstacle to efficient supervision as a consequence both of potential shirking by principals in their monitoring function and of a lack of incentive for senior bureaucrats to monitor their respective bureaus.

In addition, the limited transferability of membership rights weakens two sources of control or influence over senior bureaucratic behaviour that are available to stockholders in proprietary firms. Politicians and senior bureaucrats cannot withdraw the capitalized value of the expected rent stream from their investment as a response to undesirable monitoring arrangements. Nor can voting power easily be concentrated among the principals with a view to removing senior bureaucrats from office.

Nonetheless, monitoring incentives remain, albeit in a truncated form. Legislators, tied to specific special interest constituencies whence they receive electoral support and campaign finances, provide a flow of policy benefits to those interest groups. The committee system is geared to serving this function in all systems of representative government. The committees typically are accorded a truncated property right over a designated range of bureaucratic activities, including some control over bureau budgets. Bureaus that fail to deliver services favourable to the constituency interests of those politicians charged with overseeing their activities are unlikely to receive favoured budget allocations. In this respect, monitoring may be quite effective, be it from the cabinet ministers of a parliamentary government, or from the appropriations committees of the U.S. Congress.

Of course, such monitoring as occurs predictably will be directed to the advantage of special interest groups, and not necessarily to the benefit of majority voters. Once again, representative governments, in the absence of rules, may utilize discretion in ways that do not serve the interests of the majority model of democracy. To the extent that they are seen to do so, there is a case for restricting discretion via constitutional rules and/or via an appropriate division of power between the executive, the legislature and the judiciary.

Canadian Constitutional Design

Prior to 1982, the Canadian constitution was designed on the basis of four important features (Penniman, 1975; Sproule-Jones, 1974). First, the *British North America Act* of 1867, as amended by the United Kingdom parliament and as interpreted by the highest judicial authority (since 1949 the Supreme Court of Canada) set out the legislative, spending and taxing authority of the federal and provincial governments. Second, the United Kingdom parliament, by convention, would not amend the Treaty of Westminster unilaterally, notwithstanding the fact that it was an ordinary statute of the Westminster parliament. Third, the Queen and her representatives (the governor general and lieutenant governors) did not withhold, by convention, royal assent to federal or provincial statutes. Fourth, the courts granted complete legislative supremacy to the federal and provincial governments alone, subject only to the common law doctrines of ultra vires and natural justice.

The Canadian Constitution established the framework for a federal system of government, entrenched in the 1931 Statute of Westminster which bestowed political independence upon Canada subject to the British North America Act itself. Thus, by constitutional document, government powers were divided between two jurisdictions and the notion of unitary government was rejected. Parliament was composed of two chambers, namely, the House of Commons (elected) and the Senate (appointed by the House of Commons). Each of the ten provinces had its own elected parliament with negotiating rights vis-à-vis the federal government and with decentralized decision-making powers of its own.

The constitutional design cannot be properly evaluated without reference to geography and to political and ethnic antecedents. Geographically, Canadians are dispersed over some 3,000 miles along the east-west sliver lining the southern border, without any natural geographical centre around which social interactions cohere. Moreover, the country's regions differ sharply in physiographic and economic character. This heterogeneity itself makes for striking economic differences between the separate provinces, differences that have posed persistent problems for those committed to nationwide economic union.

The country's dominant British and French antecedents endowed Canada with two diverse political traditions: the French settlers left a legacy of community and unity which tended in the direction of decentralization, and even political isolation; the British legacy included not only the institutional framework of a parliament system, but also the values that had evolved with it, namely, a strong emphasis on property and civil rights and a distrust of minority government. Indeed, as Breton has indicated, the non-elected Senate, in large part, is a reflection of the non-elected House of Lords. Also, the ambivalent attitude of some Canadians toward federalism may, to some degree, reflect their sympathy with the British unitary system of parliamentary government.

The Canadian Political System

For purposes of electing representatives to the House of Commons, Canada is divided into 282 federal constituencies. Each constituency sends one representative to the Ottawa legislature, elected by the plurality or "first-past-the-post" principle. This electoral system, bequeathed from Britain, tends to exaggerate the political representation of parties with the majority vote in two-party systems. Under certain ideal conditions, whose details need not concern us here, a cube rule operates in such circumstances, with seats in the House reflecting the cube of the proportion of the votes that each party receives; even where, as in Canada, these ideal conditions do not hold, the tendency toward exaggerated majorities is clearly present. The voting mechanism is damaging for smaller parties in a multi-party election, which tend to be significantly underrepresented in the House by comparison with those under a system of proportional representation. In a country such as Canada characterized by a number of small but homogeneous ethnic minorities, such an electoral system may provide for majority tyrannies in the absence of constitutional constraints.

In the Canadian system, which operates without primaries, parliamentary aspirants have virtually no chance of election unless adopted by a substantial political party. Candidates normally are chosen in conventions organized by local constituency associations. Thus, acceptability to those who exercise power at the constituency level of the parties is a necessary condition for a successful federal political career.

Unlike members of Congress in the United States, elected representatives in Canada are much more closely bound to the collective decisions of their party caucuses. The executive is not elected by popular vote as such, but holds office by virtue of commanding the support of the

House of Commons, of which it is an integral part. Its power flows from its capacity to command a majority of the members; either because the government party holds a majority of the seats, or because it has the support of members of other parties.

One consequence of a parliamentary system in a highly heterogeneous society like Canada is that regional, ethnic and social compromises cannot be effected by executive-legislative logrolling or vote trading. Nor can legislators take independent positions in support of the special interest groups that make up their electoral constituencies, as is typical in the United States. Instead, compromises are derived largely through the competitive interactions within a multi-party system and via intricate trades between the federal and provincial political parties.

The Senate is nowhere nearly as effective as its U.S. counterpart in effecting logrolled compromises, although its composition reflects regional characteristics. Senators are appointed by the government; usually they owe their status to their various contributions to the governing party. The Senate, like the House of Lords in the United Kingdom, is relatively powerless by comparison with the U.S. senate. Its principal value to government is as a source of patronage and as a useful vehicle for retiring ineffective cabinet colleagues.

The federal structure of Canada, in particular the division of powers that has evolved between the federal government and the provinces, is an important constraint on the discretionary powers of the federal government. Each province has a parliamentary system of its own; these systems are serviced by parties only tenuously related to the national parties themselves. This separation of provincial from federal political parties is a rather recent development, and reinforces the above-mentioned division of powers between the federal and provincial governments. It also, in practice, enables provincial governments to invade the federal decision-making process to support special interest constituencies.

In view of the considerable authority accorded to Canadian provincial governments in relation to important economic and social issues, many important political decisions are reached through federal-provincial negotiations. Many of these are effected by officials and then simply endorsed by the governments concerned. The dangerous consequence, at least for majority democracy, is that governments, at both federal and provincial levels, are left merely with plebiscitory powers to accept or to reject agreements effected de facto by ministers and their permanent officials. The scope for agenda manipulation in such circumstances is considerable.

A further feature of the Canadian political system is that, like many others, it allows, in practice, considerable discretionary power to the federal bureaucracy. Each federal bureau technically operates under the authority of a minister, and is responsible to the cabinet which, in turn, is responsible to Parliament. In practice, however, as earlier analysis has indicated, bureaucracy is endowed with significant discretion based upon substantial independent powers. Such powers may be deployed in ways inimical to the interests of the majority voters.

Canada is a multi-party political system, with three major political parties. However, no minority party has ever formed a government. In this sense, the Canadian federal political market is best analyzed as a two-party system. All parties contesting elections for the House of Commons in Ottawa also seek office in at least some of the provinces. But the relationship between the parties in the two jurisdictions varies considerably, even when the same party name is employed. For example, the National Liberal Federation of Canada is legally and practically quite separate from the Parti libéral du Québec. In some cases, there is no provincial equivalent of a federal party; separate organizations, in such circumstances, may offer strong political support.

The Conservative party, under the leadership of Sir John A. Macdonald, helped to forge the Canadian Dominion in 1867. The party was committed at an early stage to the union of Canada and to the centralization of the Canadian political system. Its support was drawn from the propertied electorate, and it was closely allied to the commercial, social and religious establishment.

The hegemony of the Conservative party was challenged successfully toward the end of the 19th century by the Liberal party under the leadership of a French Canadian, Sir Wilfrid Laurier. For most of the 20th century, the Liberal party has dominated Canadian politics, forming the government for a large proportion of that time. Neither major political party has deep ideological roots, and both reflect the pro–private enterprise preferences of the Canadian median voters. The Liberal party typically positions itself somewhat to the left of the Conservative party in political space, though the pressures of the vote motive encourage convergence at election times.

Toward a Political Economy of Canadian Federal Government

Canada is a federation in the strict sense of Breton and Scott (1980). The responsibility for public policies is divided between two jurisdictions, and entrenched in a constitutional document. Changes in assignment of powers are costly to implement, as the recent constitutional debate clearly indicates.

Early American proponents of federalism, notably the authors of *The Federalist Papers*, sought a political framework designed to reinforce individual liberties by checking the powers of democratically elected governments. Fearing that the vote motive alone would prove to be an inadequate check on the coercive powers of the unitary form of government, Madison and others argued in favour of the fragmentation of such powers among government units operating at different jurisdictional levels. They predicted that competition among such units would enhance individual liberties and would do so to a greater degree within a federal than within a balkanized system of government.

Federalism is especially effective in promoting competition at the provincial level of government. At this level, voter mobility (the exit option) is less costly than at the national level. Provincial governments that use discretionary power to discriminate against voter minorities may induce outward migration of voters to provinces that offer more attractive environments. Although this "club" safeguard may be facilitated also by balkanized unitary governments, typically the latter do not facilitate migration to the extent provided for by federalism. Moreover, federalism offers additional voice safeguards to coerced citizens who may appeal to the federal level for protection.

Of course, the cost of exit is never low, and the adjustment mechanism is accordingly restricted. It is unlikely that coerced minorities would achieve optimal relocations, even in a federal system, for occupations tend in many instances to be location specific and to restrict geographical mobility. In addition, there are a limited number of clubs in Canada (provinces and territories) among which disenchanted voters may pick and choose. Moreover, the fact that the French language is not widely used outside Quebec (except in parts of New Brunswick and in Ottawa) severely restricts the mobility of francophone Quebeckers.

If federalism is to be favoured by reference to the criteria of liberty, adaptability to risk and diversity, these advantages are not without cost. They are purchased at a price measured in foregone scale economies, foregone external benefits both in production and in consumption, and by some sacrifice in the efficiency of public goods supply at the provincial level. There may also be a reduction in empathy, even an increase in animosity, between citizens across the jurisdictional boundaries.

Breton and Scott, among others, have argued that bargaining between the federal government and the provinces is usefully analyzed as a bilateral monopoly process, albeit tempered by interprovincial rivalry. Bargaining is predictable over the allocation of powers, with the provinces trading authority in return for federal grants and other benefits. Given the complex and costly nature of such bargaining, there is no reason to expect efficient solutions.

Bargaining is one aspect of the federal system. Another is the monitoring of the performance of provincial governments by the federal government in matters such as the provision of publicly funded health care, where the provinces implement programs in collaboration with the federal authorities. Once again, the principal-agent relationship manifests itself. The federal government has many sanctions, economic and non-economic, with which to discipline "aberrant" provincial governments. In the absence of constitutional constraints, the vote motive ensures that such sanctions will be employed.

Interjurisdictional tensions are nowhere more apparent than in fiscal relationships between the federal and provincial governments (Buchanan, 1960). In particular, if the provinces are required independently to finance certain traditionally assigned functions, fiscal inequalities will arise if their respective fiscal capacities are not equivalent. Also, and even in the limiting case of identical fiscal capacity (per capita income and wealth distributions) the burden of taxation or the rate of provision of public services may not be the same. For fiscal decentralization offers scope for provincial governments to vary the fiscal packages that they supply to their citizens.

Thus, the concept of fiscal equity does not require equality of fiscal treatment. Rather, it implies an equality of fiscal capacity — the ability to provide equivalent services at an equivalent burden of taxation. To the extent that fiscal capacities in this sense are unequal, a case exists for an interjurisdictional transfer system operated at the federal level. In principle, such transfers would be so designed as to eliminate the fiscal capacity incentive for individuals to migrate from the less to the more highly endowed jurisdictions. Indeed, without such a transfer system, political pressures either toward centralized unitary government or toward balkanization of the federal system may prove to be inexorable. If the decentralized authority of provincial jurisdictions is to be protected, fiscal equity, in the view of some public choice analysts (Buchanan, 1960), constitutes a case for unconditional transfers rather than for grants-in-aid tied to specific expenditure programs.

In any event, public choice theory does not suggest that principles of fiscal equity will dominate once a transfer system is operative. Special interest groups will invade the process; legislators will look to their constituencies. Rent seeking will eliminate much of the transfer benefits en route from donors to recipients, and much of what actually is transferred will be diverted to advantages for special interest groups. In the absence of rules, it is predictable that principles will be washed aside by the realities of institutional public choice, however determined the majority vote and however supportive the election manifestoes of the competing political parties.

The constitutional basis for fiscal federalism in Canada was set out in sections 91–95 of the *Constitution Act, 1867*, as interpreted by the courts. The terms of the act were sufficiently flexible, however, to encourage both federal and provincial governments to justify political initiatives in apparently precluded areas. The major but not the sole avenue for federal initiatives was the power to spend on any policy out of general revenues, unless legislation authorizing such expenditures amounted to a regulatory scheme falling within provincial powers. The major but not the sole avenue for provincial initiatives has been the property and civil rights clause of section 92. The major vehicles for joint federal and provincial initiatives have been (a) concurrent jurisdiction in the areas of agriculture and immigration; (b) parallel legislation and administrative regulation; (c) the delegation of legislative powers by one government to a body created by another government; and (d) fiscal transfers and grants, or contracting-out options for such transfers and grants.

Inevitably, in such circumstances, constitutional arrangements have been jointly negotiated between the federal government and the ten provincial governments, acting exclusively as a club. The club has tended to act together to exclude all other governments (such as local governments), associations or individuals from negotiations over constitutional arrangements. Specifically, all bids by the municipalities since 1969 for co-equal constitutional status with federal and provincial levels of government and for direct federal funding for urban areas have been thwarted. Moreover, until 1982, all attempts to entrench a bill of rights in the *British North America Act* were denied by the failure to achieve unanimous provincial government consent for a constitutional amendment. The unanimity convention was eliminated by the Canadian Supreme Court during the recent constitutional debate.

The *British North America Act* initially assigned fiscal powers between federal and provincial governments in sections 91 and 92, confining the provinces to direct taxation and offering the federal government exclusive rights to impose import duties and wholesale or manufacturing sales taxes. Subsequently, however, the courts interpreted direct taxation to include taxes not only on real property and on personal income, but also on corporate income and retail sales. Moreover, other sections of the act offered the federal government almost unlimited taxation and legislative powers which, in various circumstances, would override sections 91 and 92.

World War II led to the emergency appropriation of personal and corporate income taxation powers by the federal government. But even before that the experience of the 1930s, when the tax base of the provinces collapsed just as the relief payments constitutionally assigned to them were expanding, had pointed to the desirability of concentrating more fiscal power in the hands of the federal government. Federal relief expenditures together with federal refinancing of the maturing debt played a role in the process of fiscal centralization.

By 1947, seven provinces had agreed to a federal tax-rental offer under which income taxes and death duties were to be collected by the federal government. Quebec and Ontario refused to sign this agreement, but the latter province signed a more favourable agreement in 1952. By 1957, all the provinces, except Quebec, had surrendered their corporate and personal income taxes for collection by the federal government and were dependent upon reallocation schemes which tended to redistribute in favour of the less wealthy provinces. In addition to federal grants, the provinces and municipalities were left with retail and property taxes, the revenues from which were growing at a rate much slower than that of the national economy, while finding themselves responsible for most of the increase in public expenditures.

The system of Canadian equalization payments (unconditional cash transfers) was designed in principle to induce fiscal equity in the sense outlined above. The equalization system is based on a measure of the ability of a province to raise fiscal revenues according to some representative tax system. The system incorporates a specified number of tax bases into a representative tax system. A population-weighted average tax rate is computed and applied to the base in order to obtain an estimate of the average per capita receipts for all provinces. Payments are transferred to provinces with below average receipts. These transfers, which are totally unconditional, are added to tax abatements made available by the federal government.

Following World War II, shared-cost programs became an increasingly important area of federal-provincial governmental interaction in Canada. Programs such as hospital insurance, medicare, extended health care, postsecondary education and the Canada Assistance Plan fell constitutionally under provincial jurisdiction. However, federal involvement in such programs was justified as standardizing public services and reducing interprovincial wealth differentials. Only Quebec resisted and retained provincial autonomy. As the cost of such programs increased during the early 1970s, so the federal government began to cap its contributions to postsecondary education and to medicare expenses. In 1977, a block-funding agreement was implemented whereby hospital insurance, medicare and postsecondary education would not be subject to matching grants but would be funded from a special abatement of personal income taxes and corporate income taxes together with a variety of cash transfers from the federal government. A similar arrangement followed for the Extended Health Program, leaving only the Canada Assistance Plan as the remaining shared-cost program.

Thus, as economic growth rates fell and federal budget deficits increased, strained relationships between the federal government and the provinces were increasingly evident. The four poorest provinces (Newfoundland, New Brunswick, Nova Scotia and Prince Edward Island) increasingly became dependent on the federal government; other provinces, (notably Alberta and Quebec) systematically pressed for greater autonomy. Provincial holdouts and threats of secession became common bargaining ploys. It is noteworthy, however, that the equalization principle, albeit somewhat tarnished, survived as a principle of fiscal equity. The explicit rules governing transfers appear to have protected the system from the pressures of institutional public choice, even under threat of balkanization of the Canadian federal system. It is unlikely, however, that the transfer system is proof against rent seeking social waste as special interest groups vie for its opportunities.

The Constitution Act, 1982: A Public Choice Perspective

The debate within Canada over the repatriation of the Constitution in suitably amended form and the provision of a Charter of Rights and Freedoms forcibly demonstrates the relevance of public choice theory for understanding the issue of rules versus discretion in constitutional design (Courchene, 1984; Breton, 1984; Winer, 1984; Sproule-Jones, 1984). As such it forms an ideal topic for the concluding section of this paper.

The "agreement" of November 1981, Quebec dissenting, which paved the way for the 1982 act, was the outcome of a titanic battle over both the political and the economic future of Canada. Politically, the battle lines were drawn with Ottawa, New Brunswick and Ontario on one side, and the eight remaining provinces on the other. Economically, the debate centred around the issue of whether the economic union of Canada should be supported by centralizing constitutional rules, or whether provincial governments should retain their discretionary powers, if necessary balkanizing the economic union in the interests of their own constituents. As public choice theory would predict, the outcome was a logrolling compromise, once the veto power for Quebec was eliminated by a Supreme Court decision that unanimity was not necessary to effect constitutional changes.

Although the Charter of Rights and Freedoms potentially is an extremely important document checking the sovereignty of federal and provincial parliaments, it should not be viewed as establishing the basic structure of society in the sense defined by Rawls. For the charter certainly did not precede the parliamentary system in Canada; self-evidently it was a logrolling compromise between the existing federal and provincial governments. The existing constitution thus determined the Charter; rather than the Charter establishing the framework for subsequent constitutional evalution, as is required for "justice as fairness."

The initiative of the federal government in offering a Charter as a part of the process of repatriating the Constitution played a decisive role in the compromise solution, because the Charter constituted an evident threat to the sovereignty of provincial governments. Citizens would be offered specific safeguards against the abuse of discretionary power, and these safeguards would operate through the mediation of the Charter, which would be given its real strength by a national body, the Supreme Court of Canada.

The eight provinces that opposed Ottawa on constitutional change opposed for a variety of motives; but the Charter was one of the more important. Several of the eight premiers, recognizing the threat to parliamentary supremacy, opposed it in defence of their own discretionary power. Others opposed it because the Charter would identify citizens more closely with their national government, thereby loosening provincial loyalties. More generally, a Charter threatened the privileged positions of politicians and bureaucrats. As Breton argues, it is easy to understand why politicians and bureaucrats do not draft strong charters.

In any event, in this instance the vote motive dominated special interests as the 1980–81 debate proceeded. In proposing the Charter, the federal government encouraged the view initially that everything except linguistic rights would be negotiable. That position was inevitable in the dynamics of constitutional change which involved a struggle between competing conceptions of federalism. However, once the electoral popularity of the Charter became evident, the federal government assigned to it a much more central role than had initially been anticipated and the Charter was approved as part of the constitutional accord.

The role of the Supreme Court in interpreting the Charter now is crucial. Already several hundred cases await judicial interpretation. Once again, the issue of parliamentary supremacy is centre stage. If the Supreme Court allows Parliament to deflect its judgments, the newly established separation of powers will quickly disappear. If it holds to the letter of the Charter, government discretion will be significantly restricted, and the role of rules in the Canadian Constitution will be enhanced.

Although many of the specific rules proposed by the federal government in support of economic union had to be abandoned in order to achieve the final compromise of 1981, the repatriated Constitution, together with the Charter of Rights and Freedoms, constitutes a major victory for the federal system of government. The relevance of rules binding sovereign parliaments has been acknowledged. The procedures now available ensure the potential for constitutional amendment should the popular will in favour of rules once again override the obstruction of those who now gain from existing political discretion. Those who favour strong economic union will be especially concerned to promote further the rights to migrate freely and to transfer property and goods freely throughout Canada, for these rights are *crucial* to the effective unification of a federal economy. The Charter of Rights and Freedoms failed to guarantee those rights universally in its 1982 form, and thus left individuals susceptible to significant discretionary power of the provincial governments.

Notes

This study was completed in December 1984. I should like to acknowledge valuable comments received from participants of two meetings of the Research Advisory Group on Social and Economic Ideas and Issues held in April and July 1984. I am also grateful to James M. Buchanan, Robert Elgin, Robert D. Tollison, Gordon Tullock and Michael Walker for helpful suggestions. The paper also reflects the comments of three referees. Robert Elgin ably assisted my research on this subject throughout the summer of 1984. My especial thanks are due to Joan Smith of the Center for Study of Public Choice whose secretarial support for this project went well beyond the call of duty. The Centre for Socio-Legal Studies and Wolfson College, Oxford, also extended its research facilities in support of this project. Finally, I must thank David Laidler, whose critical contributions and unfailing support were essential to the effective completion of this project.

1. This term is taken from the title of a forthcoming text by Brennan and Buchanan.
2. For a detailed critique see Rowley and Peacock (1975).
3. On the principal-agent relationship see Fama (1980).
4. For a more detailed review of this viewpoint, see Brennan and Buchanan (1983).
5. For a review of this, see Buchanan and Wagner (1977).
6. See also Wagner (1984).
7. The use of the term "spatial," in this context, derives from geographical-style location theory first introduced into economics by Hotelling (1929). His early reference to the possible political applications of this notion triggered the literature on public choice.

Bibliography

Black, D. 1958. *The Theory of Committees and Elections*. London: Cambridge University Press.

Boulding, K.E. 1971. "Environmental Quality: Discussion." *American Economic Review* (May): 167–68.

Brennan, G., and J.M. Buchanan. 1980. *The Power to Tax: Analytical Foundations of a Fiscal Constitution*. London: Cambridge University Press.

———. 1983. "Predictive Power and the Choice Among Regimes." *Economic Journal* 93 (March): 89–105.

———. 1985. *The Reason of Rules*. New York: Cambridge University Press. Forthcoming.

Breton, A. 1974. *The Economic Theory of Representative Government*. New York: Macmillan.

———. 1984. "An Analysis of Constitutional Change: Canada 1980–82." *Public Choice* 44 (1): 251–72.

Breton, A., and A. Scott. 1980. *The Design of Federations*. Montreal: Institute for Research on Public Policy.

Breton, A., and R. Wintrobe. 1982. *The Logic of Bureaucratic Conduct*. London: Cambridge University Press.

Buchanan, J.M. 1960. "Federalism and Fiscal Equity." In *Fiscal Theory and Political Economy*, edited by J.M. Buchanan. Durham, N.C.: University of North Carolina Press pp. 170-89.

———. 1975. *The Limits of Liberty: Between Anarchy and Leviathan*. Chicago: University of Chicago Press.

Buchanan, J.M., and D.R. Lee. 1982. "Politics, Time and the Laffer Curve." *The Journal of Political Economy* 90 (August): 816–19.

Buchanan, J.M., and R.E. Wagner. 1977. *Democracy in Deficit: The Political Legacy of Lord Keynes*. New York: Academic Press.

Buchanan, J.M., R.D. Tollison, and G. Tullock, eds. 1980. *Toward a Theory of the Rent-Seeking Society*. College Station: Texas A&M University Press.

Courchene, T.C. 1984. "The Political Economy of Canadian Constitution-Making: The Canadian Economic-Union Issues." *Public Choice* 44 (1): 201–50.

Davis, O.A., M.J. Hinich, and P. Ordeshook. 1970. "An Expository Development of a Mathematical Model of the Electoral Process." *American Political Science Review* 64 (2): 426–48.

Downs, A. 1957. *An Economic Theory of Democracy.* New York: Harper and Row.

———. 1966. *Bureaucratic Structure and Decision-Making.* New York: Rand Corporation.

Enelow, J.M., and M.J. Hinich. 1984. *The Spatial Theory of Voting.* London: Cambridge University Press.

Fama, E.F. 1980. "Agency Problems and the Theory of the Firm." *Journal of Political Economy* 88 (April): 288–302.

Gordon, Scott. 1980. *Welfare, Justice and Freedom.* New York: Columbia University Press.

Hamilton, A., J. Jay, and J. Madison. 1937. *The Federalist.* New York: Modern Library.

Hobbes, T. 1943. *Leviathan.* London: J.J. Dent.

Hotelling, H. 1929. "Stability in Competition." *The Economic Journal* 39: 41–57.

Hume, D. 1963. "Of the Independency of Parliament." In *Essays Moral, Political and Literary,* vol. I, edited by T.H. Green and T.H. Grose. Oxford: Oxford University Press.

Kant, I. 1965. *The Metaphysical Elements of Justice.* Indianapolis: Bobbs.

Locke, J. 1955. *Second Treatise of Civil Government.* Chicago: Regnery Gateway.

Mill, J.S. 1977. "Considerations on Representative Government." In *Essays on Politics and Society,* vol. 19 of *The Collected Works.* Toronto: University of Toronto Press.

Niskanen, W.A. 1971. *Bureaucracy and Representative Government.* Chicago: Aldine.

Olson, M. 1965. *The Logic of Collective Action.* Cambridge: Harvard University Press.

———. 1982. *The Rise and Decline of Nations.* New Haven: Yale University Press.

Pareto, V. 1909. *Manuel d'Économie Politique.* Paris: Girard and Brière.

Penniman, J.R. 1975. *Canada at the Polls.* Washington, D.C.: American Enterprise Institute.

Rawls, J. 1972. *A Theory of Justice.* Oxford: Oxford University Press.

Rousseau, J.J. 1913. *The Social Contract.* London: J.M. Dent.

Rowley, C.K. 1974. "Pollution and Public Policy." In *Economic Policies and Social Goals,* edited by A.J. Culyer, pp. 284–312. London: Martin Robertson.

———. 1983. "The Failure of Government to Perform its Proper Task." *Ordo* 34: 39–58.

———. 1984. "The Relevance of the Median Voter Theorem." *Journal of Institutional and Theoretical Economics* (March): 104–35.

Rowley, C.K., and A.T. Peacock. 1975. *Welfare Economics: A Liberal Restatement.* London: Martin Robertson.

Rowley, C.K., and R. Elgin. 1985. "Towards a Theory of Bureaucracy." In *Public Choice, Public Finance and Public Policy,* edited by D. Greenaway and G.K. Shaw. Oxford: Basil Blackwell.

Smith, A. 1937. *The Wealth of Nations.* New York: Modern Library.

Smithies, A. 1941. "Optimum Location in Spatial Competition." *Journal of Political Economy* 44: 429–39.

Sproule-Jones, M. 1974. "An Analysis of Canadian Federalism." *Publius* (Fall): 109–36.

———. 1984. "On the Analysis of Constitutional Change in Canada." *Public Choice* 44 (1): 279–83.

Tullock, G. 1965. *The Politics of Bureaucracy.* Chicago: Public Affairs Press.

———. 1967. *Towards A Mathematics of Politics.* Ann Arbor: University of Michigan Press.

———. 1974. *The Social Dilemma.* Public Choice Society Book and Monograph Series. Blacksburg, Va.

Wagner, R.E. 1984. *Agency, Economic Calculation and Constitutional Construction.* Miami: Florida State University Working Paper.

Wicksell, K. 1896. *Finanz Theoretische Untersuchungen.* Jena: Gustav Fischer.

Winer, S. 1984. "Comment on Papers by Thomas Courchene and Albert Breton." *Public Choice* 44 (1): 273–78.

4

The Growth of the Public Sector in Canada

Dan Usher

This paper has two related objectives: to summarize explanations of the increase in government involvement in the economy, and to present a broad statistical picture of the growth of government in Canada.

Explaining the Growth of Government

Explanations of the growth of government involvement in the economy can be classified under headings of what might be called the theory of rational self interest behaviour by the majority of voters, and conspiracy theory.[1] Theories based on rational, self-interested behaviour of the majority of voters start with the premise that there is a "best" size of government at any given time, depending on the demands for and the costs of the services that government does or could provide. Changes in the size of government are then attributed to changes in the underlying costs and benefits, that is, to shifts over time in the demand or supply curves of public services. The obvious, though trivial, example is the shift in the demand curve for soldiers when a country goes to war. Conspiracy theories attribute observed growth to the machinations of self-seeking, power-hungry bureaucrats and politicians, to the influence of special-interest groups in the private sector, and to fiscal illusion by which voters can be enticed with "free goods" because they cannot see the connection between expenditure and taxation. Theories based on the rational self-interest of voters will be examined first because the force of conspiracy theories depends on whether there is anything left to be explained after as much as possible has been attributed to the self-interest of the average citizen as a consumer of government services.

Rational Self-Interest Theories

The notion of rational, self-interested behaviour on the part of a majority of voters is inevitably somewhat vague, for there are many potential majorities in any given population. This difficulty has a family resemblance to the well-known ambiguity in the concept of the social optimum or common good, that there is no obviously right way for conflicting interests among citizens to be reconciled. This difficulty is common to all evaluation of social policy, and it is no more or no less a problem in the present context than in any other. In discussing theories of the growth of government, I simply assume that something corresponding to the interest of a majority of voters can be identified.

Particular care must be taken to distinguish between size and growth, that is, between reasons why government is large and reasons why government is growing. For instance, it is no explanation of the growth of government to say that government has to provide public goods. What needs to be explained is why people want more public goods today than at some time in the past. My examination of theories of the growth of government will proceed in stages: first an enumeration of benefits and costs of public expenditures, and then a list of reasons why certain benefits or costs may be changing over time.

BENEFITS AND COSTS

The benefits from public expenditure are simple and well known: avoidance of the free-rider problem in the provision of public goods, redistribution of income, reassignment of income, and internalization of externalities.[2]

The most important instance of the free-rider problem concerns the protection of citizens from foreign enemies and from one another. The army and the police benefit everybody, but nobody's contribution has a significant impact upon the total provision, and it is in each person's interest to evade his share of the cost. Everyone has an incentive to free ride at the expense of his neighbours. The public sector must therefore compel each citizen to contribute his share of the cost of the army and the police. Provision of roads is similar insofar as it is impractical to collect tolls on the use of roads. Another example is pure research, which is a worldwide public good because knowledge acquired by research in Canada may convey benefits to the people in other countries as well.

Redistribution may be designed to improve the lot of the permanently poor at the expense of the permanently rich, or it may be thought of as insurance for everyone. I do not know when I shall become unemployed or whether the ups and downs of fortune throughout my life will leave me, on retirement, with sufficient resources to provide for my old age.

Private insurance is considered inadequate. I therefore join with my fellow citizens to procure insurance through the intermediary of the public sector in the form of unemployment insurance and the universal old age pension.

Government may influence the distribution of income in two quite distinct ways. It may seek to narrow the gap between all rich and all poor (what I am calling redistribution) or it may seek to increase the income of the members of a particular group of people who may or may not be among the poorer half of the nation. For want of a better term to distinguish these two types of influence on the incomes of citizens, the latter may be called a "reassignment." Among the various kinds of reassignment of income are rent control, agricultural price supports or acreage allotments, and subsidies to farms or firms. One may speak of reassignment of income as a reason for government participation in the economy without committing oneself as to whether the reassignment is ultimately beneficial to the economy as a whole. It is sufficient to observe that governments do knowingly reassign income from time to time.

The fourth reason is to make the economy more efficient — in effect to increase national income per head — by closing the gap between private and social costs or benefits of private activity, that is, by correcting for externalities in the private sector: the factory does not bear the social cost of the smoke emitted from its chimney; firms cannot capture the full benefit of training supplied to their workers; education of the young inculcates good citizenship; innovators cannot capture the full benefit to the community of new products or processes; the shadow, or accounting, price of labour may be less than the market wage in areas of considerable unemployment. Government is said to correct for such externalities when it taxes, subsidizes, regulates, encourages, mandates or prohibits behaviour for which the private and social marginal product would differ in the absence of such intervention.

Though redistribution, reassignment, and correction for externalities are conceptually distinct, they are often mixed up in practice. Some groups are subsidized because they are poor, despite the fact that no subsidies are offered to others who are equally poor. Reassignment is often justified as though it were redistribution (as when rent control for wealthy occupants of posh apartments is justified with reference to poverty-stricken old ladies, or when subsidies accruing to owners of firms are justified with reference to poorly paid workers), which is why it is especially important to have distinct terms for redistribution and reassignment. Corrections for externalities typically benefit one group at the expense of another so that, once again, it is possible to clothe the interests of some groups in the language of the general good, in this case efficiency rather than equalization.

Two considerations are particularly important in assessing the role of the government in the reassignment of income and in correcting for externalities. The first is statistical. Whereas provision of public goods and transfers to persons require public expenditure and are reflected in the time series of government expenditure as a percentage of national income, the attempt to favour a particular group of people or to equalize private and social product may leave no statistical trace within the national accounts. An industry may be promoted through investment tax credits, tariffs on competing imports, subsidization of inputs, regulation of entry of new firms, or low rates of corporation income tax. Government involvement in the economy through tax expenditures and regulation cannot be captured by the usual measure of the growth of the public sector, though it may be recorded by other measures to be discussed below.

The other consideration has to do with the formation of economic policy. It is a serious mistake to suppose that the mere identification of externalities is sufficient justification for public policy. Externalities are not like weeds in the garden which should be eliminated the moment they appear. The reason is that externalities cannot as a rule be eliminated costlessly. Government is a large, clumsy, expensive machine which must be employed for some purposes but which should not be employed unless the prospective benefit exceeds the prospective cost.

The word "cost" has a special meaning in this context. It is not just the financial cost of the service that the public sector provides. It is the entire cost of employing the public sector, including certain costs of government over and above the minimum required to induce firms to produce whatever it is the public sector supplies. These costs of government include administrative cost, agency cost, deadweight loss, expenditure on rent seeking, and political cost.

"Administrative cost" consists of the time and effort in deciding what the public sector should do and in overseeing its activities.[3] Consider, for example, the acreage allotment for the production of tobacco. If this remains constant over time, the administrative cost is the cost of policing the regulation to ensure that no tobacco is grown on land not designated for the purpose. If the allotment is adjusted from time to time, the administrative cost must include the labour cost of the deliberations that precede any given change — the meetings of interdepartmental committees, the research to support the positions of the different departments, the time spent discussing the issue in the Privy Council and the cabinet, and so on.

The "agency cost" has to do with the relative efficiency of the public and private sectors.[4] In any organization, there is an incentive on the part of each agent in the hierarchy to serve his own interest rather than the interests of the organization as a whole. The manager of a firm seeks to augment his income and perquisites at the expense of the stockholder. The worker exerts himself no more than is necessary to hold his job. On analyzing the incentives in the public and private sectors, it is difficult to avoid the conclusion that the agency problem is more serious in the public sector, for there are no good substitutes in the public sector for competition among firms or for takeovers by dissident stockholders. Casual observation suggests that employees work longer hours and with greater intensity in the private sector, though there are pockets of energy and efficiency in the public sector as well. Statistical comparisons of the cost of production between public and private sectors in the provision of air transport, refuse collection, and a few other services have tended to show that public provision is usually more expensive, twice as expensive according to the author of one survey of this literature.[5]

"Deadweight loss" is the difference between the revenue raised by taxation and the full cost to the taxpayer inclusive of the loss of output from the diversion of resources from taxable to non-taxable activities.[6] Suppose, for instance, that the corporation income tax is 50 percent (so that an investment with a private value of one dollar has a social value of two dollars) and that a rise in the rate of tax sufficient to generate an extra $100 of tax revenue reduces total investment by $40, diverting that amount to consumption instead. Since the social valuation of $40 of private investment is $80, the full cost to the taxpayer is $140, of which $100 is reflected in tax revenue and the extra $40 is deadweight loss. All taxes entail marginal deadweight loss of one kind or another: the income tax by reducing the incentive to work and save, the tariff by redirecting production and consumption, the excise tax by reducing consumption of the taxed good, and bond financing by crowding out private investment. Furthermore, the diversion of resources from relatively productive, highly taxed activities to relatively unproductive, less taxed activities is magnified by out-and-out tax evasion which causes resources to be used up unproductively by the evader in covering his tracks and by the tax collector in bringing the evader to justice.

Deadweight loss is an important consideration in the comparison of costs and benefits of public sector projects. To continue with our example, a project that costs $100 (in the usual accounting sense of the word "cost") and is to be financed by a small increase in the rate of the corporation income tax should only be undertaken if the value of its benefits exceeds $140. Although estimates of the social cost of tax revenue turn out to be very sensitive to the assumptions of the analysis, recent studies have suggested that the number could easily be as high as 2.0, signifying that a project costing $100 should yield $200 worth of benefits to be acceptable.[7]

"Rent seeking" refers to the waste of resources when firms compete for privileges given at the discretion of the public sector.[8] Suppose that the world price of sewing machines is $100 per machine and that Canada imports 10,000 machines when the tariff is 30 percent so that the domestic price is $130 per machine. Sewing machines will still sell at $130 if the tariff is replaced by an import quota of 10,000 machines because the domestic demand for sewing machines is unchanged. If the government auctions the quotas, their price will settle at $30 and the revenue from the auction will be $300,000, precisely what the revenue from the tariff would have been. If the government chooses to assign the quota to one or more deserving firms, the importers fortunate enough to receive a part of the quota will make a clear profit of $30 per machine. In the latter case, it would pay firms to devote resources to proving their worthiness by hiring lobbyists, employing ex-civil servants, cultivating members of Parliament and showing themselves to be progressive, modern, and socially responsible. A firm seeking quotas would be willing to spend up to $30 per machine. Such rent-seeking expenditure is a waste of resources to society as a whole, for the return to the successful firm is entirely at the expense of another firm that would have been assigned the quota instead. Rent seeking can be expected to arise whenever public policy benefits one group at the expense of others — in adjustments to tariffs, in grants to firms to promote socially beneficial types of investment, in restrictions on the output of farm products, and in tax policy. The more extensive the scope of public policy and the more it tends to favour this or that firm, group, or class at the expense of the rest of the economy, the more costly rent seeking is likely to be.

The political cost of government participation in the economy is impossible to quantify but nonetheless real.[9] Political cost is the tendency toward disintegration of our system of government when elected officials or civil servants have to decide among competing claims of interested groups of citizens. For instance, public provision of medical care requires the government to determine the wages of doctors, and unemployment insurance requires the government to determine the income of the unemployed. Industrial policy is more insidious, for it typically requires the government to decide whether investment will take place here or there, fostering a political climate in which local issues become more important in an election than national issues, the party in power has a strong incentive to favour one region over another, and the disfavoured region has no recourse but the threat of separation. This is compounded by an increase in the temptation to bribery, legal or otherwise, as part of the process of rent seeking, and by what is called political overload — the proliferation of questions that must be resolved by the cabinet, the corresponding reduction in the time available for the consideration of any given issue, and the increased likelihood that decisions will be poorly thought out or excessively delayed.

In principle, these five costs of government are additive, but they appear in different amounts and proportions from one type of expenditure to the next. Pure public goods typically give rise to administrative cost, agency cost and deadweight loss but not rent seeking, except insofar as one group gains more than others from the presence of the public good. Subsidies are particularly conducive to rent seeking, especially where the recipients have to be chosen one by one.

Benefits and Costs of Government Expenditure

Benefits	Costs
Provision of public goods	Administrative cost
Compensation for externalities	Agency cost
Redistribution of income	Deadweight loss
Reassignment of income	Rent seeking
Insurance	Political cost

Thus, in considering what to place upon the agenda of the public sector and what to exclude, the appropriate procedure is to weigh the benefits and costs associated with each program proposed and to accept only those programs for which the balance is favourable.

REASONS FOR THE GROWTH OF GOVERNMENT

Growth may occur as a movement from disequilibrium to equilibrium or because the equilibrium itself is shifting over time. In any given year, there may be an imbalance between benefits and costs of government expenditure, and a lapse of time may be required for the appropriate shift in institutions to take place. It is not impossible that the observed growth of the public sector over the last 50 years is the simple consequence of the fact that the public sector should have been larger 50 years ago and that only now has the right size been discovered. Not impossible, but most unlikely. It seems more reasonable to attribute the growth of government to changes in the balance of benefits and costs over this period. Thus the generic explanation of the growth of government expenditure would be that changes in technology, economic organization, or society have increased benefits or decreased costs in some or all of the categories listed above. I shall speak of changes in benefits as being "on the demand side" and of changes in costs as being "on the supply side." These are considered in turn. Four distinct types of demand (in the sense of taste or want, and not in the sense of an ultimatum) may be identified.

There is first a set of demands arising out of the growing complexity of the economy and leading to an increase in expenditure on the correction of externalities, provision of public goods and redistribution. Environmental protection is the obvious instance. We are constantly inventing new substances that seem to be beneficial to the immediate user, but may be harmful in the long run to the user or to the population as a whole, and are likely to be employed excessively unless their use is regulated. As more and more potentially lethal substances are discovered and as growth of population and per capita income leads to a potential increase in their use, there is an ever greater requirement for regulatory activity.

Changes in the technology of production may lead to an increase in government expenditure by requiring relatively more of the types of goods and services that government ordinarily provides. Consider transportation. As the economy becomes more integrated, Canadians spend increasingly more time on roads and in the air, and an ever larger share of the national product is devoted to the upkeep and construction of roads and airports. Having chosen in the 1930s to run Air Canada as a national airline, the Canadian government committed itself to controlling a segment of the economy that was destined to expand considerably in the years to follow.

Growing complexity of the economy has also been put forward as an explanation for the introduction of unemployment insurance and the old age pension. These institutions would have been of little value in the days when people lived on the land and families took responsibility for the care of the aged. All that has changed with the decline of farming, the advent of the nuclear family, and the increased vulnerability of the worker to technical obsolescence and to the ups and downs of the market. So, the argument goes, people face increasingly greater risks which can only be pooled by the appropriate public policy.

These are the difficult arguments to assess. It is undeniable that technology has become steadily more complex and that new modes of production require new modes of participation by the public sector. It is not obvious that the public sector need become larger or more interventionist on balance, for old forms of intervention may no longer be advantageous. Is it absolutely necessary for Air Canada to remain as a public corporation? Perhaps the unprecedented growth of per capita income since the 1930s has rendered it possible for the prudent worker to acquire sufficient assets to ride out periods of unemployment without public provision of unemployment insurance. Similarly, if Canada did not already have a program of family allowances, I would think it unlikely that we would be inclined to introduce one now.

The point of all this is that there is no solid case for the proposition that increasing complexity of the economy requires larger and more influential government on balance. Public sector intervention in the economy needs to be justified or explained item by item.

Second, it is often alleged that there is a high income elasticity of demand for public goods and regulatory activity; as we become richer we want better parks and public amenities of all kinds rather than more cars, radios, food, and so on.[10] What this argument requires is that the income elasticity of demand for public goods and services be greater than unity. It is difficult to say whether this is really so.

Third, the growth of expenditure on redistribution has been attributed to a change in the composition of the electorate. I have so far reasoned as though there were a single common interest of the population as a whole, an interest which is in some sense the average of the particular interests of the different voters. I discuss conflict of interest among groups of voters under the heading of conspiracy theories below, but there is another political explanation having to do with the extent of franchise.[11] Think of the government as providing public goods and transferring income from rich to poor. When franchise is restricted to the rich, voters are inclined to oppose the redistribution of income, and government is restricted to providing the army, schools, roads, and a few other public goods. As franchise increases, there appear more and more voters whose receipts from transfers would be expected to exceed their share of the tax required to finance transfers. The percentage of the national product paid out in transfers therefore increases over time with the increase in the proportion of poor among the eligible voters, and the ratio of public expenditure to national income increases as well. This theory, while not illogical, is probably out of date. It could explain growth of public expenditure in the 19th and early 20th centuries, but it is hard to see how it can explain the growth of government since the First World War, because franchise has been effectively universal over this period.

A variant of the political theory of the growth of government expenditure connects the incentive to redistribute income with the skewness of the income distribution.[12] In this theory, the amount of redistribution is that desired by the median voter, the voter halfway up the scale of rich and poor. He gets his way because he can choose to enter a majority coalition in the legislature with the 50 percent of voters who are poorer than he and want more redistribution or with the 50 percent of voters who are richer than he and want less. The amount of redistribution desired by the median voter — the amount that maximizes the difference between his receipts and his tax bill — depends on the gap between the median income and the average income in the economy as a whole. The theory is not unreasonable as a partial explanation of the amount of redistribution (or the progressiveness of the tax system) at any moment in time but it is questionable as an explanation of growth, for the income distribution has become less, not more, skewed in most Western countries in the course of this century.

Just as explanations of the growth of government from the demand side have to do with the benefits of government activity, so explanations from the supply side have to do with changes in costs. One such explanation is that improvements in the technology of tax collection have lowered the marginal deadweight loss per unit of tax revenue. In the 19th century, it would have been literally impossible to collect as large a percentage of the national income as governments routinely collect today; tax rates as high as those in force today would have driven the economy back to barter or provoked such massive tax evasion that total revenue would have been less than what was actually collected at the rates in force at that time. Only now, with our modern methods of accounting, communication and computing, can we collect as much as 50 percent of the national income in taxation in peacetime without destroying the economy altogether. [13]

Another way of putting this point is that the Laffer curve has shifted right. At any moment of time, there is an inverted U-shaped curve connecting tax rates and tax revenue. When taxes are low, an increase in tax rates yields an almost proportional increase in tax revenue. As tax rates rise, the extra revenue from a one percent increase in the rate diminishes (and the marginal deadweight loss increases accordingly because the social cost of taxation is proportional to the rate rather than to the revenue) until eventually a point is reached where an increase in the rate yields no extra revenue at all. At the point where total revenue is maximized, the marginal deadweight loss per unit of revenue is effectively infinite, for increases in tax rates make taxpayers worse off without augmenting tax revenue. Improved methods of computing and accounting may have enabled government to appropriate a large share of the national income at a marginal cost that citizens are willing and able to bear. A reduction in the social cost of acquiring public revenue may generate an increase in the equilibrium amount of public expenditure, even if the demand for publicly supplied goods, services and transfers remains stable over time.

Another supply-side explanation of the growth of public expenditure concerns the relative price of public and private goods. [14] Suppose that the only public good is protection, that the amount of protection is proportional to the number of police, and that the efficiency of the police force in supplying protection has remained constant over time, despite the increase in the efficiency of the economy in producing food, clothing, cars, and other private goods. If this were so, the price of protection would rise relative to the price of private goods, a larger share of the national income would be required to maintain the proportion between protection and private goods and there would be an incentive to economize on protection to some extent. Whether this constitutes an explanation of the growth of government expenditure depends on the price elasticity of the demand for protection. The ratio of government expenditure to national income rises or falls according to whether the elasticity is less than or greater than unity. In short, a gradual fall in the productivity of labour in public goods, compared with its productivity in private goods, *may* account for a rise in the percentage of the national income devoted to the purchase of public goods, but *need not* do so.

The issue is complicated by the fact that the output of services cannot ordinarily be observed. The number of policemen each year is known. Whether the amount of protection is increasing is not known because there is no objective measure of output per policeman. This does not matter if the only concern is with the ratio of government expenditure to national income, for government expenditure is a value, not a quantity. Inability to measure output accurately does matter when it comes to evaluating theories connecting growth of government to changes in the relative price of public and private goods.

That completes the list of rational explanations of the growth of government. Are these explanations sufficient to explain the phenomenon? Is there anything more to be explained by conspiracy theories? The answers to these questions would seem to be "yes" and "possibly." Observed growth might be explained by the considerations set out above; I would be inclined to put particular weight upon the reduction in the cost of government made possible by improvements in accounting, communication, computing, and tax collection.

Conspiracy Theories

Growth of the public sector is sometimes attributed to a drive by bureaucrats to expand their spheres of influence.[15] This is a difficult proposition to accept, not because bureaucrats are more altruistic than the rest of us, but because it takes no account of forces pushing in the opposite direction and because it is an explanation of size rather than of growth. There is even some question as to whether the civil servants would gain from the growth of government. Practitioners of most trades seek to reduce entry so as to maintain high wages. Why would bureaucrats not be inclined to do so too? Furthermore, bureaucracy is expensive, and the taxpayer as voter has an incentive to elect representatives committed to holding down the tax bill by limiting the number of civil servants employed. At any moment there is a balance of forces, some tending to increase the civil service, some tending to reduce it. Like the rest of us, civil servants are greedy and power-hungry. What needs to be explained is why the alleged desire on the part of civil servants to expand their spheres of influence is more successful today than in the past. Evidence discussed below suggests that the number of civil servants has grown less rapidly than total government expenditure.[16]

Growth of the public sector has also been attributed to special interest groups in the private sector that exert pressure on politicians to grant favours in the form of tariffs, subsidies, or helpful regulations. Interest groups may subvert legislators or combine with other well-organized interests into a majority coalition in the legislature.[17] Once again, the difficulty with this theory is that it explains size rather than growth. If special interest groups can influence government today, then why could they not do so yesterday? If they could do so yesterday, then why has government grown?

A possible explanation may lie in the interaction between the politics of interest groups and the growth of the public sector for other reasons.

Socialized medicine makes doctors' incomes particularly dependent on the good will of the public sector, converting doctors into a pressure group with a special incentive for collective action. The old age pension transforms the entire population of over 65 into virtual wards of the state with an incentive to vote for high taxation and high public spending. Growth of the civil service and the educational establishment recruits voters into what might be called the high-tax coalition of those who have more to gain as recipients of salaries paid by the government and of transfer payments than they stand to lose from the taxes to finance public expenditure.

Government is sometimes seen as growing according to its own inexorable law, regardless of the interest of the governed or of their rulers. Two such hypotheses are of particular interest. The first is that size of government remains more or less constant in peacetime, but increases permanently during a war.[18] Government expenditure always grows in wartime. The hypothesis is that the decline once the war is over is never sufficient to restore the prewar ratio of public expenditure to total income. The evidence on this hypothesis is mixed. The hypothesis tends to hold quite well for Britain where it was first proposed. It appears to do less well for other countries. In Canada and the United States, the time series of public expenditure as a fraction of national income shows a continuous rise with no major breaks, except during the war years themselves.

It has also been suggested that the size and composition of government expenditure may be the consequence of great waves of public opinion as to how society ought to be organized — opinion with a life of its own, independent of the interests of the citizens who hold that opinion. Toward the end of the last century, the jurist Dicey explained the development of law in England as the consequence of a movement of public opinion through three stages: a conservative stage at the beginning of the century, a brief utilitarian period in the middle, and a socialist phase at the end.[19] Looking over the history of Canadian public expenditure since the Second World War, it is hard to avoid the conclusion that Canadians, like many other people at that time, began the period in a mood of what might be called idealistic Keynesianism in which a substantial redistribution of income and a more interventionist government were believed to be warranted for the establishment of a just society and for the stabilization of the economy. Subsequently, from about 1960 to the present, the influence of government upon the economy seems to have grown in ways that are much more difficult to explain or justify. There has been less emphasis on redistribution of income per se, and greater inclination on the part of the public sector to direct the economy by regulation, subsidy, public ownership of firms, and provision of services that cannot be classified as public goods. This tendency, which does not appear to be grounded in any firm view of how the economy should be organized and which, for want of a better term, might be referred to as "mindless intervention," is not necessarily recorded in any summary statistic of the size of government as a whole.

Measuring the Growth of Government Involvement in the Economy

The growth of government expenditure from 1926 to 1983 is illustrated in Figure 4-1. The primary data in the graphs are from the national accounts. All series are expressed as percentages of "gross national income," defined as gross national expenditure less indirect taxes, plus subsidies, plus an imputation for the services of public sector capital. The rationale for and exact definitions of these terms are contained in the Appendix.

The figure is most easily read from the bottom up. The lowest graph, **government expenditure on civilian goods and services**, begins at about 8 percent of gross national income in 1926, rises a bit in the Depression, falls to a low of about 5 percent during World War II, rises steadily to a peak of 22 percent in 1975, falls slightly, and then rises to an all-time high of 24 percent in 1982. The final rise need not signify a new upward trend; it may be due primarily to the fall in national income in a bad year. The graph above is **government expenditure on civilian and military goods and services**. The distance between these graphs is military expenditure alone. At its peak in 1944, military expenditure accounted for a full 40 percent of gross national income! Four years later, in 1948, it was down to 1.6 percent. It rose to a postwar high of 8 percent in 1953, thereafter declining to under 2 percent in the early 1980s. The next graph, **total government expenditure less interest on the public debt**, may be informative because interest on the public debt is really a deferred tax on past expenditure — a payment from A to B, through the intermediary of the public sector, to compensate for the fact that B paid more than his share of government expenditure and A paid less some years before. Notice how the gap between this graph and the previous one has widened since 1950, mostly because of transfer payments and subsidies. The top graph is **total government expenditure inclusive of interest on the public debt**. Between 1965 and 1983, the interest on the public debt grew from 4 percent to over 8 percent of gross national income. This increase is primarily the consequence of the rise in the money rate of interest required to compensate for the fall in the real value of bonds denominated in money, and not a reflection of increased government involvement in the economy.

Public sector employment can be said to increase or decrease depending on how it is viewed. Public sector employment can be defined narrowly to include civilian employees of federal, provincial and municipal government, or it can be broadly defined to include teachers, post

FIGURE 4-1 Public Expenditures as Percentages of Gross National Income

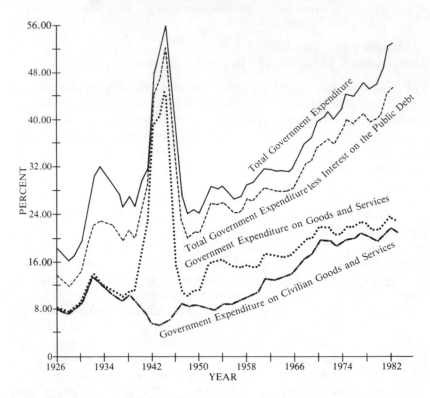

Source: Tables 4A-1 and 4A-2, based on Statistics Canada, *National Income and Expenditure Accounts,* 13-531, 13-201 (Ottawa: Statistics Canada). Cansim and Communications from Statistics Canada.

office workers, the hospital sector and employees of public enterprises. Data sources may not always agree or be equally useful; a choice must be made from among labour force surveys, taxation statistics, civil service records, and so on. Also, to make the numbers meaningful in a growing economy, they must be expressed as a proportion of some economy-wide measure. The customary measure is total employment, but that may not be appropriate in a context where an increasing proportion of the population is participating in the labour force. Is a larger civil service required if people enter the labour force younger or if more women choose to work? It is arguable that the number of government employees is best expressed as a percentage of the population. As may be seen from the top graph of Figure 4-2, the number of civilian employees in federal, provincial, and municipal government has grown steadily from 2.82 percent of the *population* in 1961 to 4.18 percent in

FIGURE 4-2 Indicators of the Government's Role in the Economy

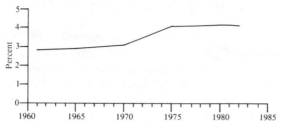

Government employment as a percent of total population

Transfers to persons as a percent of gross national income

Subsidies as a percent of gross national income

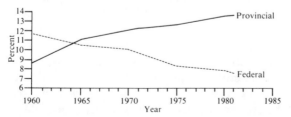

Assets of government business enterprise as a percent of total capital stock

Source: Tables 4A-3, 4A-4 and 4A-5.

1980. The provincial and municipal governments have grown quite rapidly, while federal employment, inclusive of armed forces, has remained constant as a share of total population. Total non-military government employment accounted for 10.5 percent of total *employment* in 1982.

The next two graphs in Figure 4-2 show transfers to persons increasing from under 2 percent of gross national income in 1926 to 13 percent in 1983, and subsidies growing from virtually nothing in 1926 to just under 3 percent in 1981. Both series grew steadily except for a modest increase in transfer payments in the Depression and a substantial increase in subsidies during World War II. It is significant that capital assistance to firms, after hovering at under one-third of one percent of gross national income throughout the 1970s, has more than doubled in 1982 and accounted in that year for a full three-quarters of one percent of gross national income.

Series such as these are reasonably faithful indicators of the growth of government as purveyor of public goods, employer of civil servants, and redistributor of income, but they are less than ideal as indicators of the growth of government influence upon the economy because such influence is increasingly exerted through Crown corporations, in regulations, in tax law favouring one line of activity over another, and in loan guarantees to firms.[20] One can pull together scraps of information confirming or disconfirming the common impression that government influence upon the economy is growing more rapidly than is suggested by the statistics of expenditure and employment. The bottom graphs in Figure 4-2 show assets of federal and provincial government business enterprises, expressed as a percentage of the total mid-year net stocks of non-residential capital in Canada. The reader should be warned that the available data are less than ideal for the purpose at hand. A government business enterprise is defined as a firm with more than 50 percent of the stock owned by the government. Minority holdings of government are therefore ignored, even in circumstances where the government's minority position is sufficient to assume undisputed control. Thus, the Canada Development Corporation is counted as part of government business enterprise in some years but not in others, for its ownership has changed over time.

Federal and provincial loans and loan guarantees to the private sector have increased significantly since World War II from 4.3 percent of GNP in 1950, to 11.8 percent in 1960, to 15.5 percent in 1970, and to 18.5 percent in 1980. However, loans and loan guarantees had been quite large in the Depression, 3.2 percent of GNP in 1930 and 15.6 percent in 1939.[21]

The number of federal and provincial regulatory statutes in force increased from 150 in the year 1870, to 726 in the year 1949, to 1,748 in the year 1978, and the growth of these statutes seems to be accelerating.[22] It is difficult to say what effect, if any, the growth in the number of regulations may be having upon the conduct of firms. One all-inclusive statute may give the government more power over the market than a large number of statutes, each covering a narrow range of the economy and specifying precisely what government may or may not do.

Government influence on agricultural income has grown considerably, but appears to have stabilized in the last few years. The percentage of farm cash receipts channelled through marketing boards increased from 14 percent in 1962 to 55 percent in 1972 and has remained about the same thereafter; it was 55 percent in 1983 as well.[23] The proportion of subsidies of one kind or another in aggregate net farm increased from 8.4 percent in 1965 to 36.2 percent in 1977 and then declined to 25.4 percent in 1978.[24]

Appendix
The Price of Government Output and the Measurement of the Share of the Public Sector in the Economy

The usual measure of the share of government in the economy is the ratio of total government expenditure to gross national product as these terms are defined in the national accounts.[25] This measure is somewhat misleading in that it does not quite answer the question in peoples' minds when they ask about the share of government in the economy. The purpose of this Appendix is to explain why the usual measure is misleading and to justify the modification employed in constructing the graphs in Figure 4-1 in the preceding text. The statistics are presented in Tables 4A-1 and 4A-2 at the end of this Appendix.

Imagine an economy with a public good called guns and a private good called butter. By definition, the share of government, s, is given by the expression:

$$s = \frac{pG}{B + pG} \tag{1}$$

where G is the number of guns produced, B is the number of pounds of butter, and p is the relative price of guns in terms of butter. Obviously, for any given values of B and G there is a one-to-one relation between p and s. If p were zero, signifying that guns could be acquired at no alternative cost in terms of butter, then s would be zero too. At the other extreme, as p becomes infinitely large, then s becomes infinitely large as well. This expression does not lead to a unique measure of the share of government in the economy because there are several ways to define p. Just as the "price" of an ordinary commodity might be measured as the amount (gross of all taxation) paid by the ultimate consumer, the amount (net of all taxation) paid by the original producer, or the amount paid when the commodity is purchased in a particular market; so, too, might the services of government be valued according to a demand price, a supply price or a market price. Call these prices p^1, p^2 and p^3.

Suppose the technology of the economy were such that one hour of labour is sufficient for the production of one gun or one pound of butter. In that case, the supply price, p^2, would have to equal 1. The market price, p^3, would equal the supply price if there were no excise taxes on guns or butter (or if the excise taxes were equal) and if all public revenue were raised by an income tax. The market price would be less than the supply price if there were an excise tax on the private good alone; an excise tax at a rate t increases the market price of the private good to $1 + t$, thereby decreasing the relative price of the public good to $1/(1+t)$. The demand price, p^1, is the marginal rate of substitution in use between public and private goods. It is not reflected in any market price because public goods are supplied by the government. A government representing the interests of the governed chooses a quantity of public goods at which the demand price, p^1, covers both the direct cost in terms of butter of the labour that must be diverted from butter to produce an extra gun and the butter-equivalent of the deadweight loss associated with the contraction of the tax base in response to the increase in tax rates required to finance the extra expenditure. Thus p^1 exceeds p^2 when the optimum quantity of public goods is produced. One would expect that $p^1 > p^2 > p^3$ which implies that $s^1 > s^2 > s^3$ where s^1, s^2 and s^3 are the corresponding measures of the share of government in the economy.

Still abstracting from depreciation, our next step is to confront s^1, s^2 and s^3 with statistics in the national accounts. The statistical counterparts of s^2 and s^3 are straightforward, but that of s^1 is not.

The statistical counterpart of s^3 is

$$s^3 = \frac{\text{government expenditure}}{\text{national expenditure}} \tag{2}$$

where the usual terms "gross" and "net" are left out of the denominator because there is as yet no distinction between them. The statistical counterpart of s^2 is

$$s^2 = \frac{\text{government expenditure}}{\text{national income}}$$

$$= \frac{\text{government expenditure}}{\text{national expenditure} - \text{indirect tax} + \text{subsidies}} \tag{3}$$

where "indirect taxes less subsidies" is almost always positive in practice. The statistical counterpart of s^1 is

$$s^1 = \frac{\emptyset \text{ government expenditure}}{\emptyset \text{ government expenditure} + \text{income originating in the private sector}} \tag{4}$$

where "income originating in the private sector" is the difference between "national income" and "government expenditure" and where ϕ is the marginal social cost of public funds which, as discussed in footnote 7, is generally believed to exceed 1 and has recently been estimated to be as high as 3.5.

Which of these shares is correct? That is to say, which of the above expressions corresponds most closely to what we mean when we speak of the share of the government in the economy? The measure s^3 is commonly employed in studies of the share of government in the economy, but it is in many respects the least satisfactory. First, it is not true, as would be the case if guns and butter were two private goods, that their relative price — the ratio of actual prices paid by the purchasers of these goods — reflects the consumer's rate of substitution in use. That rate is reflected in p^1 rather than p^3. It is not reflected in p^3 because guns and butter are purchased by different agents with different frames of reference. I believe the measure s^3 would appear considerably less attractive if this were recognized.

There is, in addition, a hidden bias in s^3. To identify the bias, suppose the entire public expenditure were financed by an excise tax on private goods. Let the rate of the tax be t and the supply of the labour be N, of which N_G units of labour are employed making public goods and N_B units of labour are employed making private goods. Clearly in such a world, p^3 has to be less than p^2 because the market price of the private good is buoyed up by the excise tax, i.e. $p^2 = p^3(1+t)$. For the government's budget to balance, the following equations must hold: i) $N = N_G + N_B$, ii) $N_G = tN_B$ = expenditure on public goods, and iii) $(1+t)N_B$ = expenditure on private goods. Consequently

$$s^3 = \frac{\text{expenditure on public goods}}{\text{national expenditure}}$$

$$= \frac{N_G}{N_G+(1+t)N_B} = \frac{tN_B}{tN_B+(1+t)N_B} = \frac{t}{1+2t} \quad (5)$$

which has a maximum value of 1/2. When public revenue is raised by an excise tax on private goods, this measure of the share of government in the economy cannot exceed 1/2, regardless of the proportion of resources devoted to the production of public goods and no matter how high the tax rate becomes! The reason for this seemingly anomalous result is that the excise tax incorporates the value of public goods into the market value of private goods, so that the latter is always the larger of the two.

Suppose instead that public revenue is raised through an excise tax at a rate t and an income tax at a rate i. In that case, i) $N = N_G + N_B$, ii) $N_G = iN + tN_B$ = expenditure on public goods, iii) $(1+t)N_B$ = expenditure on private goods, and

$$s^3 = \frac{N_G}{N_G+(1+t)N_B} = \frac{i+t}{1+2t-it} \quad (6)$$

which approaches N_G/N as t approaches zero, and approaches $t/(1 + 2t)$ as i approaches zero. Note particularly that the common value of s^2 and s^3 when $t = 0$ can be expressed either as N_G/N or as i, that is, either as the share of resources employed in the public sector or as the rate of income tax that would be required to finance the public sector for given values of N_G and N. The share of resources and the required rate of the income tax are the same in the simple example, though they will diverge in response to additional considerations to be introduced below.

I think that s^2 is the most appropriate measure of the "share of government in the economy" in that it conveys the information one has in mind when one uses the term. One wants to know the share of total productive capacity devoted to the production of public goods. That is precisely the value of s^3 when public revenue is raised by an income tax and it is the value of s^2 always, for N can be thought of as national income when, as assumed above, the wage of labour is 1, and tN_B can be thought of as "indirect taxes less subsidies." A case can be made for the use of s^1, but I do not consider that here.

Three more considerations must now be introduced: transfers, depreciation, and the return to capital in the public sector. Transfers can be incorporated straightforwardly into the expression for s^2. Once again, the expression would be interpreted as the rate of income tax required to finance the entire public expenditure. Depreciation is not so easily incorporated. A case can be made for measuring public and private expenditure net of depreciation. The argument is that people are concerned, not with the gross outputs of guns and butter, but with the amounts of guns and butter left over after provision for the maintenance of the capital stock. On the other hand, the rate of income tax required to finance the public sector depends on gross rather than net expenditure, and a gross measure of the services of capital is consistent with the treatment of the services of labour. Quantities of labour input are weighted by wages regardless of whether workers retire or lose their skills over time. I employ gross rather than net statistics in the final measure of the share of government in the economy. Only part of the return to capital in the public sector is included in the national accounts. There is an imputation for "consumption of own capital" but no imputation for the rate of return over and above the cost of depreciation. This creates a downward bias in the ratio of gross public expenditure to gross national expenditure as measure of the share of the government in the economy, a bias that might be corrected by adding an imputation for the net earnings of capital in the public sector. I attempt to do so, though the method is not completely satisfactory. The procedure is to scale up the measure of depreciation in the public sector by the ratio of the earnings of capital to depreciation in the private sector. One can think of this procedure as an attempt to measure government expenditure as it would be if public capital were rented.

I have shown that s^2 can equally well be interpreted as the share of the nation's resources employed by or distributed by government, or as the rate of income tax required to finance public expenditure. These interpretations diverge when publicly owned capital must be accounted for. It is now important to distinguish between (a) the rate of the income tax that would be required to finance public expenditure if there were no other taxation and if there were no response on the part of taxpayers to the change in the tax structure; and (b) the sum of the share of resources devoted to public sector output plus the share of income redistributed by government. The first of these measures would seem to be appropriate if one's main concern were with the taxes that have to be raised to finance public expenditure. No imputation would be required for the services of publicly owned capital; nor need one take account of depreciation of public sector capital. The second of these measures would seem to be appropriate if one's main concern were with public sector usage of the nation's resources. In that case, an imputation for the services of publicly owned capital would certainly be required. It is arguable that interest on the national debt might be excluded on the grounds that it is a financial residue of provision of goods and services in the past.

The final measure of the share of government emphasizes resource usage rather than the required rate of the income tax. It is defined as

$$s^4 = \frac{\text{gross government expenditure}}{\text{gross national income}} \tag{7}$$

"Gross government expenditure" is defined as "total government outlay" (17, 16 to 17, 15)[26] plus "imputed net rent on government-owned capital" which is estimated with the aid of the assumption that the ratios of capital income to depreciation are the same in the public and private sectors. Imputed net rent on government-owned capital is therefore measured as "government capital consumption allowance" (18, 2) scaled up by a parameter defined as one less than the ratio of "total income of corporate and government business enterprise" (20, 7) to "corporate and government business capital consumption allowance" (22, 5). "Gross national income" is defined as "gross national expenditure" (2, 19), less "indirect taxes less subsidies" (1, 10), plus "imputed net rent on government-owned capital" as defined above. Consequently in 1983,

$$s^4 = \frac{\left[\begin{array}{c}\text{"total govern-}\\\text{ment outlay"}\\\text{(176,118)}\end{array}\right] + \left[\begin{array}{c}\text{"imputed rent}\\\text{on government-}\\\text{owned capital"}\\\text{(18,375)}\end{array}\right]}{\left[\begin{array}{c}\text{"gross national}\\\text{expenditure"}\\\text{(390,340)}\end{array}\right] - \left[\begin{array}{c}\text{"indirect taxes}\\\text{less subsidies"}\\\text{(41,417)}\end{array}\right] + \left[\begin{array}{c}\text{"imputed rent}\\\text{on government-}\\\text{owned capital"}\\\text{(18,375)}\end{array}\right]}$$

where the numbers in parentheses are millions of dollars and where "imputed rent on government-owned capital" is measured as

$$
\begin{array}{c}\text{``government}\\\text{capital}\\\text{consumption}\\\text{allowance''}\\(6{,}733)\end{array} \times \left[ \cfrac{\begin{array}{c}\text{``total income of}\\\text{corporate and}\\\text{government}\\\text{business enterprise''}\\(103{,}291)\end{array}}{\begin{array}{c}\text{``corporate and}\\\text{government business}\\\text{capital consumption}\\\text{allowance''}\\(27{,}818)\end{array}} - 1 \right]
$$

According to this measure, the share of government in the economy in 1983 was 52.94 percent. Ideally total government outlay should be net of indirect tax on sales of goods to the public sector. No allowance has been made for this item in the calculation because it is difficult to obtain a breakdown of indirect tax between sales to the public sector and sales to the private sector. This item is probably quite small, for sales to the public sector are often exempt from tax.

TABLE 4A-1 Canadian Government Expenditure and Related Data

	Total Government Expenditure			Non-Defence Gov't Expenditure on Goods and Services	Transfers to Persons	Subsidies	Gross National Income Inclusive of Imputation for Services of Gov't Owned Capital
	Inclusive of Imputation for Services of Gov't Owned Capital	Less Interest on the Public Debt	On Goods and Services				
	($ millions)						
1926	861	630	390	375	81	2	4,676
1930	1,019	775	502	478	118	7	5,249
1935	1,140	860	442	415	226	23	3,869
1940	1,766	1,493	1,048	505	211	53	6,032
1944	6,141	5,718	4,929	630	262	267	10,940
1950	4,087	3,543	1,928	1,435	1,032	64	16,930
1955	7,111	6,447	4,036	2,276	1,731	86	25,769
1960	10,517	9,424	5,281	3,735	3,103	314	34,420
1965	15,436	13,761	8,358	6,799	3,449	457	49,392
1970	30,174	26,924	16,630	14,762	7,028	756	76,572
1975	67,980	61,442	33,380	30,600	17,163	3,858	153,805
1980	129,334	112,679	59,405	54,571	30,997	7,352	282,073
1981	151,708	129,895	69,245	63,634	35,271	8,694	316,979
1982	173,821	147,754	77,768	70,966	43,584	8,226	332,469
1983	194,385	166,269	84,104	76,880	50,027	8,627	367,190

Source: Statistics Canada, *National Income and Expenditure Accounts*, Cat. Nos. 13-531, 13-201, Cansim and Communications from Statistics Canada (Ottawa, various years).

TABLE 4A-2 Canadian Government Expenditure as a Percentage of Gross National Income

	Total Gov't Expenditure	Total Gov't Expenditure Less Interest on the Public Debt	Total Gov't Expenditure on Goods and Services	Non-Defence Gov't Expenditure on Goods and Services	Transfers to Persons	Subsidies
1926	18.41	13.47	8.34	8.02	1.73	0.04
1930	19.40	14.76	9.56	9.11	2.25	0.13
1935	29.46	22.22	11.42	10.73	5.84	0.59
1940	29.28	24.75	17.37	8.37	3.50	0.88
1944	56.14	52.27	45.05	5.76	2.39	2.44
1950	24.14	20.93	11.39	8.48	6.10	0.38
1955	27.59	25.02	15.66	8.83	6.72	0.33
1960	30.55	27.38	15.34	10.85	9.02	0.91
1965	31.25	27.86	16.92	13.77	6.98	0.93
1970	39.41	35.16	21.72	19.28	9.18	0.99
1975	44.20	39.95	21.70	19.90	11.16	2.51
1980	45.85	39.95	21.06	19.93	10.99	2.61
1981	47.86	40.98	21.85	20.08	11.13	2.74
1982	52.28	44.44	23.39	21.35	13.11	2.47
1983	52.94	45.28	22.90	20.94	13.62	2.35

Source: Table 4A-1.

TABLE 4A-3 Assets of Government Enterprises

	Assets of Federal Government Enterprises	Assets of Provincial Government Enterprises	Total Mid-Year Non-Residential Capital Stock in Canada	Federal Assets as a Share of Capital Stock	Provincial Assets as a Share of Capital Stock
	($ millions)			(percent)	
1960	7,990	6,091	68,586	11.65	8.88
1965	10,174	10,766	97,310	10.46	11.06
1970	15,353	18,941	153,328	10.01	12.35
1975	25,096	39,010	308,029	8.14	12.66
1980	46,985	80,149	588,594	7.98	13.61
1981	50,917	93,178	681,817	7.48	13.67

Source: Statistics Canada, Federal Government Finance, Cat. No. 61-203 (Ottawa, various years). Statistics Canada, Provincial Government Finance, Cat. No. 61-204 (Ottawa, various years). Data provided by Statistics Canada.

TABLE 4A-4 Government Employment in Canada

	Federal Civilian (1)	Armed Forces (2)	Provincial (3)	Municipal (4)	Total Non-military Gov't Employment (1) + (3) + (4)	Population of Canada
	(thousands)					
1961	204.4	120.0	168.4	140.8	513.6	18,238
1965	207.8	114.2	197.1	159.8	564.7	19,501
1970	258.6	90.2	225.6	201.1	685.3	21,182
1975	365.0	79.2	330.9	247.2	943.1	22,569
1980	349.0	81.2	401.0	274.1	1,024.1	23,912
1981	360.1	83.1	399.4	276.9	1,036.4	24,221
1982	357.8	82.9	401.6	287.1	1,046.5	24,513

Source: Data on government employment supplied by Statistics Canada for the years 1970 to 1982. Figures for 1961 and 1965 are from R.M. Bird, Financing Canadian Government: A Quantitative Overview (Toronto: Canadian Tax Foundation, 1979), Table A4.

TABLE 4A-5 Government Employment in Canada as Percent Share of Population of Canada

	Federal Civilian	Armed Forces	Provincial	Municipal	Total Non-military Gov't Employment
1961	1.12	0.66	0.92	0.77	2.82
1965	1.07	0.59	1.01	0.82	2.90
1970	1.22	0.43	1.07	0.95	3.24
1975	1.62	0.35	1.47	1.10	4.18
1980	1.46	0.34	1.68	1.15	4.28
1981	1.49	0.34	1.65	1.14	4.28
1982	1.46	0.34	1.64	1.17	4.27

Source: Table 4A-4.

Notes

This paper was completed in November 1984. I would like to thank Barbara Clift of Statistics Canada for data and advice.

1. The best and most comprehensive work on the growth of government expenditure in Canada is that of Richard Bird and his associates at the Canadian Tax Foundation. See Bird (1970, 1979) and Bird, Bucovetsky, and Foot (1979). All contain extensive bibliographies. The last book is the best current introduction to the subject.

2. These issues would be discussed in detail in any good textbook of public finance; see, for instance, Boadway and Wildasin (1984).

3. Economists know far too little about the administrative cost of public sector programs. The one published Canadian study I am aware of is by Mendelson (1979), who estimates that the administrative cost of unemployment insurance and workmen's compensation amount to about 9 percent of the money disbursed by these programs. The cost of the old age pension is in the order of one-half of one percent. His estimates do not include the cost of collecting the revenue to finance these programs or their share of the cost of Parliament, Treasury Board, and so on.

4. On agency cost, see Becker and Stigler (1974) and Jensen and Meckling (1976).

5. Spann (1977); see also Borcherding, Pommerehne, and Schneider (1982).

6. Deadweight loss would be discussed in any textbook of public finance; Boadway and Wildasin's book is adequate.

7. There is a wide variation among estimates of the marginal cost of public funds because such estimates are very sensitive to assumptions about the magnitudes of the underlying elasticities of demand and supply. In the earliest empirical paper on the subject, Campbell (1975) estimates marginal social costs of taxation to be about $1.25 per dollar of public expenditure. Browning (1976) estimates the comparable figure for the United States to be between $1.09 and $1.16. The papers differ in that Campbell estimates the loss from the reorientation of consumption brought about by excise taxation, while Browning is concerned with the labour-leisure choice as affected by the income tax. Stuart (1984) derives a series of estimates varying, according to the assumptions about elasticities of labour supply and other aspects of the economy, between $1.07 and $2.33. Browning and Johnson (1984) estimates the marginal cost of transfers to be as high as $3.49. The estimate of a factor of two is from my own paper (Usher, 1982), which cites a number of other papers on this topic.

8. This argument originated in Tullock (1967); for a more thorough treatment, see Krueger (1974).

9. The classic on this topic, Frederick Hayek's old tract *The Road to Serfdom* (1944).

10. This phenomenon is known as Wagner's Law. It is discussed at length in Bird (1979, chap. 4).

11. See Meltzer and Richard (1981).

12. See Peltzman (1980).

13. See Kau and Rubin (1981).

14. This argument has been put forward by Baumol (1967) in an article with the unlikely title of "Macroeconomics of Unbalanced Growth: The Anatomy of Urban Crisis." Beck (1976) has assembled evidence purporting to show that "real" growth of the public sector has been very much less rapid in this century than "nominal" growth, as a percentage of GNP.

15. For example, Niskanen (1971); the thesis of his book is that government is comparable to a firm which maximizes sales subject to a budget constraint; the book contains no adequate explanation of the nature of the constraint. A development of this idea, which is more interesting than the original, is advanced by Brennan and Buchanan (1980), who assume that governments maximize revenue over and above the cost of the public goods necessary to keep the economy going. Given such behaviour by government, their problem is to determine which constitutionally imposed tax base is best for the taxpayer-citizen.

16. See Bird et al. (1979).

17. This proposition, exaggerated to the point of parody, is the central theme of Olson (1982).

18. See Peacock and Wiseman (1961).

19. Dicey (1898).

20. A great deal of literature on regulation, Crown corporations, loans and loan guarantees and equity ownership in private sector firms is summarized in Howard and Stanbury (1984).

21. See Economic Council of Canada (1982).

22. See Economic Council of Canada (1979, Tables B2–1 and B2–2).

23. See Agriculture Canada (various years).

24. See Forbes, Hughes, and Worley (1982, Tables 3–5); as "subsidies," I am including what the authors call "federal subsidies" and "direct payments through commodity programs."

25. To measure the share of government as the ratio of public expenditure to GNP is customary but not universal. Deviation from this practice has been in two directions. First, it has been proposed that both the numerator and the denominator of the ratio be expressed in real terms, with government expenditure deflated by a price index of public output and GNP deflated by a price index of total output. This correction tends to reduce the estimated growth of the public sector considerably because the estimated price index for the public sector has risen very much faster than the index for the entire economy; see Beck (1976). In my opinion, the deflated ratio is not appropriate as an indicator of the share of the public sector in the economy, or of the growth over time in that share. The matter is discussed fully in Heller (1981). Second, there has been a good deal of discussion of whether the increase of income should be net or gross of indirect taxes; see Meerman (1974). Much of the literature on this question has developed in the context of measuring the distribution among income classes of the burden of tax and the benefits of public expenditure. Opinions about the appropriate measures have often depended on who is seen to bear the burden of indirect taxation.

26. Numbers in parentheses refer to table and item in the Canadian national accounts, as published by Statistics Canada, cat. no. 13–201, annual.

Bibliography

Agriculture Canada. Various Years. *Marketing Board Statistics*. Ottawa: Agriculture Canada.

Baumol, W. 1967. "Macroeconomics of Unbalanced Growth: The Anatomy of Urban Crisis." *American Economic Review* 415–26.

Beck, Morris. 1976. "The Expanding Public Sector: Some Contrary Evidence." *National Tax Journal* 29: 15–21.

Becker, G.S., and G.J. Stigler. 1974. "Law Enforcement Malfeasance and Compensation of Enforcers." *Journal of Legal Studies* 3 (January): 1–18.

Bird, Richard. 1970. *The Growth of Government Spending in Canada*. Toronto: Canadian Tax Foundation.

———. 1979. *Financing Canadian Government: A Quantitative Overview*. Toronto: Canadian Tax Foundation.

Bird, Richard, Meyer Bucovetsky, and David Foot. 1979. *The Growth of Public Employment in Canada*. Montreal: Institute for Research on Public Policy.

Boadway, Robin, and David Wildasin. 1984. *Public Sector Economics*. 2d ed. Boston: Little, Brown.

Borcherding, T., W. Pommerehne, and F. Schneider. 1982. "Comparing the Efficiency of Private and Public Production: Evidence from Five Countries." *Zeitschrift for Nationaloekonomie, Supplementum* 2: 127–56.

Brennan, G., and J. Buchanan. 1980. *The Power to Tax*. Cambridge: Cambridge University Press.

Browning, Edgar. 1976. "The Marginal Cost of Public Funds." *Journal of Political Economy* 84 (April): 283–98.

Browning, Edgar, and William Johnson. 1984. "The Trade-Off Between Equity and Efficiency." *Journal of Political Economy* 92: 175–203.

Campbell, Harry. 1975. "Deadweight Loss and Commodity Taxation in Canada. *The Canadian Journal of Economics* 8: 441–77.

Dicey, A.V. 1898. *Lectures on the Relation between Law and Public Opinion in England during the Nineteenth Century*. London: Macmillan.

Economic Council of Canada. 1979. *Responsible Regulation: An Interim Report*. Ottawa: Economic Council of Canada.

_____. 1982. *Intervention and Efficiency: A Study of Government Credit and Credit Guarantees to the Private Sector*. Study prepared for the Economic Council of Canada. Ottawa: Minister of Supply and Services Canada.

Forbes, J.D., J.K. Hughes, and J.K. Worley. 1982. *Economic Intervention and Regulation in Canadian Agriculture*. Study prepared for the Economic Council of Canada. Ottawa: Minister of Supply and Services Canada.

Hayek, Frederick. 1944. *The Road to Serfdom*. Chicago: University of Chicago Press.

Heller, Peter. 1981. "Diverging Trends in the Shares of Nominal and Real Expenditure in GDP: Implications for Policy." *National Tax Journal* 34 (March): 61–74.

Howard, J.L., and W.T. Stanbury. 1984. "Measuring Leviathan: The Size, Scope and Growth of Government in Canada." In *Probing Leviathan*. Vancouver: The Fraser Institute.

Jensen, M.C., and W.H. Meckling. 1976. "The Theory of the Firm's Managerial Behaviour: Agency Costs and Ownership Structure." *Journal of Financial Economics* 3: 305–60.

Kau, J., and P. Rubin. 1981. "The Size of Government." *Public Choice* 37: 261–74.

Krueger, A. 1974. "The Political Economy of a Rent Seeking Society." *American Economic Review* 64: 291–303.

Meerman, Jacob. 1974. "The Definition of Income in Studies of Budget of Incidence and Income Distribution." *Review of Income and Wealth*: 515–22.

Meltzer, A., and S. Richard. 1981. "A Rational Theory of the Size of Government." *Journal of Political Economy* 89 (October): 914–27.

Mendelson, M. 1979. *The Administrative Cost of Income Security Programs, Ontario and Canada*. Occasional Paper 9. Toronto: Ontario Economic Council.

Niskanen, W. 1971. *Bureaucracy and Representative Government*. Chicago: Aldine, Atherton.

Olson, M. 1982. *The Rise and Decline of Nations: Economic Growth, Stagflation, and Social Rigidities*. New Haven: Yale University Press.

Peacock, A.T., and J. Wiseman. 1961. *The Growth of Public Expenditure in the United Kingdom*. New York: National Bureau of Economic Research.

Peltzman, S. 1980. "The Growth of Government." *Journal of Law and Economics* 23 (October): 209–87.

Spann, R. 1977. "Public versus Private Provision of Government Services." In *Budgets and Bureaucrats: The Sources of Government Growth*, edited by J. Borcherding. Durham, N.C.: Duke University Press.

Statistics Canada. Various Years. *Federal Government Finance*. Cat. No. 61-203.

_____. Various Years. *National Income and Expenditure Accounts*. Cat. Nos. 13-531, 13-201.

_____. Various Years. *Provincial Government Finance*. Cat. No. 61-204.

Stuart, Charles. 1984. "Welfare Cost per Dollar of Additional Revenue in the United States." *American Economic Review* 74: 352–62.

Tullock, G. 1967. "The Welfare Costs of Tariffs, Monopolies and Theft." *Western Economic Journal* 5: 224–32.

Usher, Dan. 1982. *The Private Cost of Public Funds: Variations on Themes by Browning, Atkinson and Stern*. Discussion Paper 481. Kingston: Queen's University, Institute for Economic Research.

5

Economic Rationality and the Political Behaviour of Canadians

CLAUDE MONTMARQUETTE

Introduction

On average, approximately one-half of the total expenditures in the economy are made by governments. Whether at the local, provincial or federal level, the significant role played by governments and the "political market" phenomenon is a reality which is generally recognized today. But despite our awareness of this significance, our knowledge of how the political market functions is relatively poor.

It is necessary to understand the reasons for the emergence of government and the political market, and also to discover the economic mechanisms that govern the political market's operations. By addressing these questions, the economist brings a dimension of rationality to the political behaviour of individuals — a rationality that so often seems to be lacking in public debates. One need look no further than the emotional debates that have occurred over the years on the question of Quebec separatism to be convinced of this lack of rationality. The economic perspective proposed in this paper goes further than an examination of hypothetical behaviour of individuals: instead, it takes as its starting point the Canadian political reality and gives an account of the elements inherent in this economic logic that no one is able to break through, whether they be *péquistes*, federalists or Orangemen.

This economic logic tells us that government expansion, brought about by rapid economic growth, by the development of an imposing bureaucracy and by other circumstances, has resulted in the emergence in Canada of a sizable political market combining all the elements which determine supply and demand within a public sector. In turn, the dynamics of the political market have created a political situation in which a large number of Canadians no longer find an acceptable consensus. If the rationality of the individual decisions of median voters or members of pressure groups dominates the political market, the only solution to the political crisis in Canada, in the absence of any rules aimed at controlling this market, is the economic crisis that forces government and political markets to reduce their size.

In the second section of this paper, I begin to justify this conclusion by offering a general examination of the question of omnipresent government and the emergence of political markets in market economies.

The third section focusses on an explanation of the Canadian situation based on the hypothesis of economic rationality in the political behaviour of Canadians, and on the economic principles inherent in the functioning of the political market.

The final section of the paper includes a review of the main results contained in the preceding sections, and draws the necessary conclusions regarding Canadian unity and political consensus, and the economic survival of Canada.

Omnipresence of Government and the Political Market in Market Economies

THEORIES ON THE SUPPLY AND DEMAND OF PUBLIC GOODS AND SERVICES

According to Bénard (1983, p. 514), the classical approach to discussing the role of government in a market economy involves defining and including "public goods" in the analysis of the Pareto optimum and general equilibrium theories.[1] From Samuelson's definition (1954) of a pure public good (one that is indivisible and nonexclusive) to the definition of an impure or mixed public good (one that is divisible and exclusive), this approach consists of extending to public goods the neoclassical model of the functions of supply and demand of private goods. This approach assumes that preferences for public goods are revealed and that a Pareto optimum exists, namely a situation in which it is impossible to improve the lot of one consumer without adversely affecting the lot of another. In many of these models (see Bénard for specific references), the role of government is limited to calculating and acting as an information centre, such as in the model developed by Wicksell and Lindahl. In other models, "decisions regarding public goods are no longer taken through simple exchanges of information between the centre (government) and the periphery (consumer/taxpayers), but through the polls." (Bénard, p. 525)

At this point, we come up directly against the problem involved in revealing accurate individual preferences that certain authors, such as Green and Laffont (1979), have attempted to resolve by analyzing the conditions in which the sincere vote is the dominant strategy. (It should be noted that these votes consist of directly choosing the quantities of public goods to be supplied, and not in electing political representatives.)

The pursuit of the Pareto optimum, which some authors consider to be the normative approach to the role of government in the economy, requires unanimity among consumers/citizens/taxpayers. Although the rule of unanimity is theoretically possible, it is difficult to achieve. Furthermore, while this approach defines in the abstract the optimum level of government, it does not define this optimum in statistical terms (for example, the level of government expenditures in relation to the gross national product, one of the conventional measurements of the government's relative size in empirical studies). Nor does it offer an explanation for the growth of government in market economies which has taken place over the past twenty-five years.[2] To clarify these points, an approach considered more positivist and empirical has been selected for this paper.

In fact, a wide variety of the literature offers various explanations for government expansion in market economies. One of the oldest explanations is based on Wagner's income effect (1893), which linked the growth in government to the increased demand for public services created by economic growth in the country. Recently Meltzer and Richard (1983) suggested modifying Wagner's law to take into account not only income, but also the distribution of income, which element combines with the price effect in the median voter's approach in Bergstrom and Goodman (1973) and Borcherding and Deacon (1972), serving as a complement to Wagner's law.[3]

Peacock and Wiseman's widely known theory (1967) associated the expansion of the public sector with conflict or crisis situations, which allowed government to reach a taxation level that it retained in the post-crisis periods. This theory has been the subject of a number of econometric tests (see in particular Diamond, 1977) which have established the theory's validity in general.

Baumol (1967) is another point of reference in this literature. This author pointed out that in the public sector, which is primarily a producer of services, productivity increases less rapidly than in other sectors of the economy, particularly in the industrial sector, which can benefit from technical advances. When nominal public sector wages are in line with those of progressive sectors of the economy, the relative cost of public services increases, leading to an increase in the level of government expenditures in relation to the gross national product.

Other studies attribute government growth to political factors. In a model considered a classic with this approach, Downs (1957) shows how politicians determine the level of government expenditures in order to maximize the probability of their being elected or reelected. For example, according to Migué (1976), by directing sums of money toward small, electorally important groups and spreading the costs among all tax-payers, politicians push the government machinery toward continual budget increases.[4] Based on the same political determinants but/or different economic agents, Niskanen (1971)[5] considers that, as long as the bureaucracy possesses some power, it will seek to increase the size of government.

From an economic point of view, all of these theories and their variations fall in line with either the demand side or supply side of public goods and services. Specifically, when we refer to the maximization of the interests of bureaucrats or politicians, we are discussing the supply of government services; when we speak of the preferences of citizens, groups of citizens or the median voter, we are identifying the demand for government services.

The "demand" dimension has recently attracted greater attention on the part of researchers. In particular it should be noted that the literature emphasizes discussions, at a theoretical level, of citizens' desire to see government intervene in the distribution of income:[6] this explains, at an empirical level, the rapid growth over the past years of the transfer component of government expenditures.[7] For Meltzer and Richard (1981, 1983), when median income increases along with the ratio of average income to median income, the effect on income and the distribution of income leads the median voter to increase his demands for transfers. In Peltzman's view (1980), the argument is defined in terms of intragroup income equality between low-income voters and middle-income voters: the greater the degree of income equality between the potential recipients of transfer payments, the easier it is for them to form a coalition strong enough to ensure that their demands are met.

By taking into account various factors in the labour market, Dudley and Montmarquette (1984) showed how the median voters, under certain conditions, are led to demand public expenditures that will provide them with jobs or transfer resources if they are unemployed. Dudley (1983) demonstrated the same result under uncertain conditions. Finally, Becker (1983) widened the theoretical debate to include pressure groups that have their sights set on political redistribution of income.

The Concept of the Political Market

The foregoing discussion shows clearly that several models or approaches are capable of explaining the relative size and growth of government in market economies. In fact, many of these models have been empirically verified and have generally presented statistics compatible with the basic data of the problem. This shows us that the elements of supply and demand of a public sector must be considered simultaneously in any explanation of the role and size of the public sector in a market economy. It is therefore interesting to focus on the models that allow an interaction between the supply and demand of public services, in order to arrive at the concept of a *political market* analogous to the economic market.[8]

Three models in particular have captured our interest. They appear to provide an especially useful complement to an overall explanation concerning the existence and functioning of the public sector in a market economy. The first model, which was not specifically mentioned in the preceding section, is the one developed by Buchanan and Tullock (1962). It is often presented in the literature as the junction between the normative models of general equilibrium with the Pareto optimum, which require the rule of unanimity, and the so-called positivist models of public choice, which are defined according to the rule of the majority rather than unanimity in the decision making relating to public services.

Their analysis presumes that individuals are motivated by the desire to maximize their preferences, and that they are willing to negotiate the costs and benefits of collective action when they see the possibility of mutual gain. Buchanan's and Tullock's important contribution was to insist on the concept of rationality of individual preferences in political choices,[9] and to show that, in the absence of the rule of unanimity, we come across the process of vote trading (so-called log rolling) and the concepts of political entrepreneurs and vote brokers — the key elements of a political market. In other words, in the political market there is trading between the agents concerned, as well as option costs, equilibrium prices, and middlemen to promote trading and make the market work.

Another model that brings together the elements of supply and demand of public services is that of the median voter. Following the work pioneered by Hotelling (1929), Bowen (1943) and Black (1958), it was shown that under certain conditions, including symmetrical voter preferences on a single electoral issue, the median voter becomes the target voter of politicians seeking election so that, ex post, we are in a position to observe the ex ante preferences of this voter. This model is important because it allows for a discussion of pure public goods. It avoids the problem of "free riders" in the revelation of preferences for public goods, and avoids having to resort to a collective utility function which conflicts, in a democracy, with the famous Arrow theorem (1951).[10]

Finally, another study integrating supply and demand deals with pressure groups, and was brought to the fore by Becker (1983). He presents a theory on the political redistribution of incomes and other government policies resulting from the competition among pressure groups seeking political favours. Assuming a Cournot-Nash strategy, where added pressure from one group does not affect the political expenses of other pressure groups, a political equilibrium is defined that depends, among other factors, on the efficiency of each group in applying political pressure and on the marginal influence of the added pressure on this market. According to Becker (p. 396), politicians and bureaucrats attempt to carry out the political allocations that result from the competition among pressure groups; they can also possess important political power, particularly when pressure groups are not in a position to repudiate them. This model complements the median voter model insofar as impure or mixed public goods are concerned.

The Functioning of the Canadian Political Market

There is no doubt that the theories of Wagner, Niskanen, Downs, Peacock, Wiseman and others are pertinent to the explanation of the growth of governments in Canada, as shown by the empirical studies on the subject using Canadian data.[11]

We believe, however, that to gain an understanding of the political situation in Canada as a whole, and Quebec in particular, a most interesting explanation would be one based on the pressure group model (Becker), the median-voter model (Borcherding and Deacon; Bergstrom and Goodman), and the consensus-calculation model (Buchanan and Tullock).

The Pressure Group Model

The idea of pressure groups is obviously not recent in economic literature. Mancur Olson (1965) showed how small producer groups that are able to organize without excessive costs can profit considerably from government intervention. Pressure is exerted by particular groups for the benefit of these groups.

Becker (1983) recently complemented this approach by presenting a theory on the competition existing among pressure groups that want to acquire political influence. Emphasizing the idea of group competition to obtain government favours, the author points out once again that government is often concerned with private interests rather than collective interests. Another interesting aspect of Becker's theory is that it seeks to determine the conditions of efficiency of such interventionist groups. Some of these conditions appear to be closely linked to the efficiency of pressure groups on the economic market; this economic efficiency allows them to increase their expenses in order to exert political pressure.

This last point tells us something about the interaction between the economic market and the political market in an economy. It allows us to qualify the popular view of certain anglophones in Quebec and elsewhere who see francophones seeking political means to compensate for their lack of financial and intellectual participation in the economic markets. In short, there is interplay here between the political market and the economic market. Thus, when Quebec changed from a rural to an urban industrial economy, the government facilitated the transition for the majority of the population by encouraging the development of the education system. From then on, group interests were created, spurred by the acquisition of human and physical capital which eventually made francophone political pressure effective.

It should be pointed out that two recent studies, which are not related to the Quebec context, support the idea that the efficiency of pressure groups in the political market is closely linked to their efficiency in the economic market. In a study dealing with several countries, Sowell (1983) argues that influential minority groups in the political market have first developed the necessary skill and attitudes to operate efficiently in the economic market. Tullock (1983) defends essentially the same view in his study on the economics of redistribution: those who are most well informed and well organized profit more from government redistribution policies than those who are not.

It is clear that efficient pressure groups subsequently orient political decisions toward their own specific interests, which often conflict with the interests of others.

In Quebec, the quiet revolution (the periods of acquisition of human capital and participation of Québécois entrepreneurs in the economic markets) preceded the era — so disparaged by certain pressure groups — of Bill 101: that is, the unequivocal establishment of rules of the language game and an infrastructure promoting the specific capital of Quebec francophones.

This attitude of exploiting the political market to defend one's interests is universally rational. Political decisions are won by the pressure groups that are the most efficient in market competition. This kind of political market exploitation explains both the recent political behaviour of Quebec francophones, and the political behaviour of the anglophone merchants in Montreal who, in order to promote their private interests, founded the Annexation Association which, irony of ironies, associated them with the francophone rebels of 1837![12]

The Median-Voter Model

The pressure group theory involves private interests. For example, some groups are particularly affected by legislation and taxation and invest private resources in an attempt to reduce their tax burden, often regardless of what their taxes produce. Economists who do not accept the idea of a social utility function, and who associate pressure groups with private interests, must look elsewhere to explain the demand for "public goods" according to Samuelson's definition. On this question, the theory of the median voter is very accommodating. In fact, under certain conditions, such as symmetrical voter preferences on a single electoral issue, the median-voter model shows that the preferences of this voter determine public choices.

As Borcherding and Deacon expressed very well (1972, p. 892), it follows that we are able to observe ex post the ex ante preferences of the median voter, which frees us from the problem involved in observing the preferences of a free rider, as noted in the preceding section.

While this model enables the economist to situate the problem of "public goods" in the familiar context of the maximization of an individual utility function under conditions of budgetary constraint, it also allows the role of political entrepreneur to be introduced into the political market.

Thus, it is in the interest of politicians to identify the median voters and to take into consideration not only their preferences for "pure" public goods, but also their preferences for other public goods. Clearly, the median-voter model is simplistic in the context of a far more complex political reality, but if we nevertheless accept that this model can serve as a valid representation of reality, we can establish a certain profile of the median voter for Canada as well as for Quebec. At the national level, given the Quebec electorate's monolithic tendency toward the Liberals and the West's same tendency toward the Conservatives, the median voter, at the federal level, would likely be located in the industrial southwest of Ontario. In Quebec, if we consider the majority of Parti Québécois supporters, they are francophone, between 25 and 34 years old, with over 12 years of education. In all likelihood, a person fitting this description is also the median voter at the provincial government level. In such a context, the political situation in Quebec can be explained.

Quebec francophones could profit from the production of "pure public goods" at the Canadian level because, according to the term's definition, (a good which can be consumed by more than one person at a time), the size of the Canadian population diminishes the production cost of pure public goods compared to the production cost of the same goods in Quebec.[13] However, the choice of pure public goods produced at the federal level to respond to the preferences of the federal median voter does not necessarily correspond to the choice of the Quebec median voter. Furthermore, insofar as the number of "pure" public goods is relatively restricted (Dudley and Montmarquette, 1984; Montmarquette, 1978), and the demand for these public goods can vary according to culture (language), a specific francophone demand therefore exists for the production of public goods and services compatible with their interests and with francophone human capital in particular.[14] There is thus a demand for goods, services and regulations that favour the Quebec median voter, which results in a supply offered by politicians who respond to this demand.

It should be pointed out that this interaction between supply and demand in the political market could very well create the dynamics that would justify Cairns' opinion (1977) that Canadian regionalism exists not only because of regional preferences, but also because of regional political institutions. But regardless of where the cause lies, the whole thing is a result of rational behaviour, on both sides, of the various agents in question.

It is rational behaviour for francophones to support demands that Ottawa make a maximum effort and change the rules of the game in their favour. It is also rational that a group of individuals get elected by demanding that Ottawa accept their claims. The same rationale led Ontarians, behind their median voter, to be separatist, demanding, for example, the establishment of tariffs to protect and develop Ontario industry[15]; it has also led Albertans to safeguard their oil revenues in a Heritage Fund. Finally, it is the same rationale that encourages political parties to modify their electoral platforms if they believe they can thereby win or maintain power.

The Consensus Calculation Model

In the third model, or perhaps more appropriately, in the third universal dimension of political markets and therefore the Canadian political market, it is necessary to specify what kind of consensus Canadians can achieve and how such a consensus can be obtained in the absence of unanimity, which is impracticable.

If we avoid the rhetorical themes about the development of a great nation, the idea of creating a consensus or accepting certain rules of the game, as Buchanan and Tullock (1962) explained, lies in the fact that individuals will find it advantageous to accept certain rules in advance (which occasionally will be their disadvantage) when the expected benefits are greater than the costs.

The content of the present Canadian consensus, if simplified as much as possible, concerns the use of a common currency and the definition of borders beyond which the free movement of goods and people is no longer assured.

In practice, according to Hayes (1982) and Gherson (1983), the free movement of goods is hindered between the provinces, who erect barriers, grant subsidies to businesses, and practice "buy local" policies to reduce high unemployment in their economies or to promote their own economic growth. Furthermore, according to Carter (1983) and Courchene (1978), the policies of the Canadian central government can themselves hinder free trade in the country by tolerating, and even encouraging, the maintenance of provincial barriers, such as provincial marketing offices for agricultural products and provincial preferential buying policies.[16] As Migué maintained (1983), these policies especially hinder free trade by altering regional prices, that is by offering too much or too little of a good or service, according to the preferences of residents of the regions.

It is necessary to acknowledge that certain barriers exist to hinder the free movement of people as well. For example, it is difficult for an essentially unilingual francophone Québécois to emigrate to another area of Canada. It is also recognized that it has become more difficult for unilingual anglophones to move to Quebec since the adoption of certain language laws in that province. Federal intervention in these areas is still relatively timid and may be termed a qualified success, if we are to rely on the annual reports of the federal Commissioner of Official Languages and, more recently, the disputes over recognition of Franco-Manitoban language rights.

Furthermore, Winer and Gauthier (1982) showed how the federal equalization policy delayed migration to the West, and how unemployment insurance delayed emigration from the Atlantic provinces — two population movements made necessary by economic conditions that a "free" movement of people would have allowed to happen. This is a situation of conflicting objectives, underlining the fact that when choices are restricted something must always be given up so that something else can be gained.

In other words, certain federal policies of stabilization, redistribution and production of public goods can conflict with each other. Added to the difficulty of reaching a consensus is the fact that, as Carter explained (1983, pp. 613, 614), "Economic models of government action do not allow the elimination of uncertainty regarding the optimal political structure in a confederation such as Canada." Specifically, according to this author, the centralization costs involved in achieving economies of scale in the production of pure public goods, the costs of coordinating stabilization and redistribution policies, and the costs of transactions related to revealing and meeting the demand for public goods can exceed the benefits of centralization. Furthermore, Carter (p. 601) stresses quite correctly that, when calculations seem to indicate a certain degree of centralization is necessary, as is often the case for currency, it is not clear that the optimal solution is defined according to national borders.

Therefore, given the difficulties involved in defining and achieving even a minimum consensus needed to guide the different political markets, how can we hope to reach a consensus on *all* government expenditures, which constitute approximately 50 percent of the economy's expenditures, not counting government decisions which do not result in actual money expenditures? Faced with this multitude of collective decisions, is it possible for a controlled political market to exist where log rolling, in the absence of the rule of unanimity in decision making, leads to an optimal situation? For society, the costs of transactions are enormous, and it is difficult to evaluate the efficiency of the political market. For many, if not all individuals, it is in their interest to be a part of this market and hold a position of strength. Given the complexity of the market, there is room for efficient entrepreneurs and brokers, so much so that suppliers of public services can profit from it. This leads to the rational explanation for the emergence of a political group that gains the support of the Quebec median voters by promising to obtain the maximum for them. Also, because the uncertainty of this market is quite considerable, anyone can claim and propose almost anything in the short term. Depending on the situation, the federal government is detrimental to Quebec, or vice versa; unemployment will be beaten now; inflation will be curbed, and so on. In fact, all the governments in Canada attempt to occupy more and more space in the political market, and their strategy often consists of acquiring negotiating tools to discuss the Canadian consensus subsequently. Quebec's demands for international recognition provide a good example of this strategy. It is said that Quebec's objective is only to obtain recognition in order to gain international acceptance of its political positions.[17] But the real objective might just as well be to annoy the federal government in order to induce it to acquiesce on another issue. The federal government responds by leaping into the age-old battle for francophone rights . . . and the war is on.

In the final analysis, who can determine the advantages of these situations? Who profits from them? In economic markets, prices and wages, profits and losses control the markets. But how can political markets be brought under control?

In our view, this is the challenge of obtaining a Canadian political consensus, and it will not be reached through such formal ceremonies as those surrounding the repatriation of the constitution!

Conclusion

Rapid economic growth, the development of an imposing bureaucracy, and a variety of other circumstances has led to the development of a strong government presence at all levels of society in Canada. This presence involves not only government expenditures but also the multiple decisions, regulations and interventions that affect almost all facets of Canadian life. Out of the government machinery has emerged a political market that has brought together supply and demand in the public sector. In turn, the dynamics of the political market with its median voter, pressure groups and search-for-a-majority consensus have created a political situation that no longer seems acceptable to a large number of Canadians.

In light of this situation, two choices are possible. One is to allow economic conditions to modify the political markets: that is, economic decline, by theoretically reducing the size of government, will diminish the importance of the political market and the problems related to it (here we have images of the British nightmare). The other is to find the means to reach a political consensus, and to control the political market before the implacable logic of economics does it for us.

Contrary to the idea that it is important first of all to define the elements of a Canadian political consensus (in fact, it would be possible to limit the definition to the free movement of goods, people and currency), we believe that the definition of the elements of such a consensus will be valid only once the political market has been brought under control.

Before putting forward various proposals on this question, let us recall a number of points related to the political market which follow directly from our discussion on the previous pages. First, it is essential to realize that the concept of "pure" public goods, according to Samuelson's definition, is more theoretical than empirical. A number of years ago, using a definition of a pure public good taken from Musgrave and Musgrave (1973), which allows for the possibility of non-unique consumption and where excludability does not apply, I estimated that only 15 percent of total government expenditures made in Canada in 1973 could be considered "pure" public goods (Montmarquette, 1978). More recent studies have confirmed this result (Montmarquette, 1983; Dudley and Montmarquette, 1984). In short, governments above all produce *private goods which are publicly financed.*[18]

Second, in political markets, just as in labour, financial and other economic markets, the rationale of individual or group private interests takes precedence over other explanations of the behaviour of individuals.

Finally, in the absence of the rule of unanimity in decision making, the political market is neither more efficient nor more equitable than economic markets. It has ultimately been the choice of society to decide resource allocation and distribution according to the strength of influential political groups (or the median voter), rather than making them functions of the potential productivity of individuals. Economic markets can be reproached for excluding nonproductive individuals and for being incapable of producing pure public goods (which are few in number in any case). On the other hand, given the presence of a political market, company managers must choose, for example, between spending their time improving the goods produced by their companies, or increasing political contacts to improve their company's competitive position, regardless of the quality of the product.[19] The consequences of these choices for economic development are different, and it is for this reason that we believe there is no real choice in the long term. The same conditions which existed during the establishment of government and the political market will play against the market because of the inevitable economic stagnation that results when resources are dissociated from the productive efforts of economic agents. In short, to a certain extent we broaden the relationship that Olson recently established (1982) between pressure groups and the economic decline of countries to include the entire political market.

In the medium term, there are possibly other solutions, and, following the example of authors such as Friedman and Friedman (1980), and Brennan and Buchanan (1980) who are calling for constitutional amendments to limit governments' powers to tax, spend and regulate, I believe that every means should be considered to bring the political markets under control.

In other words, discretionary government powers must be limited and politicians must be obliged to be *visibly responsible* for their decisions. For example, automatic tax increases must be avoided, whether caused by inflation or increases in productivity. If the government commits itself to certain expenditures, it must be forced to identify accurately the recipients of these benefits and determine who will have to finance them. This last remark applies equally to government decisions that do not involve money expenditures. Since it will take time for governments to develop the necessary expertise and credibility, strict rules limiting government expenditures will have to be defined in the meantime.

It is also necessary to promote competition, through the private sector, in the production of mixed, and even pure, public goods offered by governments. A study carried out by Spann (1977) showed that U.S. public production proved more costly than private production in fire fighting and garbage pickup. Competition between governments is often recommended either to limit the central government's taxation powers and guarantee civil liberties (West and Winer, 1980), or to ensure efficiency in the production of public goods and services (Epple and Zelenitz, 1981; Dilorenzo, 1983). This approach is doubtful, however, since the survival of a non-local government is obviously not linked to the profits it makes or the losses it suffers. In other words, the concept of vertical competition (as opposed to horizontal competition between local governments) would appear not to be applicable in situations where the market is not under control, and where it is difficult to vote with one's feet.[20] As to guaranteeing civil liberties through competition, this is just as much an argument in favour of limiting the size of government as the converse. What I am proposing has greater similarities to a regulated monopoly situation in which the sole criterion of minimizing administrative and organizational costs in the manner of Breton and Scott (1978) determines the relative size of the different levels of government; I recommend that the absolute size of governments be limited to the production of pure public goods.

Canada has been trying for twenty years to resolve the problem of Canadian unity through political markets. I believe that these markets are the cause and not the solution to the problem, and that they seriously threaten the only consensus acceptable to all Canadians, which is economic prosperity. It is about time to realize that an unrestrained political market hinders efficient resource allocation and that, in the absence of rules of unanimity in decision making, a certain inequity persists in the distribution of these resources. The economic market presents difficulties as well but, in the medium and long term, it will mean economic survival.

Notes

This study is a translation of the original French-language text which was completed in December 1984.

I wish to thank Marie-Claude Coté and Marie-Christine Thirian for their assistance in this work. I am also grateful to Professors Bernard Bonin, Ken Norrie and François Vaillancourt for their comments on an earlier version of this text. Several remarks by anonymous referees were appreciated as well.

1. The following few paragraphs on this question are largely based on the article by Bénard (1983) on the economic analysis of public expenditures.
2. See Nutter (1978).
3. The median-voter model is described further on.
4. In the long term, such a situation only occurs in the event of a permanent fiscal illusion. On this question, see Carter (1982).
5. See also Breton (1974), Buchanan and Tulloch (1977) and Fiorina and Noll. (1978).
6. It is interesting to note that this approach is not as recent as is generally believed. In 1835, Alexis de Tocqueville had already noted the demands of non landowners asking for transfers of resources.
7. For a statistical discussion of the relative importance of governmental transfers, see Beck (1982).
8. It is important to point out the study by Breton (1974) on supply and demand of policies. His study, which we do not discuss in this text, formalizes several elements of interactions between the demand by citizens and the supply by politicians and bureaucrats that we wish to explore to better understand the Canadian situation. Finally, Gordon (1977) also refers to this idea of supply and demand of governments, but he emphasizes in particular the demand side and a normative approach to the role of government.
9. It should noted that this approach differs from the approach generally taken in political science where the individual representative is primarily concerned with the public interest or the common good rather than with his or her own private interest.
10. Some might judge the restrictions of the median-voter model as severe as the hypotheses which according to Sen (1970) allow the escape from Arrow's impossibility theorem.
11. See, for example, Auld (1976), Bird (1970, 1971), Gunderson (1979), Montmarquette (1978).
12. See Carter (1983, p. 609).
13. This question is extensively discussed in Dudley and Montmarquette (1979).
14. The existence of regional preferences is not limited to Quebec. Thus, Simeon and Blake (1980), after analyzing certain gallup polls, concluded (p. 81) that each provincial population wants to realize different things. See also Rawlyk and and Perlin (1979) on Atlantic regionalism.
15. This caused Robert Nixon (cited in Dumas (1983)), the former Liberal leader of Ontario, to say that the reason for Ontario's strength is the fact that it had the first separatist government in Quebec.
16. For other examples, see Ontario Economic Council's (1978) study; Courchene (1980, p. 573) also notes the presence of barriers to free movement of capital with heritage funds of the provinces and fiscal mechanisms to retain this capital.
17. Bertin (1981, chap. 9) discusses in this regard political gains associated with the search for positions outside the nation-state.
18. The expression is by Aranson and Ordeshook (1981).

19. See Migué (1980) for examples of protection and privileges granted by the public administration.
20. Bélanger (1984) discusses this question and the overall problem of the "competition of federalism."

Bibliography

Aranson, P.H., and P.C. Ordeshook. 1981. "Regulation Redistribution and Public Choice." *Public Choice* 37: 60–100.

Arrow, K.J. 1951. *Social Choice and Individual Values*. New York: Cowles Foundation.

Auld, D.A.L. 1976. *Issues in Government Expenditures Growth*. Montreal: C.D. Howe Research Institute.

Baumol, W.J. 1967. "Macroeconomic of Unbalanced Growth: The Anatomy of Urban Crises." *American Economic Review* 57 (June): 413–26.

Beck, Morris. 1982. "Toward a Theory of Public Sector Growth." *Public Finance/Finances Publiques* 21: 163–77.

Becker, G.S. 1983. "A Theory of Competition Among Pressure Groups for Political Influence." *The Quarterly Journal of Economics* 3 (August): 371–400.

Bélanger, Gérard. 1984. "The Division of Powers in a Federal System: A Review of the Economic Literature, with Applications to Canada." In *Division of Powers and Public Policy*, volume 61 of the research studies prepared for the Royal Commission on the Economic Union and Development Prospects for Canada. Toronto: University of Toronto Press.

Bénard, Jean. 1983. " Les progrès récents de l'analyse économique des dépenses publiques." *Revue d'économie politique* 93 (4) (July–August); 509–50.

Bergstrom, T.C., and R.P. Goodman. 1973. "The Private Demands for Public Goods." *American Economic Review* 63 (June): 280–96.

Bertin, Gilles. 1981. "Les objectifs extérieurs des États." Paris: *Economica*.

Bird, R.M. 1970. *The Growth of Government Spending in Canada*. Toronto: Canadian Tax Foundation.

———. 1971 "Wagner's Law of Expanding State Activity." *Public Finance* 26 (11): 1–24.

Black, D. 1958. *The Theory of Committees and Elections*. Cambridge: Cambridge University Press.

Borcherding, T.E., and R.T. Deacon. 1972. "The Demand for the Services of Non-Federal Governments." *American Economic Review* 62 (December): 891–901.

Bowen, H.R. 1943. "The Interpretation of Voting in the Allocation of Economic Resources." *Quarterly Journal of Economics* 58 (February): 27–48.

Brennan, G., and J.M. Buchanan. 1980. *The Power to Tax: Analytical Foundations of a Fiscal Constitution*. New York: Cambridge University Press.

Breton, Albert. 1974. *The Economic Theory of Representative Government*. London: Macmillan.

Breton, A., and A. Scott. 1978. *The Economic Constitution of Federal States*. Toronto: University of Toronto Press.

Buchanan, J.M., and G. Tullock. 1962. *The Calculus of Consent: Logical Foundations of Constitutional Democracy*. Ann Arbor: University of Michigan Press.

———. 1977. "The Expanding Public Sector: Wagner Squared." *Public Choice* 31 (Autumn): 147–50.

Cairns, Alan. 1977. "The Governments and Societies of Canadian Federalism." *Canadian Journal of Political Science* (10 (4) (December): 695–726.

Carter, R. 1982. "Beliefs and Errors in Voting Choices: A Restatement in the Theory of Fiscal Illusion." *Public Choice* 39: 343–60.

———. 1983. " Séparation, annexion et fédéralisme : au-delà des préceptes normatifs usuels." *L'actualité économique/Revue d'analyse économique* 59 (3) (September): 596–619.

Courchene, T.C. 1978. "Avenues of Adjustment: The Transfer System and Regional Disparities." In *Canadian Confederation at the Crossroads*, edited by T.J. Courchene, P. Lewis, P. Lortie and M. Walker. Vancouver: Fraser Institute.

_____. 1980. "Toward a Protected Society: The Politization of Economic Life." *Canadian Journal of Economics* 8 (4) (November): 556–77.

De Tocqueville, Alexis. 1835. *Democracy in America*. Oxford: Oxford University Press. (Reprint of the 1835 edition, 1965).

Diamond, J. 1977. "Econometric Testing of the "Displacement Effect" — A Reconsideration." *Finanzarchiv* 5 (3).

Dilorenzo, Thomas J. 1983. "Econometric Competition and Political Competition, An Empirical Note." *Public Choice* 40: 203–209.

Downs, A. 1957. *An Economic Theory of Democracy*. New York: Harper and Row.

Dudley, L. 1983. "On the Motives for Public Spending Under Uncertainty." Unpublished manuscript. Montreal: Université de Montréal.

Dudley, L., and C. Montmarquette. 1979. "Frontières nationales et taille du gouvernement: le choix des paramètres d'intervention gouvernementale." In *Économie du Québec et Choix Politiques*, edited by C. Montmarquette, pp. 3–35. Montreal: Presses de l'Université du Québec.

_____. 1984. "The Effects of Non Clearing Labor Markets on the Demand for Public Spending." *Economic Inquiry*. (April): pp. 151–70.

Dumas, P. 1983. "Quand l'Ontario était autonomiste, séparatiste, voire violente . . . ." *La Presse*, Section Plus, 4, November 19, 1983.

Epple, Dennis, and Allan Zelenitz. 1981. "The Implications of Competition Among Jurisdictions: Does Tiebout Need Politics?" *Journal of Political Economy* 89 (6) (December): 1197–1217.

Fiorina, M.P., and R.G. Noll. 1978. "Voters, Bureaucrats and Legislators: A Rational Choice Perspective on the Growth of Bureaucracy." *Journal of Public Economics* 9 (2): 239–54.

Friedman, M., and R. Friedman. 1980. *Free to Choose*. New York: Harcourt Brace Jovanovich.

Gherson, G. 1983. "Provinces Bar the Way to Free Trade." *The Financial Post*, "Report on the Nation No. 65," November 1983.

Gordon, S.H. 1977. "The Demand and Supply of Government: What We Want and What We Get." Discussion Paper 79. Ottawa: Economic Council of Canada.

Green, J.R., and J.J. Lafont. 1979. *Incentives in Public Decision Making*. Amsterdam: North-Holland.

Gunderson, M. 1979. "Earnings Differentials between the Public and Private Sectors." *The Canadian Journal of Economics* 2 (May): 228–42.

Hayes, J.A. 1982. *Economic Mobility in Canada: A Comparative Study*. Ottawa: Minister of Supply and Services Canada.

Hotelling, H. 1929. "Stability in Competition." *Economic Journal* 39 (March): 41–59.

Meltzer, A., and S. Richard. 1981. "A Rational Theory of the Size of Government." *Journal of Political Economy* 89 (5) (October) 914–27.

_____. 1983. "Tests of a Rational Theory of the Size of Government." *Public Choice* 41: 403–18.

Migué, J.L. 1976. " Le marché politique et les choix collectifs." *Revue économique* 27 (6) (November): 984–1007.

_____. 1980. " La régulation au service de clans." International conference on the management of non-commercial state activities, Paris, Université de Paris 9, Dauphine, May.

_____. 1983. " La Centralisation, Instrument de Balkanisation au Canada." *L'Analyste* 2: 662–67.

Montmarquette, C. 1978. "Taille relative des gouvernements: causes et conséquences." Discussion Paper 122. Ottawa: Economic Council of Canada.

———. 1983. "Public Goods and Price Indexes." In *Price Level Measurement*, edited by E.W Diewert and C. Montmarquette, pp. 665–78, Ottawa: Statistics Canada.

Musgrave, R.A., and P.B. Musgrave. 1973. *Public Finance in Theory and Practice.* Montreal: McGraw-Hill.

Niskanen, W.A. 1971. *Bureaucracy and Representative Government.* Chicago: Aldine-Atherton.

Nutter, G.W. 1978. *Growth of Government in the West.* Washington, D.C.: American Enterprise Institute.

Olson, M. 1965. *The Logic of Collective Action.* Cambridge, Mass.: Harvard University Press.

———. 1982. *The Rise and Decline of Nations.* New Haven: Yale University Press.

Ontario Economic Council. 1978. *Government Regulations.* Issues and Alternatives Series. Toronto: The Council.

Peacock, A.T., and J. Wiseman. 1967. *The Growth of Public Expenditures in the United Kingdom.* London: George Allen and Unwin.

Peltzman, S. 1980. "The Growth of Government." *Journal of Law and Economics* 23 (October): 209–88.

Rawlyk, G., and G. Perlin. 1979. "The Nova Scotia Elite and the Problems of Confederation." Report of the "Conference on the Political Economy of Confederation," Kingston, November 10–12, 1978, sponsored by the Economic Council of Canada and the Centre for Intergovernmental Relations at Queen's University.

Samuelson, P.A. 1984. "The Pure Theory of Public Expenditure." *Review of Economics and Statistics* (November): 387–89.

Sen, A.K. 1970. *Collective Choice and Social Welfare.* Edinburgh: Oliver and Boyd.

Simeon, R., and D.E. Blake. "Regional Preferences: Citizens' View of Public Policy." In *Small Worlds: Provinces and Parties in Canadian Political Life*, edited by D.D. Elkins and R. Simeon, pp. 77–105. Toronto: Methuen.

Sowell, T. 1983. *The Economics and Politics of Race: An International Perspective.* New York: William Morrow.

Spann, R.M. 1977. "Public Versus Private Provisions of Governmental Services." In *Budgets and Bureaucrats*, edited by T.E. Borcherding, pp. 71–89. Durham, N.C.: Duke University Press.

Tullock, G. 1983. *Economics of Income Redistribution.* Boston, Mass.: Kluwer-Nijhoff

Wagner, A. 1893. *Grundlegung der Politischen Oekonomie.* 3d ed. Leipzig.

West, E.G., and S.L. Winer. 1980. "Will Federal Centralization Help the Poor?" *Canadian Public Policy* 6 (4): 662–67.

Winer, S.L., and D. Gauthier. 1982. *International Migration and Fiscal Structure: An Economic Study of Determination of Interprovincial Migration in Canada.* Study prepared for the Economic Council of Canada. Ottawa: Minister of Supply and Services Canada.

6

Government, Special Interest Groups and Economic Growth

ANDRÉ BLAIS
JOHN MCCALLUM

Introduction

Should Canada follow the lead of Britain and the United States in seeking to reduce the role of the public sector or "down size" government, in current parlance? Or are the challenges of the 1980s likely to be such as to require an increased role for government? Or would it be better to expand the role of government in some areas and reduce it in others? Certainly these are among the more hotly debated questions of the day, and our hope in this study is to examine some of the evidence that may have a bearing on these issues.

Specifically, by studying the experience of a relatively large number of industrial countries, we hope to be able to answer a number of questions regarding the links between government activities and economic growth. After taking account of other factors affecting growth rates, is it possible to conclude that large governments (or growing governments) have had favourable or unfavourable effects on growth? If so, can we go further and determine what aspects of government activities (e.g., transfer payments, deficits, or taxation) have played an important role? And, finally, can we identify the channels through which these effects have occurred–for example, through negative effects on incentives to work, save or invest, or through positive effects arising from public investment or from the government's ability to foster confidence in the stability of the economic system? Certainly we will not be able to provide a comprehensive set of answers to all of these questions. Nevertheless, the results do point quite clearly to certain conclusions that may have a bearing on the ongoing debate over the desirable place of government in the 1980s.

While the role of government in the process of economic growth is the major focus of this study, considerable attention is also paid to the role of special interest groups as emphasized in Mancur Olson's influential book *The Rise and Decline of Nations*. Indeed, it will be seen that the two topics are closely related, since special interest groups are likely to influence economic growth mainly by exerting an impact on the economic policies of governments.

It may be useful to note some of the more important strengths and limitations of this study at the outset. Certainly economic growth is a complex and imperfectly understood phenomenon, and this study cannot possibly identify *all* the factors that may influence economic growth nor can it analyze *all* the potential effects of government on the growth process. Modern government, it may be argued, is no less complex, with a multiplicity of programs and activities that may influence the economy in many different ways. Rather, as in economics itself, the object of the exercise is to identify a relatively small numer of key factors out of an almost limitless range of possibilities. A more specific limitation of the study is the exclusion of some aspects of government behaviour that may indeed be crucial to the growth process because of measurement problems and data limitations. For these reasons we largely ignore such hard-to-measure but potentially important activities as government regulation, and focus instead on measurable indicators relating to the scale of government activities in various areas. (The impact of regulation is, however, addressed indirectly via the role of special interest groups.) Furthermore, if only because of data limitations, we are obliged to test the impact of fairly broad categories of government activity (e.g., social expenditures) rather than more specific activities or programs (e.g., family allowances). This last point means that while the study may have broad implications for the general thrust of government policy in the future, it is certainly not a substitute for detailed studies of specific government programs or policies.

On a more positive note, we feel that our research does represent a significant improvement over previous work of this kind. In particular, it goes well beyond the simple correlations between the size of government and rates of economic growth that are to be found in the literature,[1] both in taking account of other factors affecting economic growth and in testing the impact of a number of different dimensions of government activity. Hence the study differs from much of the research prepared for the Royal Commission in that it is primarily an attempt to increase our knowledge of the linkages connecting economic growth, size of government, and special interest groups, rather than a survey of the existing literature in this area.

The first section of the study provides an overview of the main facts relating to economic growth and the size of government. The first part of this overview provides historical perspective on Canada's performance, and the second part surveys international experience. The next step is to develop an analytical framework for studying why growth rates differ across countries. This is the task of the second section, which considers the key factors affecting economic growth. Two of these factors, the roles of government and special interest groups, are discussed at some length. The upshot of the discussion is a set of hypotheses which are subjected to empirical tests in the third and fourth sections. The tests are based on a statistical or econometric analysis of the growth experiences of 16 industrial countries over three subperiods between the years 1960 and 1979. Our tests, therefore, are based on a sample containing 48 observed growth rates, and the basic question we ask may be set out as follows: after taking account of other factors affecting economic growth, has there been a statistically significant relation between economic growth and first, one or more dimensions of government activity and, second, one or more variables measuring the importance of special interest groups. The third section presents a discussion of the nature of these tests and the variables that we use to represent the roles of government and special interest groups, while the fourth presents the results of the tests. The fifth and final section offers an interpretation of our findings and a discussion of policy implications.

Finally, in an effort to improve the flow of the main body of the text, we have relegated much material to a series of appendices. These appendices are listed in the table of contents, and their relationship to the text will be indicated in the course of the analysis.

Overview of the Facts

While most of this study is concerned with a comparative analysis of postwar economic growth, it may be useful to begin with a brief review of Canada's experience in a longer term historical perspective. It is sometimes observed that the unprecedented growth and economic stability of the postwar period coincided with the growth in the size and role of government. This has led some analysts to suggest that this may not have been a pure coincidence of timing but that postwar government policies may have been responsible.[2] While it is clear that many other factors have been at work, it might nevertheless be interesting to determine whether in fact the postwar period has been one of unprecedented growth and stability. That is the focus of the first part of this overview, and the second part provides a review of the basic facts of economic growth and size of government in an international context during this period.

Postwar Growth in Historical Perspective

Annual growth rates of manufacturing output over the past 123 years for the United States (1860–1983) and over the past 64 years for Canada

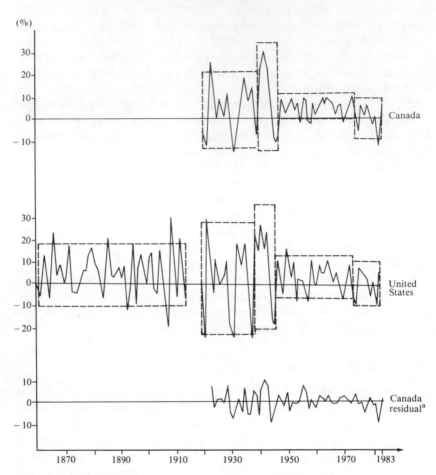

Note: Dashed lines indicate ± 1.5 standard deviations from the mean of each period.

[a] Actual growth rate minus growth rate predicted by U.S. growth.

(1919–83) are plotted in Figure 6-1. These were the longest time series based on annual data that we were able to find. The dotted lines in the charts divide the chart into the following periods: the pre-World War I period 1860–1913 (available for the United States only); the inter-war period 1920–39; the World War II period 1940–46; the pre-OPEC "golden age" covering the years 1947–74; and the most recent period 1975–83. The degree of stability or volatility of economic growth in each of these periods can be readily seen.

What is one to conclude from these graphs? Certainly on the basis of the Canadian experience since 1920, it can be concluded that the years since World War II have been remarkably stable in relation to the preceding quarter century. Economic growth has become more volatile and considerably lower since 1974, but the increase in volatility is rather small in comparison with the experience of the interwar period. In a sense, however, this does not tell us a great deal, as we do not know whether it was the postwar that was remarkable for its instability. The U.S. experience between 1860 and 1913 suggests that both conjectures are true, as economic growth during this earliest period was much more stable than during the interwar period but considerably more volatile than over the postwar period 1947–83. (The standard deviations for the United States for the periods 1861–1913, 1920–39, and 1947–83 were respectively 9.4, 16.7 and 6.3.) It would seem, then, that the postwar experience has been unprecedented in terms of economic stability, at least on the basis of the growth rate of manufacturing output since 1860.

It is also interesting to note a number of points of comparison between Canadian and U.S. growth rates (discussed in more detail in Appendix A). First, Canada's growth rate has generally been somewhat higher than that of the United States, the only exception being the most recent period, 1975–83. Second, as measured by its standard deviation, Canada's growth was 30 percent less volatile than that of the United States in the interwar period and 40 percent less volatile over the period 1947–74. The degree of volatility was approximately equal in the two countries for the periods 1940–46 and 1975–83. Third, there has been a remarkably strong and stable relationship between growth rates in the two countries — about 75 percent of the variations in Canada's growth rate can be explained by the U.S. experience. The part of Canadian growth that *cannot* be explained by U.S. growth (the residual) is plotted at the bottom of Figure 6-1. While the relatively small amplitude of this residual is perhaps indicative of Canada's high degree of dependence on the U.S. economy, it is clear that by no means all of Canada's growth experience can be explained by events south of the border. In particular, 1982 stands out as a year in which a 2 percent output decline could have been expected on the basis of U.S. conditions, whereas in fact manufacturing production fell by 12 percent.

These similarities and differences between Canadian and U.S. economic growth certainly warrant much more study. In the present context, however, the key point to record from this brief survey is that the past three to four decades stand out as years of very exceptional if not unprecedented economic stability. This is a point to which we return later in the paper.

International Experience

The primary focus of this study is on the decades of the 1960s and 1970s, and the basic facts of economic growth over this period are set out in Table 6-1. Where possible, data are provided for 18 industrial countries.

TABLE 6-1 Economic Growth in 18 Countries, 1960–80

	Real GDP	Total Employment	Productivity[a]	Working Age Population	Participation Rate	Employment Rate[b]
			(average annual percentage growth rates)			
Australia	4.0	2.0	2.0	2.1	0.2	0.3
Austria	4.3	0.1	4.2	0.2	-0.1	0.1
Belgium	4.0	0.6	3.4	0.5	0.3	-0.2
Canada	4.6	2.8	1.8	2.3	0.7	-0.2
Denmark	3.5	1.1	2.4	0.6	0.6	0.0
Finland	3.9	0.1	3.8	0.8	-0.4	-0.3
France	4.5	0.5	4.0	0.9	-0.1	-0.3
Germany	3.6	-0.1	3.7	0.4	-0.3	-0.1
Ireland	4.1	0.5	3.6	1.0	-0.4	-0.1
Italy	4.3	0.1	4.2	0.6	-0.4	-0.1
Japan	7.5	1.1	6.4	1.3	-0.2	0.0
Netherlands	3.8	0.7	3.1	1.4	0.6	-0.2
New Zealand	3.2	2.0	0.8	n.a.	n.a.	n.a.
Norway	4.3	1.3	3.0	0.6	0.7	0.0
Sweden	3.2	0.8	2.4	0.3	0.5	0.0
Switzerland	2.7	0.4	2.3	0.7	-0.3	0.0
United Kingdom	2.4	0.2	2.2	0.2	0.2	-0.2
United States	3.5	2.1	1.4	1.7	0.5	-0.1
Unweighted mean	4.0	0.8	3.2	0.9	0.0	-0.1

Source: OECD, Historical Statistics, 1960–81.
a. Real GDP per person employed (column 1 minus column 2).
b. The employment rate is defined as 100 minus the percentage unemployment rate.

As the table indicates, aggregate growth was exceptionally high in Japan, well above average in Canada and France, and well below average in Switzerland and the United Kingdom. On the other hand, productivity growth was impressive in Austria, France, Italy, and Japan but poor in the United States and Canada. Canada, then, combines an extremely high growth rate of total employment with a very low growth rate of productivity.

Changes in employment data are broken down into three sources: changes in the population of working age, changes in the proportion of the population that wishes to work (the participation rate), and changes in the proportion of the work-seeking population that manages to find a job (the "employment rate," defined as 100 minus the percentage unemployment rate). The sum of the three is approximately equal to the growth rate of total employment. As the table indicates, the sources of Canada's exceptional employment growth included not only the highest growth rate of working-age population of any country, but also exceptionally rapid growth of the participation rate over the two decades. It is interesting to observe that, as a whole, changes in the employment rate (or unemployment rate) played an almost negligible role in influencing differences across countries in the growth rate of total employment.

Information on the size of government and changes in the size of government in the same 18 countries is provided in Table 6-2. Figures on total outlays of all levels of government, expressed as a percentage of gross national product, are given for 1960 and 1979 and for the change between these two years. In addition, the table provides the same information on the two largest subcomponents of government expenditure: current expenditures on goods and services (or "consumption expenditures") and transfer payments to persons (or "social security payments"). The difference between total outlays and the sum of these two components consists mainly of government capital expenditures, interest on the public debt, and government subsidies.

It can be seen that, for the average country, total outlays increased by 16.4 percentage points, from 28.3 percent of GNP in 1960 to 44.7 percent in 1979 On average, this increase was divided quite evenly between increases in consumption expenditures (6.2 percentage points) and increases in social security payments (6.6 percentage points), with all other categories of expenditure increasing by an average of 3.6 percentage points. Countries with outstandingly large increases in total outlays were Denmark, Sweden, and the Netherlands, all of which recorded increases of 24 percentage points or more. At the other end of the scale were the United States, France, the United Kingdom, Australia and Canada, with increases of 11 percentage points or less. There has, therefore, been considerable diversity across countries with respect to both increases and levels of government outlays. In terms of the level of

TABLE 6-2 The Size of Government in 18 Countries, 1960–79

| | Size of Government (as percent of GNP) | | | | | | Change in Size of Government 1960–79 (percentage points) | | |
| | 1960 | | | 1979 | | | | | |
	Consumption Expenditures	Social Security Payments	Total Outlays	Consumption Expenditures	Social Security Payments	Total Outlays	Consumption Expenditures	Social Security Payments	Total Outlays
Australia	9.4	5.7	22.1	16.1	9.0	33.2	6.7	3.3	11.1
Austria	12.8	10.4	32.1	18.1	19.3	49.0	5.3	8.9	16.9
Belgium	12.4	11.3	30.3	17.7	20.9	49.5	5.3	9.6	19.2
Canada	13.6	8.0	28.9	19.5	9.9	39.8	5.9	1.9	10.9
Denmark	13.3	7.4	24.8	25.0	15.4	53.2	11.7	8.0	28.4
Finland	11.9	5.1	26.7	18.4	9.4	38.5	6.5	4.3	11.8
France	13.0	13.6	34.6	14.9	22.7	45.5	1.9	9.1	10.9
Germany	13.4	12.5	32.5	19.6	16.8	47.7	6.2	4.3	15.2
Ireland	12.5	5.5	28.0	19.5	11.9	49.8	7.0	6.4	21.8
Italy	12.8	9.8	30.1	16.2	15.7	45.2	3.4	5.9	15.1
Japan	8.0	3.8	18.3	9.8	10.0	32.0	1.8	6.2	13.7
Netherlands	12.8	14.0	33.7	18.1	25.4	58.0	5.3	11.4	24.3
New Zealand	10.7	n.a.	n.a.	15.9	n.a.	n.a.	n.a.	n.a.	n.a.
Norway	12.9	9.0	29.9	19.5	15.5	50.9	6.6	6.5	21.0
Sweden	15.8	8.0	31.1	28.4	17.8	61.1	12.6	9.8	30.0
Switzerland	8.8	3.9	17.2	12.9	10.6	29.9	4.1	6.7	12.7
United Kingdom	16.6	6.9	32.6	19.9	11.4	43.4	3.3	4.5	10.8
United States	16.9	5.3	27.6	17.4	10.4	32.9	0.5	5.1	5.3
Unweighted mean	12.1	8.3	28.3	18.3	14.8	44.7	6.2	6.6	16.4

Source: OECD, Historical Statistics, 1960–82.

expenditure, it can be seen that Canada was very close to the average in 1960, but because of this country's below-average increase in the size of government between 1960 and 1979, our position in 1979 was some 5 percentage points below the all-country average (but 6.9 percentage points above the level recorded for the United States).

Why Growth Rates Differ: Analytical Framework

In discussing the reasons why growth rates have differed across countries, it is useful to begin with a standard growth accounting framework. The essence of this approach is to begin by adding up all the measurable contributors to economic growth, such as the growth of hours worked, improved education, and capital accumulation. The difference between actual growth and the sum of all the measurable contributors to growth is a residual often labelled "technical progress." In the simplest case where labour and capital are the only inputs to production, the result of such an exercise can be written in the form:

$$G = TP + \alpha \dot{K} + \beta \dot{L} \tag{1}$$

where G is the growth rate of total output, TP is the rate of technical progress, and $\dot{K}$ and $\dot{L}$ are respectively the growth rates of capital and labour. Under constant returns to scale, the coefficients α and β sum to one. Hence, the overall growth rate G depends on the growth rates of factor inputs ($\dot{K}$ and $\dot{L}$) and changes in technology or economic efficiency (TP). As already mentioned, this latter term is calculated as a residual.

Now, the problem with this approach is that it tells us nothing about the causes of changes in the contributing factors. It represents at best a point of departure in understanding economic growth, because a true understanding requires explanations of why rates of technical progress, capital accumulation, and employment growth have differed across countries and over time. Our approach is to begin with the growth accounting framework and then to formulate and test hypotheses regarding the determinants of rates of technical progress, capital accumulation, and employment growth. In particular, we test the hypothesis that three factors have played important roles in influencing rates of technical progress and capital accumulation. These three factors are: a measure of the technological gap between the country in question and the United States (GAP): a measure or measures of government activities or size ($GOVT$); and a measure or measures of the importance of special interest groups (SIG).

The rationale behind each of these will be discussed in some detail shortly, but for the moment we focus attention on the general framework for the analysis. Given that the three factors just mentioned are determinants of technical progress and capital accumulation, we may rewrite equation (1) with the factors replacing the terms for technical progress (TP) and capital accumulation ($\dot{K}$). In linear form, the result may be written:

$$G = a_0 + a_1 GAP + a_2 GOVT + a_3 SIG + a_4 \dot{L} \qquad (2)$$

This equation says that economic growth depends on the technological gap, the government, special interest groups, and the growth rate of employment.

Three limitations of this formulation should be noted. First, it can be seen that we are treating technical progress and capital accumulation as a single composite variable. We are not, for example, attempting to identify the role of government in influencing each of these items separately. While in principle it may be desirable to distinguish between the determinants of technical progress and of capital accumulation, it was not possible because data on the capital stock were available for only a limited number of countries and time periods. To the extent that new techniques are embodied in new capital equipment, it could be argued that this composite approach is appropriate on theoretical grounds.

A second and possibly more important limitation is that the rate of growth of employment ($\dot{L}$) is here treated as an independent or exogenous variable. For at least two reasons it would be desirable to include an explanation of employment growth in our analysis and tests. First, government activities, which are the central concern of the paper, may influence labour supply decisions and hence employment and growth. Second, much of the growth literature, and especially the work of Nicholas Kaldor and his followers, holds strongly to the view that employment growth has not generally been exogenous or supply-constrained but has in fact responded to the growth process itself. Potential supply constraints, it is argued, can be and have been countered by some combination of immigration, induced changes in participation rates, and shifts from agriculture to other sectors of the economy. In the light of these points, our procedure early on was to develop equations for employment growth as well as output growth and then to estimate the complete model simultaneously. We still believe that this is the appropriate procedure in principle but, because the employment side of the model performed rather poorly empirically, and in order to avoid unnecessary clutter in the main body of this paper, we have relegated the employment-related aspects of the analysis to appendices. A complete theoretical model, including equations for employment growth, is set out in Appendix B, and empirical results are discussed in Appendix D. The tests and discussion of the text will focus on explaining aggregate output growth, with employment growth taken as given.

The third limitation is the more general point that there have undoubtedly been other factors which have had a bearing on economic growth but which we have not included in our formulation. Such factors might include the resource base of the country, people's attitudes to work and entrepreneurship, the population of the country, the degree of openness of the economy to foreign trade, and the relative importance of the agricultural and service sectors. We did test for a role for the last three of these factors, which are relatively easy to measure, but with negative results. However, no attempt was made to provide tests of the roles of the resource base and of attitudes.

We turn now to a discussion of the mechanisms through which our three principal factors (the technological gap or catch-up factor, the government, and special interest groups) may influence economic growth.

Convergence Factor

The basic hypothesis is that the large technological lead of the United States at the end of World War II created the potential for other countries to realize high growth rates by copying or importing more advanced U.S. technology. In one form or another, this idea has been advanced by writers including Abramovitz (1979, 1983), Cornwall (1977), Gomulka (1971), Rowthorn (1975), and Scarfe (1977). On the other hand, Boltho (1982) criticizes this "convergence" thesis on the grounds that while technological disparities had always existed in the past, they did not in general result in convergence-related growth. Indeed, Abramovitz (1979) shows that there was divergence rather than convergence during the interwar period, since 1950 productivity levels in most European countries and Japan were actually lower relative to those in the United States than they had been in 1913. Hence while it is true that the convergence factor generates a *potential* for relatively high growth rates in lagging countries, it should be acknowledged that other conditions must also be satisfied if that potential is to be realized.

As noted by Abramovitz (1983, p. 80), one of these other conditions is that "the several countries are sufficiently advanced in their human and institutional preparation." Another essential factor is a relatively stable economic environment that is free of major wars and economic crises. It is this last point that is emphasized by both Abramovitz and Boltho in comparing world economic growth rates in the interwar and postwar periods. These considerations suggest, first, that the convergence thesis should be applied to a relatively homogeneous group of countries (e.g., OECD members) and second, that there is no conflict between Boltho's emphasis on the stability of the postwar economic environment and the proposition that within the context of that stable environment the convergence factor may help to account for cross-country differences in growth rates. Other things being equal then, relatively backward countries might be expected to have relatively high growth rates. As will be seen in more detail below, the degree of relative "backwardness" is readily approximated by a measure of the initial gap between per capita GNP of the country in question and that of the United States.

Government

The main arguments advanced in support of a relationship between government activity and economic growth are summarized in Table 6-3. Government activities are classified into seven major categories: taxation, transfer payments, final consumption expenditures, investment expenditures, deficits, regulation, and stabilization policy. The second column identifies the possible linkages between the various activities of governments and the various determinants of economic growth. For example, larger government deficits may result in higher interest rates which in turn may result in lower private investment. This information will be used in the empirical tests later in the paper, but it is certainly *not* the intention to survey the vast literature relating to all the items listed in the table.

We focus first on the possible negative effects of government on economic growth. In the area of taxation, government policy may have negative effects on work incentives and hence on labour supply or participation rates. In addition, if tax rates are high, saving may be adversely affected, and this in turn may translate into lower investment. This result is questionable, however, because (a) rise in saving may, in the short run, result in lower aggregate demand rather than higher investment and (b) investment in a small open economy will not be limited by national saving to the extent that capital can be obtained with equal facility from abroad. The third effect of government in the tax field is channelled directly to investment, and the fourth runs from higher taxation to a larger underground economy to lower recorded growth rates.

Transfer payments also may have negative effects on saving, labour supply, and labour mobility. For example, publicly provided pensions may have negative effects on both saving and labour supply, while generous unemployment compensation, sickness benefits, and other such transfer payments may have negative effects on participation rates and/or positive effects on recorded unemployment rates. Some forms of transfer payments and subsidies, of which the British system of council housing is perhaps the most widely cited example, may also serve to reduce labour mobility. It is more difficult to generalize in the case of final consumption expenditures, as the implications for growth are likely to depend very much on the particular public expenditure involved (e.g., education versus "bureaucratic waste") as well as on the kind of private expenditure, if any, that is displaced (e.g., consumption by investment). However, if one believes that government is inherently less efficient than the private sector, one might expect high levels of public consumption to

TABLE 6-3 Linkages Between Government Activities and the Economy

Government Activity	Possible Effects on Growth		
	Positive or Negative	Nature of Effect	Implications for
Taxation	−	Work disincentives	Labour supply
	−	Saving disincentives	Investment (?)
	−	Investment disincentives	Investment
	−	Underground economy	Recorded output
Transfer payments	−	Mobility disincentives	Labour supply
	−	Work disincentives	Labour supply
	−	Saving disincentives	Investment (?)
	+	Social consensus/Labour peace	Investment/efficiency
Consumption expenditures	−	Government inefficiency	Allocative efficiency
Investment expenditures	+	Direct effect on capital formation	Investment in human & physical capital
Deficits	−	Crowding-out effects	Investment
Regulation	−	Higher costs, reduced competition, etc.	Allocative efficiency/ Investment
	+	Control of monopoly power, allowance for social costs	Allocative efficiency
Stabilization policy	±	Macroeconomic stability	Investment

be generally inimical to economic growth. The last two negative items in Table 6-3 record the possibility of "crowding out" of private investment and the possible allocative inefficiencies and market distortions arising from government regulation.

While most discussions in recent years have focussed on these negative linkages between government and economic growth, there are several possible positive linkages as well, as recorded in the table. First, government investment in infrastructure, education, and other areas may contribute directly to economic growth. Second, it may be argued that the welfare state or social expenditures serve to "legitimize" the system or build social cohesion or consensus, and that these less tangible factors are favourable to economic growth. Third, government regulation may in some cases increase the degree of competition or promote overall economic efficiency in cases of market failure. Finally, the government's public commitment to full employment throughout most of the postwar period may have fostered a general confidence in economic stability as noted earlier. Such confidence on the part of investors and consumers may have resulted in more stable behaviour which itself would have further contributed to economic stability. Evidence presented by Baily (1978) suggests that this may have been the case for the United States. In addition to this psychological or confidence effect, stabilization policy may have made a direct contribution to economic stability. While most economists would probably agree with this statement in the case of automatic stabilizers,[3] the question of whether discretionary changes in fiscal policy have tended to stabilize or destabilize the economy remains a matter of controversy (although evidence presented in McCallum (1983a) suggests that discretionary federal fiscal policy was definitely stabilizing, as compared with a hypothetical "fixed fiscal rule," over the course of the 1970s).

Government intervention may thus have both positive and negative effects on economic growth. The negative effects in Table 6-3 seem to outweigh the positive and this is certainly the presumption in most recent writings on the role of government. However, this presumption is not necessarily the case, and indeed it is the central object of this study to determine whether, on balance, the negative effects of government have been more or less important than the positive effects.

Special Interest Groups

The thesis presented in *The Rise and Decline of Nations* by Mancur Olson on the role of special interest groups has attracted some attention in recent years. For our purposes, Olson's argument may be summarized as follows:

- Special interest groups will in general have a negative effect on economic growth;
- "highly inclusive" groups will have policies that are less restrictive of growth than groups that control only a negligible proportion of resources in a society; and
- the power of interest groups will depend on the length of time these groups have had to develop without major disruptions such as wars or invasions.

The rationale for the first point is well known and may be stated briefly. Special interest groups seek to increase the income or economic welfare of their members. In principle, they can do this either by lobbying for politics that promote general economic efficiency and thereby increase the size of the total "pie" or they can seek to redistribute the existing pie in their favour. In practice, such groups will opt for redistribution because they can expect to receive only a small proportion of the proceeds of any increase in general economic efficiency, whereas the expected return from a redistribution in their favour may be very large. Furthermore, special interest groups will tend to ignore the social costs or efficiency losses resulting from such redistributive actions because these costs are borne by society as a whole and hence tend to be small or negligible from the point of view of any one special interest group. Cases of redistributive action are numerous: examples include special tax, regulatory, or tariff treatment and the formation of cartels or restrictive arrangements designed to limit entry to a particular industry or occupation. Such actions are likely to reduce economic efficiency and growth. It is clear from this account that there is likely to be an interaction between the role of government and the role of special interest groups, a topic that will be addressed in the last section of this paper.

The logic of the second point follows naturally from the argument of the previous paragraph. To the extent that the group in question is large in relation to society as a whole, it will naturally take some account of the economy-wide or macroeconomics consequences of its actions. For this reason, Olson's "highly inclusive" groups will tend to have less restrictive or growth-reducing policies than small groups. The third point is based largely on the argument that collective action is difficult because of the "free rider" problem. The fact that each individual person or company will prefer to sit back and allow others to organize the group suggests that the group may not in fact be formed at all or, if formed, it may be difficult to sustain over a long period of time. For these reasons, Olson argues that special interest groups will develop only gradually and that their power will tend to be greatest in countries that have enjoyed long periods of political stability, permitting freedom of association without major disruptions such as wars or invasions.

These considerations suggest that we should test the hypothesis that economic growth depends negatively on the number or influence of special interest groups, but that we should also try to distinguish between small groups and "highly inclusive" groups. The design of concrete, measurable indicators to test these hypotheses — no easy matter — is discussed in the empirical analysis of the next section.

Empirical Implementation

Now that we have developed the analytical framework and discussed the possible mechanisms linking government and special interest groups to economic growth, it remains to recast the analysis in a form that is suitable for empirical estimation. The discussion of this section begins with the choice of countries and time periods and then turns to the definitions of the variables and a brief discussion of some data problems.

Countries and Time Periods

The initial sample consisted of 18 OECD countries. Countries excluded are those that have not had democratic governments throughout the 1960s and 1970s (Greece, Portugal, Spain and Turkey), as well as Iceland

and Luxembourg which have populations of less than half a million people. The remaining countries are Australia, Austria, Belgium, Canada, Denmark, Finland, France, Germany, Ireland, Italy, Japan, the Netherlands, New Zealand, Norway, Sweden, Switzerland, the United Kingdom, and the United States. New Zealand has also been excluded from the sample because much of the data used in the regressions was unavailable for that country.[4]

There is also the troublesome and perennial question of how to treat Japan. Earlier research, e.g., Rowthorn (1975) and Whiteley (1983), suggests that conclusions are often very sensitive to the inclusion or exclusion of Japan, and this problem is likely to be particularly severe for this study as Japan is extreme not only in terms of high growth but also in terms of a small government sector. Moreover, all the countries other than Japan are either European or settled largely by Europeans, and so Japan is very definitely set apart from the rest in terms of its culture, history, traditions, and other non-economic factors. To the extent that results hinge on the inclusion of Japan, one can never know whether the findings are genuine or whether they reflect non-economic factors that are specific to Japan. While Japan is excluded on these grounds, the consequences of this exclusion will be noted in the course of the analysis. In our opinion, the results are more meaningful when Japan is excluded, and so most of our regressions will be based on 16 countries: the original 18 minus Japan and New Zealand.

Most of the regressions are based on pooled data containing the 16 countries and three time periods, 1960–67, 1967–73, and 1973–79, for a total of 48 observations. Since the model contains no cyclical variables, in principle one should choose either a single time period that is long enough that cyclical factors can be ignored or a series of time periods for which the first and last years correspond to the same phase of the business cycle. Perhaps the ideal procedure would be to base time periods on business cycle turning points that are specific to each country, so that the time periods for each would coincide only to the extent that business cycles were synchronized across countries. Unfortunately, such an approach poses major problems and is beyond the scope of this study.

As a second-best approach, we first chose the period 1973–79 on the grounds that the years 1973 and 1979 were very close to cyclical high points in most countries. Then, taking the view that the period 1960–73 was one long boom, at least in comparison with more recent years, we chose two sub-periods of approximately equal length. It should also be noted that this choice of periods has the major practical advantage that OECD historical statistics are published in the form of averages for these periods and that comparable data for individual years in the early 1960s are not always available. While most of the regressions are based on this procedure, we also estimate equations for the single period 1960–79 (16 observations), as well as conducting tests for structural breaks after 1973.

Definitions of Variables

In discussing the definitions of variables, it may be useful to begin by rewriting our basic relationship as summarized in equation (2) above:

$$G = a_0 + a_1 GAP + a_2 GOVT + a_3 SIG + a_4 \dot{L}$$

That is, we wish to test the hypotheses that rates of economic growth G for the 16 countries over the three time periods have depended on a measure of the technological gap or catch-up factor GAP, measures of the roles of government and special interest groups $GOVT$ and SIG, and the growth rate of employment L. The last task remaining before presenting the results is to define all of these variables.

Three of the variables are easily defined. The growth rate G is defined as the average annual percentage change in real gross domestic product. Employment growth L is the average annual percentage change in total employment. The gap variable is defined as:

$$GAP = - \log(y_j / y_{us})$$

where y_j and y_{us} are per capita GDP in country j and the United States respectively in the first year of the period under consideration. The essential point to note from this definition is that the value of GAP is largest for the countries with the lowest per capita GDP in relation to the United States and that GAP is always zero for the United States itself. It should also be noted that the figures on per capita GDP are taken from a study by Kravis et al. (1979), who adjust the international data for differences in price levels across countries. Hence GAP is measured in terms of real purchasing power.

Variables remaining to be defined are the government and special interest group indicators $GOVT$ and SIG, each of which requires a more extended discussion. Beginning with government, the preceding analysis (summarized in Table 6-3) suggests that significant but distinct effects on economic growth could arise from taxation, from government deficits, and from the various categories of government expenditures. In fact, we conducted tests of the role of government based on both levels and changes of all the major categories of government activity shown in Table 6-1. These indicators are set out in some detail in Appendix C, but for present purposes it is sufficient to focus attention on the two aspects of government activity that gave rise to statistically significant effects on economic growth. They are defined as follows:

- The level of social security transfer payments as a percentage of gross domestic product (social security benefits for sickness, old age, family allowances, etc., social assistance grants and unfunded employee welfare benefits paid by general government), designated as *SS*.

- The same transfer payments but adjusted to standardize for cross-country differences in the age structure of the population in determining the level of pension payments by the government, designated as *SSA*. In other words, *SS* will tend to be larger in countries in which pensioners are a high proportion of the population, whereas *SSA* is defined to neutralize for this effect so that a higher value of *SSA* reflects more generous pensions but not a larger number of pensioners.[5] This adjustment is potentially rather important, as for some countries pension payments by the government amount to more than half of total social security expenditures.

- The change in total government outlays, defined as end-of-period minus beginning-of-period total outlays as a percent of GDP, designated as *DGT*.

In brief, then, while we tested for effects of several other aspects and measures of government activity, only those just defined turned out to have a significant impact on economic growth. The reader wishing more information on the other tests and on definitions and sources is referred to Appendix C. However, before proceeding to special interest groups, one last point regarding the different measures of government spending might be made. It would not be possible to provide effective tests for different impacts of different kinds of government spending if the major spending categories were highly correlated. If, for example, countries that were large spenders on social programs tended also to be relatively large spenders in terms of government consumption or investment, then it would not be possible to discriminate between the impacts of these different categories of government expenditures. As it turns out, this is not a problem, since there is very little correlation of this kind.[6]

Measuring the Role of Special Interest Groups

The final and most difficult problem is measurement: how to measure the strength or importance of special interest groups, and how to distinguish between "highly inclusive" groups and small groups. We begin with a summary of the procedures followed by Olson (1982) and by his research associate Choi (1983).

Olson himself applied his thesis to the states of the United States, relating economic growth between 1965 and 1980 to a number of different proxies for the importance of special interest groups. One of these proxies is the degree of unionization, which is a direct measure of the size of one particular special interest group. The other measures are much less direct and rely on Olson's view that the importance of special interest groups, or the degree of "institutional sclerosis," depends on the length of time that such groups have had to develop without major disruption. On these grounds, Olson uses proxy variables defined as the number of years since statehood or the fact of being a confederate state or not. (The latter variable is based on the idea that the Civil War represented a "major disruption" for the institutions and special interest groups of the American South.) While Olson's results generally support his thesis, there is certainly room for the suspicion that his variables may be serving as proxies for other factors influencing relative growth rates.

More to the point from our present perspective is the cross-country application of the Olson thesis by Choi (1983), who constructed an index of institutional sclerosis for 18 countries. Choi's index is a nonlinear function of the number of years since the beginning of the "consolidation of modernizing leadership," adjusted to take account of the number of years of "major disruptions." One problem with this procedure is that the researcher has many degrees of freedom in constructing the index, and the results may be sensitive to alternative definitions used. Furthermore, it is odd that Choi chose to ignore the unionization variable in the light of its use by Olson for the 50 states and its ready availability at the international level. In the light of these considerations, we used two variables as proxies for the importance of special interest groups. The first of these is the Choi variable described in the previous paragraph, but in this case we also examined the sensitivity of the results to changes in the precise specification of the variable. It turned out that the results were not very sensitive to these changes, which are described in more detail in Appendix C.

The second indicator used in our tests is a composite variable designed to reflect both the degree of unionization and the extent to which unions are highly inclusive. More specifically, the variable is defined as $(b_0 + b_1 CB) UN$, where CB is a measure of the degree to which wage bargaining is centralized, UN is the percent of the work force that is unionized, and b_0 and b_1 are coefficients whose values are to be estimated econometrically. When this variable is included in equation (2) explaining why growth rates differ, we expect to find that $b_0 < 0$ and $b_1 > 0$. The explanation is as follows. Unions are special interest groups and therefore, according to the Olson thesis, high unionization should be reduced or even eliminated to the extent that unions are highly inclusive, which in the present context is taken to mean that wage bargaining is highly centralized. If this is the case, unions may be more inclined to take account of the macroeconomic consequences of their actions. The coefficient on the degree of unionization is $(b_0 + b_1 CB)$. In general this coefficient should be negative ($b_0 < 0$), but this negative effect will be less when CB is high than when CB is low ($b_1 > 0$).

One further point on measuring the role of special interest groups deserves comment. A recent article by Murrell (1984) develops a direct measure of the number of special interest groups in each of 24 industrial countries. The author finds that there is a strong positive relation between the number of special interest groups and (a) the population of the country; (b) a Choi-type variable measuring the number of years of development without major disruption; and (c) the degree of political decentralization. Ideally we would like to include this direct measure of the number of special interest groups (perhaps adjusted for population) as an explanatory variable in our own work. Unfortunately, however, such tests must be left for the future, since we only became aware of this article during the final stages of revision of this study. Nevertheless, the fact that there is a strong positive relation between the direct measure of the number of special interest groups and the indirect measures used by Olson and Choi lends support to our own use of these indirect measures.

Some Data Problems

The data present many problems and inadequacies, some of which should be briefly mentioned.

- Because no data is available on Crown corporations, off-budget operations such as government loan guarantees, or regulation, these aspects of government activity, while perhaps very important, must be excluded from the analysis.
- Cross-country differences in accounting procedures and tax expenditures may distort some of the measures of the size of government. For example, health expenditures may be treated as transfer payments if the money is first paid to households or as public consumption if the bills are paid directly by the national health insurance system. Again, child support financed by tax exemptions may have real effects that are identical to child support financed by cash payments to families, but the latter system will result in higher recorded expenditures by the amount of the cash payments. This last example applies more generally to the whole area of tax expenditures, another issue on which there is no comparable international information.
- Another form of bias rises because productivity increases in the public sector are by assumption either zero or very low. For this reason alone a negative correlation is likely between the share of the public sector in GDP and overall productivity growth. But this bias cannot be corrected by relating the size of government to the growth rate of non-government output because, to the extent that large governments are also more rapidly expanding governments, such a procedure would merely replace one negative bias with another.

In general, it is not possible to make adjustments for these problems and possible biases, but their existence should nevertheless be pointed out.

Empirical Results

This section begins with an overview of the data and then relates the results. For convenience, the basic relationship as summarized in equation (2) is repeated once more:

$$G = a_0 + a_1 GAP + a_2 GOVT + a_3 SIG + a_4 \dot{L}$$

Economic growth G depends on a measure of the technological gap or catch-up factor GAP, on measures of the roles of government and special interest groups $GOVT$ and SIG, and on employment growth $\dot{L}$. Measurable indicators have now been developed for all of these variables, and the basic data relating to growth rates, employment growth, and the size of government were surveyed in the first section of the paper. The last step before presenting the results is to provide an overview of the data relating to the output gap and special interest groups, provided in Table 6-4.

The output gap is defined as the difference between per capita GDP of the United States and that of the country in question, taken as a percentage of the U.S. figure.[7] The numbers shown in the first two columns of the table are for 1960 and 1977. The gap is defined as zero for the United States, and for the other countries the gap in 1960 ranged from 23 percent for Sweden and 27 percent for Canada to more than 60 percent for Ireland, Italy and Japan. There was significant convergence between 1960 and 1977, as the average value of the output gap fell from 39 percent in 1960 to 30 percent in 1979. According to the technological gap hypothesis, there should be a tendency for countries with the largest gaps at the beginning of each period to register the highest growth rates.

The next item shown in the table is Choi's index of institutional sclerosis as discussed above. High values of this index imply long periods of uninterrupted stability and hence, according to the Olson argument, powerful special interest groups. It can be seen that the United Kingdom has the highest value of this index, followed by the United States and Canada. The countries with the lowest sclerosis indices are Japan, Austria and Ireland, followed by Finland, France, Italy and West Germany. It might be noted that the countries with the larger output gaps tend also to have relatively low sclerosis indices. (The simple correlation coefficient between the 1960 output gap and the sclerosis index is $-.60$.) This suggests that it is important to allow for the role of the output gap when conducting tests of the relation between economic growth and institutional sclerosis. Otherwise, the sclerosis indicator may be taking credit for an impact on economic growth that is in fact the result of technological convergence. The possible importance of this point has been stressed by Abramovitz (1983) and Pryor (1983).

Our second measure of the importance of special interest groups is the

TABLE 6-4 Selected Indicators, 18 Countries

	Output Gap		Choi Sclerosis Index	Unionization Rate	Degree of Centralized Bargaining	Strike Rate[a] 1960–78	Corporatism Indicator
	1960	1977					
Australia	.36	.32	62.36	48.16	1.2	380	0.0
Austria	.55	.42	35.95	54.64	1.7	28	4.0
Belgium	.40	.22	61.19	57.22	1.0	157	0.5
Canada	.27	.09	65.26	28.23	0.0	672	0.0
Denmark	.36	.26	57.60	54.87	1.2	204	3.0
Finland	.49	.36	40.26	46.21	0.9	398	1.5
France	.40	.21	43.56	25.00	0.4	197	0.0
Germany	.31	.19	46.07	33.36	0.9	33	4.0
Ireland	.64	.57	37.34	31.92	0.6	597	0.0
Italy	.61	.53	43.60	36.82	0.5	1,109	0.5
Japan	.69	.33	20.82	24.27	0.2	106	1.5
Netherlands	.41	.30	63.21	36.33	1.0	27	4.0
New Zealand	.29	.42	54.29	38.40	1.0	186	0.5
Norway	.42	.31	56.94	64.51	1.5	57	4.0
Sweden	.23	.22	59.90	75.92	1.4	36	4.0
Switzerland	.31	.30	63.24	30.78	0.9	3	2.0
United Kingdom	.35	.39	90.08	47.96	0.4	304	0.0
United States	0	0	76.54	27.90	0.0	451	0.0

Sources: Appendix C.
a. Working days lost per thousand non-agricultural employees.

composite indicator relating to unionization and the degree of centralization of wage bargaining. The unionization variable, set out in column 4 of the table, is defined as average union membership as a percentage of all employees over the period 1965–77. The centralized bargaining variable is based on the level at which bargaining occurs, with one point awarded to "national," zero points to "enterprise," and half a point to "region or industry." There is a fairly strong positive relation ($R = +.76$) between the rate of unionization and the degree of centralization of wage bargaining. In particular, Canada and the United States stand out as the countries with the most decentralized wage bargaining, as well as very low rates of unionization in relation to most other countries. The last two columns of the table, which concern strike levels and the degree of "corporatism," are discussed later in this section.

We turn now to the results of the empirical tests. The regression equations are set out in some detail in Appendix D as are the results for employment growth and the gap variable, which were much as expected. The four major findings relating to government and special interest groups are as follows:

1. There was a positive and very strong relation between economic growth and the level of social security payments (as a percent of GNP) at the beginning of the period. This was the case whether or not social security payments were adjusted for demographic differences across countries.
2. There was a negative and very strong relation between economic growth and the Choi index of institutional sclerosis. This is interpreted as implying a negative relation between growth and the importance of special interest groups, and the strength of the result is particularly striking because the sclerosis variable remains highly significant even when full account is taken of the role of technological convergence. The result also remains intact under several alternative definitions of the index as described in Appendix C.
3. The composite variable involving the unionization rate and the degree of centralized bargaining also exerted the expected effect on economic growth. The effect of this variable, while statistically significant at conventional levels, was weaker than the effects of the social security and sclerosis variables. This result states that high levels of unionization generally have a negative effect on economic growth, but that the direction of the effect becomes positive if the degree of centralized bargaining is sufficiently high. This is consistent with Olson's thesis regarding the potentially beneficial impact of highly inclusive groups, and it is interesting to note that there are three countries for which the degree of centralization of wage bargaining is sufficiently high to yield a positive relation between economic growth and the extent of unionization (Austria, Norway and Sweden).

FIGURE 6-2 Effects of Key Variables on Growth Rates 1960-79

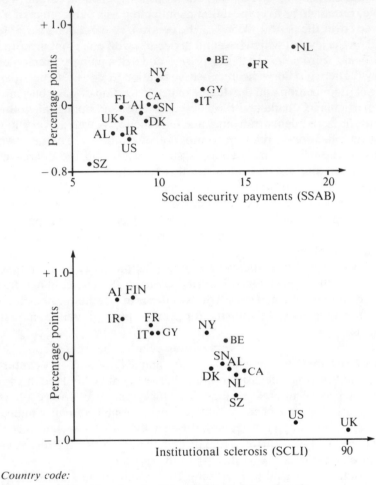

Country code:

AL — Australia; AI — Austria; BE — Belgium; CA — Canada;
DK — Denmark; FI — Finland; FR — France; GY — West Germany;
IR — Ireland; IT — Italy; JA — Japan; NE — Netherlands;
NY — Norway; SN — Sweden; SZ — Switzerland; UK — United Kingdom;
US — United States.

4. Finally, there is a negative association between economic growth and the *change* in total government spending (the variable *DGT* as defined above). However, the effect of this variable is rather small and weak.

A further perspective on our two strongest results (points 1 and 2 above), is provided by Figure 6-2. The top half of the chart plots on the horizontal axis level of social security payments (adjusted for demographic differences) as a percentage of GNP. The bottom half plots the

Choi sclerosis variable on the horizontal axis. In both cases, the vertical axes record the contribution of the corresponding variable to rates of economic growth over the period 1960–79. The contribution to growth is defined as zero for the country with the average value of the explanatory variable in question.[8] This chart provides three different kinds of information. First, it is possible to see which countries have been mainly responsible for the role of each explanatory variable. Second, one can observe the numerical importance of each of the variables from the scale on the vertical axis. Third, the charts provide a visual impression of the closeness of fit or statistical significance of the relationships.

Figure 6-2 indicates that the impact of each of the two explanatory variables has been numerically important as well as statistically significant. For example, the difference between the sclerosis index for the United Kingdom, which had the highest index, and Austria, which had the lowest (apart from Japan), was responsible for a gap of just over 1.5 percentage points in the long-run growth rates of these two countries. It can also be seen from the charts that Canada's position was below average in terms of social security payments and above average in terms of the sclerosis index. Both factors, then, were such as to reduce Canada's growth rate in relation to the 16-country average. A final point that can be observed from the figure is that the five countries with the highest social security payments were also the five original members of the European Economic Community (EEC). The sixth original member, Luxembourg, is not included in our sample. This suggests that the apparent positive role of social security payments may in fact reflect a positive effect of the EEC, although it can be seen from the chart that a positive relation remains even if the five EEC countries are excluded from the relationship. Regressions reported in Appendix D provide further evidence that the social security variable is not merely serving as a proxy for the impact of the EEC.

Two final points relating to empirical results are documented more fully in Appendix D and will be mentioned briefly in concluding this section. First, the results that we have reported remain qualitatively unchanged when Japan is included in the sample. However, the role of the social security variable becomes weaker, while the role of the sclerosis variable becomes stronger. This should not come as a surprise, as Japan had the highest rate of economic growth, the lowest level of social security payments, and the lowest sclerosis index of all the countries in our sample. The second point is that, while there was indeed a very marked slowdown in economic growth after 1973, there was no evidence of changes in the roles of any of our explanatory variables. We do not get into the subject of why economic growth slowed down around the world, but certainly the evidence does not support the view that there was any connection between the extent of a country's growth slowdown and the size or growth of its public sector.

Interpretation of the Results

This section provides an interpretation of our major findings and an assessment of the implications for policy. The analysis begins with the question of the direction of causation, or the possibility that a positive relation between, say, the welfare state and economic growth may reflect a chain of causation running from growth to the welfare state rather than the other way around. This is followed by a discussion of the implications of our results for the welfare state, special interest groups, and economic policy.

The Direction of Causation

In considering the issue of the direction of causation, a first question to ask is whether there are plausible theoretical reasons to think that the direction of causation may run in the opposite direction from what has been postulated. To give one example, the analysis of the first section indicated that there has been a strong positive correlation between economic growth in the United States and in Canada. It is clear in this case that the lion's share of the causation runs from U.S. growth to Canadian growth,[9] but in many cases the issue is less easily resolved. In the present context, the question is whether there are plausible reasons to think that high rates of economic growth might cause high levels of social security payments rather than the other way around. Certainly it could well be argued that a rapidly growing economy will by definition have a rapid increase in the total resources at its disposal, and that such a country may choose to devote a relatively large part of this increase in resources to improved social security payments. The argument, however, is much less convincing than it may at first appear. The logic of the argument suggests an association between high growth rates and large *increases* in social security payments, not between high growth rates and high *levels* of social security payments. To state the same point in a different way, the argument just presented implies that one should find high levels of social security payments in relation to GNP in *rich* countries, not in *fast growing* countries. Now, of course, the fastest growing countries will eventually become the richest countries if the process continues for long enough. But in terms of our sample of 16 countries over the period 1960–79, it has been seen that forces of convergence were at work, so that the richest countries tended also to be the slowest growing countries. Consequently, the above argument does not offer an explanation of why high growth should cause high levels of social security payments in relation to GNP in the context of industrial countries in the 1960s and 1970s.

A similar argument would seem to apply to the case of the Choi measure of institutional sclerosis that was used as a measure of the importance of special interest groups. It is true that the countries that have enjoyed relatively long periods of uninterrupted economic and political stability may tend also to be the richer countries. In fact, the negative relation between the sclerosis indicator and the output gap variable indicates that this is so. However, the results should not be biased by this point, since we allowed for the effect of the gap variable in estimating the impact of special interest groups on economic growth. Furthermore, these considerations do not in any way raise the possibility of reverse causation because the variable we seek to explain is the post-1960 growth rate, not the level, of GNP. It would be ridiculous to suggest that high rates of growth beginning in 1960 were responsible for major interruptions such as World War II that occurred before 1960.

The possibility of reverse causation is stronger in the case of the reported negative relation between economic growth and the *change* in total government spending. (The reader may recall that this result was reported above, but that it was much weaker than the results in the areas of special interest groups and social security expenditures.) Suppose, for example, that there are international emulation effects giving rise to pressures on the governments of slow growing countries (e.g., the United Kingdom) to match the increases in government services and/or transfer payments occurring in fast growing countries (e.g., France). To the extent that there is a tendency toward equality of growth rates of real government spending for this or other reasons, it follows that lower economic growth will lead to larger increases in the ratio of government spending to GNP. The reason is simply that by definition the denominator of this ratio (GNP) grows less rapidly in the low growth countries, while political pressures and other factors may make it unlikely that the numerator grows correspondingly less rapidly. Hence it is possible that causation may run from high economic growth to small increases in the size of government rather than the other way around. In any case, this aspect of the results was of marginal size and statistical significance and will not be considered further.

In brief, then, we feel relatively immune from the charge of reverse causation in the cases of social security payments and the institutional sclerosis variable. Or at least we have not been able to think of a plausible story running from economy growth to one or both of these variables, and so unless someone advances such a hypothesis, it seems appropriate to proceed on the assumption that the results do not constitute a case of reverse causation. It might also be noted that the techniques used in estimating the equations have been based on the standard procedures designed to reduce the likelihood of this problem.

The Role of the Welfare State

Perhaps the most puzzling aspect of our findings is the apparently positive relation between economic growth and social security payments, which may be taken as an indicator of the size of the welfare state. Probably the conventional view is that while the welfare state may result in greater equality and individual security, this is likely to come at the expense of economic growth and efficiency. Indeed, Katz, Mahler, and Franz (1983) do show that higher levels of taxation have been associated with higher degrees of income equality, and certainly most recent discussion has focussed on the negative effects of government intervention on growth and efficiency. Our finding that the welfare state has in general been a positive factor in economic growth therefore comes as something of a surprise.

A first point that should be acknowledged at the outset is that every aspect of the welfare state is likely to lead to inefficiencies of one kind or another in comparison with the economist's ideal world. The sum of all of the items may well give us a vast array of inefficiencies (although some may offset others). Factors giving rise to these inefficiencies were identified in Table 6-3, and there is a large literature documenting adverse effects in such areas as unemployment insurance. But economics teaches us that the whole may be greater than the sum of the parts, that the "macro-level" benefits of institutions may be greater than the "micro-level" costs. For example, a stable international monetary system may, from time to time, impose readily identifiable costs on a country by forcing it to adhere to a rigid set of rules, but the system may nevertheless have beneficial effects overall if it helps to create a stable environment that promotes economic growth. Similarly, in his study of institutional change throughout history, North (1981) analyzes the costs and benefits of institutions in terms of their capacity to foster economic growth. Institutions that appear to be inefficient from a narrow economic standpoint are shown to make a great deal of sense if one takes account of such factors as the need to monitor the performance of employees, the need for a common ideology, and the need to deal with the "free rider" problem. Given our results suggesting that on balance the welfare state has had positive effects on economic growth, the challenge is to provide possible explanations that are sufficiently powerful to outweigh the negative micro-level effects on economic efficiency.

A first possibility that comes to mind is that the welfare state may create a climate of social consensus that results in better labour-management relations, greater political stability, a higher degree of cooperation among the "social partners," and less alienation at the workplace. All of these factors may contribute to higher productivity and higher economic growth. Certainly there is at least indirect support for these ideas in the political science and economics literature. King (1983, p. 22), for example, writes that the welfare state, in the sense of maintenance by governments of certain minimum standards of material well-being, has been and is likely to be a bulwark of political stability. If it did not exist, political conservatives would have to invent it. In a similar vein, Wilensky (1983, p. 57) argues that the welfare state leaders have been able to combine good economic performance and high levels of taxing . . . with relatively little political uproar is partly explained by their capacity to achieve social consensus.

Economists have been less inclined than political scientists to investigate these issues. In recent years, however, there have been a few economic studies of the relationship between the extent of the deterioration in economic performance since 1973 and the degree of social consensus or "corporatism." Examples of studies of this kind include Crouch (forthcoming), Bruno and Sachs (1984), McCallum (1983b), and Paloheimo (1984). Deterioration in performance is measured by rising inflation and unemployment or declining economic growth; social consensus is measured by an indicator of long-run strike rates; and corporatist countries are defined as those with highly centralized unions and employer federations, low shop-floor autonomy, and widespread systems of works councils at the level of the firm. Indicators of social consensus and corporatism are set out in the last two columns of Table 6-4, and it can be seen that there is a fairly strong negative relation between the two ($R = -.76$).

The studies just mentioned have found that the post-1973 deterioration in economic performance was generally less in high-consensus/corporatist countries than in other countries. Several possible explanations of this result have been advanced. First, at a time when the rate of growth of total incomes and production slowed down, high-consensus countries were apparently better able to avoid a self-defeating inflationary scramble resulting from each group's efforts to protect its position at the expense of other groups. This explanation relates the notion of consensus to the extent of industrial or class conflict. Second, it may be that all parties would be willing to scale down their own demands as long as they were convinced that others would do likewise. In this case, the rationale for the better performance of corporatist countries is that they had the institutional means of achieving a more or less uniform scaling down, whereas countries with highly decentralized institutions had no means of achieving this result. A third rationale is the view that high-consensus countries have a greater degree of mutual trust between employers and employees, with the result that workers are more likely to believe statements by the firm to the effect that productivity growth has slowed down. In countries where such mutual trust is lacking, unions may regard such statements as an attempt by the firms to understate their ability to pay in an effort to increase profits. In such a case, there is likely to be greater resistance to reduced real wage growth in the face of a downward shift in productivity growth. This in turn is likely to result in greater inflationary pressures or a wage-price spiral.

These various rationales (which are not mutually exclusive) help to explain the observed relationship between consensus/corporatism and the degree of deterioration of post-1973 economic performance. In the present context, these considerations raise two main questions. First, do the reasons just advanced to explain why high-consensus corporatism may be desirable in the context of a *slowdown* in economic growth also imply a positive relation between consensus/corporatism and the *level* of long-run growth? In principle, the answer to this question would seem to be yes, but to a lesser degree. That is to say, low levels of industrial conflict, an institutional capacity to achieve simultaneous changes in incomes, and a high degree of mutual trust between firms and employees would seem to be desirable attributes for an economy to have at any time, but these properties are likely to be particularly valuable at a time of major adverse shocks to the economic system.

The second question to consider is whether in fact the high-consensus/ corporatist countries are also the countries with the most highly developed welfare states or the highest levels of social expenditures by government. If so, then we would have suggestive evidence pointing to channels running from the welfare/corporatist state to social consensus to above-average economic performance. This question is addressed in Figure 6-3, which plots the average level of working days lost per person employed outside agriculture over the period 1960–78 on the vertical axis, and the average level of social security payments as a percent of GNP over the same period on the horizontal axis. (Note the use of a ratio or logarithmic scale for the strike variable.) On the basis of all 17 countries there is only a very weak negative relationship between the two variables ($R = -.30$). It can be seen, however, that Switzerland is an extreme outlier, with virtually no strikes and very low social security payments. If Switzerland is excluded from the sample, there is a negative and statistically significant relation between strikes and social security payments, although the relationship is not terribly strong (R − .55). In particular, France and Italy stand out as countries with much higher strike rates than would be expected on the basis of their social security payments. (It is perhaps noteworthy that these are also the two countries with the strongest Communist parties.) A final point to observe from the chart is that the United Kingdom and its "offspring" — Australia, Canada, Ireland, and the United States — are all clustered together at exceptionally high levels of strikes and exceptionally low levels of social security payments. While it is not shown in the chart, the relationship between social security payments and the corporatism indicator is very similar to the relationship between social security payments and the strike rate.

There is strong evidence, then, that high-consensus/corporatist countries performed relatively well after the post-1973 slowdown in economic growth. However, the evidence that these attributes were also favourable in promoting longer run economic growth is much weaker. And while there is a positive relationship between the size of the welfare state and the degree of social consensus, this relationship is not very strong. On

FIGURE 6-3 Strike Rates and Social Security Payments, 1960-79

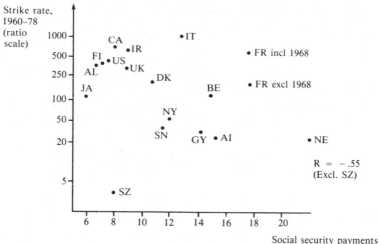

Country code:

AL — Australia; AI — Austria; BE — Belgium; CA — Canada;
DK — Denmark; FI — Finland; FR — France; GY — West Germany;
IR — Ireland; IT — Italy; JA — Japan; NE — Netherlands;
NY — Norway; SN — Sweden; SZ — Switzerland; UK — United Kingdom;
US — United States.

the other hand, it is clear that the five English-speaking countries are all characterized by relatively small welfare states, high strike rates, a low degree of corporatism, and low economic growth. All of this suggests that while there is some support for the view that the welfare state generates social consensus which in turn generates high economic growth, there is certainly room for alternative or additional explanations of the positive connection between social security payments and economic growth. One such alternative explanation interacts with the role of special interest groups and so is considered with them here.

Government and Special Interest Groups

While government as welfare state appears to have had a positive effect on economic growth, our findings suggest that government as creature of special interest groups has had a negative effect. This second aspect of our findings will undoubtedly be less controversial, and so our comments on the topic can be brief. Perhaps the basic point is that economic growth requires change and that special interest groups tend to retard or prevent change by perpetuating the status quo. Thus growth-promoting changes in industrial structure may not occur if declining industries are able to obtain special subsidies or tariff protection from the government; changes in the agricultural sector may be prevented or delayed by government-sponsored marketing boards; growth-promoting changes in the regional pattern of production may not occur as a result of federal subsidies and grants or actions by provincial governments; and unions may be able to delay or block technological change that would be favourable to economic growth. This is certainly not to deny that such changes will involve losers as well as winners or that there may be a case for slowing down the process of change on social grounds. Nevertheless, both the general argument and our empirical results do suggest that the power of each group to protect its position by lobbying the government may retard the resource reallocations that are essential to a high rate of economic growth.

The second possible explanation for the positive role of the welfare state follows from this argument. Given that special interest groups have accumulated significant power and influence over government policy, it is possible that the welfare state may help to facilitate growth and change by compensating those who would otherwise be the losers in the growth process. If potential losers know that they will receive at least partial compensation for their losses, then they may offer less resistance to the resource reallocations that are required for economic growth. Unions, for example, are likely to provide less resistance to the introduction of new technology if they know that job losers will be well compensated and if there are effective job retraining programs and good job opportunities elsewhere in the economy. Public pensions may be seen as a socially acceptable way of forcing older workers to retire, thereby giving way to younger workers who will generally be more capable of implementing new production methods. In the heyday of 19th century capitalism, growth could proceed without the safety net provided by the welfare state because most of the losers from the growth process had little or no power to resist change. From the standpoint of pure efficiency, it was not necessary to compensate losers who had no political power. Nowadays, with the rise of special interest groups and changing social norms, losers do have a measure of political power, and so policies that reduce these losses by "buying people off" may be desirable not only on social and ethical grounds but also for reasons of efficiency and growth.

Now it is also true, of course, that the same welfare state policies that succeed in compensating losers may also retard economic growth by reducing the incentives to move, to adapt, and to change. On balance, it appears that the growth-promoting role of the welfare state has outweighed its growth-retarding role, but certainly these considerations suggest that efficiency in the administration of social programs and the design of measures to minimize disincentives and misallocations are important policy objectives. Furthermore, as suggested by recent analyses of the Dutch experience (see, for example, Ellman forthcoming), it is certainly possible that welfare state policies can be carried too far. Nevertheless, the positive role of the welfare state in promoting economic growth by building social consensus and/or providing partial compensation to the losers in the growth process comes through very clearly in our empirical results.

Government and Macroeconomic Stability in Historical Perspective

The third and final aspect of our findings that deserves comment is the point that the postwar period has been a time of unprecedented economic stability. The fact that this has also been the age of big government may be pure coincidence, or it may be that big government has contributed to stability directly through automatic stabilizers and/or discretionary stabilization policy, or indirectly through effects on people's confidence in the stability of the economic system. This is not an issue on which it is possible to reach any firm conclusion. So many other factors have been at work, and it would be difficult or impossible to provide direct tests of all the possibilities involved. Some may lay great emphasis on the stability of the international monetary system, others on technological developments or "long waves" of economic development, and still others, such as Hicks (1969), on the role of population growth. The role of automatic stabilizers can be measured directly, and work by McCallum (1983a) contrasting Canada's automatic stabilizers in the 1930s and 1980s suggests that they have played an important role. But the possible channels running from government's commitment to high employment to public confidence in stability to stable behaviour by consumers and investors would be difficult or impossible to establish empirically.

What can be said, however, is that those who tend to blame government for all our economic ills have little in the way of historical precedent to support their argument. The neo-conservative notion that we could return to some golden age of noninflationary growth and stability if only the government would stop messing everything up receives little support from even a very casual reading of history. Nineteenth-century economic fluctuations appear to have been considerably more violent than those of the past thirty to forty years, to say nothing of the extreme instability of the 1920s and 1930s. From a long-run historical perspective, the disappointing experience of the past few years appears as a minor hiccup in the otherwise remarkably successful period of growth and stability since World War II. All of this *proves* nothing in terms of the role of government. But perhaps it suggests a certain scepticism with regard to the neo-conservative attacks on the government and all its works that have become so fashionable in recent years.

Policy Implications

Policy implications for Canada in the 1980s do not follow directly from the experience of 16 countries in the 1960s and 1970s. However, to the extent that inferences can be drawn from this historical experience, our results do carry certain implications for future policy. In particular, there is the implication that it may be desirable to curtail government activities and expenditures that are undertaken in response to pressures from special interest groups, while at the same time maintaining or even expanding the basic institutions and programs of the welfare state. (This is not to deny that there is a great deal of scope for improvements in the efficiency and design of current social programs.) The logic of the Olson thesis suggests, however, that it may be futile to recommend reductions in government activities caused by special interest groups, since government policies are themselves viewed as the endogenous consequence of the power of special interest groups. Government, according to this view, is not a free agent but is itself a creature of the special interest groups. This would suggest that there are two possible routes to go. One would be to accept the power of special interest groups but to try to reduce their negative effects by converting narrow groups into "highly inclusive" groups. The rationale for this approach is that only groups whose members constitute a significant fraction of society at large are likely to take account of the economy-wide implications of their actions. This would imply some form of tripartism (government, business and labour acting in concert). Alternatively, or in addition, the power of special interest groups might be reduced if the scope of government activity could be limited by constitutional means or by the pursuit of free trade policies that limited the freedom of government to respond to lobbying by special interest groups.

Appendix A
Economic Growth in Historical Perspective, Canada and the United States

The data on annual growth rates of manufacturing output in Canada were obtained from Statistics Canada, *Canadian Statistical Review*, *Historical Summary 1970* and from Department of Finance, *Economic Review*, May 1984. The U.S. series was taken from the *Economic Report of the President*, January 1983 for the postwar years and from U.S. Bureau of the Census, *Historical Statistics of the United States*, p. 11–13, for the prewar years. These series were then updated to 1983.

Appendix Table 6A-1 sets out mean growth rates and standard deviations for selected subperiods. It is noteworthy that Canada's growth rate

TABLE 6A-1 Annual Growth Rate of Manufacturing Output, Canada and the United States

	Mean Annual Growth Rate (%)		Standard Deviation	
	Canada	United States	Canada	United States
1861–1983	n.a.	4.6	n.a.	10.8
1861–1913	n.a.	5.3	n.a.	9.4
1920–83	4.6	4.1	9.1	11.9
1920–39	3.4	3.4	11.7	16.7
1940–46	9.3	8.5	16.4	18.3
1947–83	4.3	3.7	4.9	6.3
1947–74	5.5	4.3	3.7	6.2
1975–83	0.6	1.8	6.4	6.4

has been consistently higher and more stable than that of the United States, with the exception of the most recent period, 1975–83. In particular, the "golden age" of 1947–74 stands out as a period when Canada's annual growth rate was not only very high (5.5 percent) but also extraordinarily stable ($SD = 3.7$) in relation both to the United States over the same period ($SD = 6.2$) and to any other subperiod for either of the two countries. It can also be seen that the U.S. average growth rate was higher during the earliest subperiod, 1861–1913 (5.3 percent) than during the postwar period (3.7 percent). However, it is debatable whether much significance should be attached to this point, since it is usual for the manufacturing sector to grow at a more rapid rate than other sectors during the early stages of a country's development. It would be interesting to know whether the growth rate of total output or GNP was also higher over the period 1861–1913 than during the postwar period, but information on this point appeared not to be available.

Table 6A-2 sets out the results of regression equations relating Canada's growth rate to current and lagged values of the U.S. growth rate. The first column relates to the full period 1922–83, and the second column covers the same years but excludes the war period 1940–46. Columns 3 and 4 cover the two subperiods 1922–39 and 1947–83. It can be seen that the effect of U.S. growth on Canadian growth has been not only very strong but also remarkably stable.[10] The great bulk of the impact comes in the same year, and on average the Canadian growth rate has been equal to 1.8 percent plus 70 percent of a weighted average of current and past U.S. growth rates. Another noteworthy point is that Canada's growth rates have never deviated from the U.S.-determined pattern for more than two or three years at a time. This can be seen from the residual of the equation of the first column (plotted in Figure 6-1), and the point can also be inferred from the Durbin-Watson statistics which indicate the absence of *persistent* deviations of Canada's growth rate from the rate predicted on the basis of U.S. experience.

TABLE 6A-2 Regression Results for Growth Rate of Manufacturing Output in Canada

Time Period	1922–83	1922–39 1947–83	1922–39	1947–83
	(t-statistics in parentheses)			
Constant	1.84	1.75	1.88	1.58
	(2.7)	(2.8)	(1.3)	(2.2)
a_0	.64	.61	.60	.64
	(12.5)	(11.6)	(7.1)	(7.4)
a_1	.12	.11	.13	.03
	(2.5)	(2.2)	(1.6)	(0.4)
a_2	− .06	− .02	− .07	0.09
	(1.2)	(0.4)	(0.8)	(1.2)
Durbin-Watson	1.91	2.05	2.11	1.77
Standard error	4.53	3.98	5.66	3.09
$\bar{R}^2$	.74	.72	.75	.60

Note: Estimated equation was:
CG_t = Constant + $a_0 USG_{t-1}$ + $a_2 USG_{t-2}$
where CG is Canada's growth rate and USG is the U.S. growth rate.

Certainly, all of this is not to say that the American influence has been the *only* factor affecting Canada's growth rate. It is very likely, for example, that Canada has done relatively well when developments in the resource sector have been favourable, a view that is consistent with the positive residuals in the resource boom years 1955–56, 1974, and 1979. Also, as noted in the text, the negative residual of 10.0 percentage points for 1982 was the largest of any of the 62 years in the sample period, and this certainly requires an explanation. These issues are not pursued further, however, since they would take us well beyond the scope and topic of this study.

Appendix B
Theoretical Model

The theoretical model may be written as follows:

$$G = TP + \dot{K} + \dot{L} \tag{2.1}$$

$$TP + \dot{K} = a_0 + a_1 GAP + a_2 GO + a_3 SIG \tag{2.2}$$

$$\dot{L} \equiv \dot{PW} + \dot{PT} + \dot{E} \tag{2.3}$$

$$\dot{PT} = b_0 + b_1 PT_0 + b_2 GAP + b_3 G1 + b_4 \dot{E} \tag{2.4}$$

$$\dot{E} = c_0 + c_1 U_0 + c_2 (\dot{PW} + \dot{PT}) + c_3 G2 + c_4 G \tag{2.5}$$

where

G	= Growth rate of real gross domestic product
TP	= Rate of technical progress
$\dot{K}$	= Growth rate of capital stock
$\dot{L}$	= Growth rate of total employment
GAP	= Measure of technological gap
GO, $G1$, $G2$	= Government-related variables (to be specified in detail in Appendix C)
SIG	= Variable(s) relating to special interest groups
$\dot{PW}$	= Growth rate of working-age population
$\dot{PT}$	= Growth rate of participation rate
$\dot{E}$	= Growth rate of employment rate
U	= Unemployment rate
PT_0, U_0	= Beginning-of-period values of corresponding variables

Equations (2.1) and (2.2) are as developed in the text. Equation (2.3) is an identity derived from the following expression in terms of levels:

$$L \equiv PW(LF/PW)(L/LF)$$

where L is employment, PW is working-age population, and LF is the labour force. Hence LF/PW is the participation rate, and L/LF is one minus the unemployment rate (or the "employment rate"). In terms of rates of change, this identity can be written as equation (2.3) above.

The determinants of $\dot{L}$ may be analyzed by considering the determinants of each of the three components shown in equation (2.3). Beginning with $\dot{PW}$, ideally one would like to distinguish between the part of PW that is determined by the excess of births over deaths (natural increase) and the part that is determined by net migration. The determinants of each of these components could then be considered. Unfortunately, however, data limitations are such that this is impossible, and so $\dot{PW}$ is treated as an exogenous variable. The specifications for the other two components of employment growth are given by equations (2.4) and (2.5).

Beginning with (2.4), PT_0 is the level of the participation rate at the beginning of the period, and b_1 will be negative if there is a tendency for participation rates in different countries to converge over time. The GAP variable is included to allow for the possibility of cross-country differences in $\dot{PT}$ according to the stage of economic development. The variable $G1$ incorporates a role for government-related variables in influencing participation rates (discussed in Appendix C), while a positive coefficient on $\dot{E}$ would indicate the presence of discouraged worker effects (recall that positive $\dot{E}$ means a falling unemployment rate).

Equation (2.5) for $\dot{E}$ again follows for the possibility of convergence, this time via the E_0 variable. The second variable is the growth rate of the labour force, the idea being that at least in the short run, a country experiencing rapid labour force growth may have difficulty absorbing all of the additional job seekers (note that by definition labour force growth is equal to the sum of $\dot{PW}$ and $\dot{PT}$). G2 reflects a possible role for government through, for example, the generosity of the unemployment insurance system. And finally, $\dot{E}$ may be affected by the rate of growth itself.

The model, then, is given by equations (2.1) to (2.5). Endogenous variables are $G, TP + \dot{K}, \dot{L}, \dot{PT}$, and $\dot{E}$. Exogenous variables include the three government variables and the three beginning-of-period variables (GAP, PT_0, and U_0) that allow for convergence, as well as SIG and $\dot{PW}$. Appendix C sets out the definitions of these variables, and Appendix D presents empirical results.

Appendix C
Definitions of Variables

Most of the variables can be defined in an obvious and straightforward manner, and these will be presented first. Unless otherwise stated, all data come from OECD, *Historical Statistics 1960–81*, and the page numbers given below refer to that publication.

G = Annual average percent change of real GDP, p. 44.

GAP = Negative of the logarithm of the ratio of per capita GDP of country j to that of the United States, data from Kravis et al. (1979). Hence GAP is always zero for the United States and depends negatively on per capita GDP.

$\dot{L}$ = Average annual percent change of total employment, p. 26.

$\dot{PW}$ = Average annual percent change of population aged 15 to 64, p. 24.

$\dot{PT}$ = Average annual percent change of participation rate, defined as labour force growth minus $\dot{PW}$, pp. 24–25.

$\dot{E}$ = Average annual percent change of employment rate, defined as $\dot{L}$ minus labour force growth, pp. 25–26.

PT_0 = Initial year participation rate (percentage), p. 34.

U_0 = Initial year percentage unemployment rate (standardized where possible, otherwise national definition), pp. 39–41.

Variables that remain to be defined are the government variables and the special interest group indicators. For the former, it is perhaps most straightforward to begin with a list of the variables for which we have data and then to discuss the use of these variables in the various equations. All of the government variables listed below (except *DUC*) are measured as a percentage of GDP, and all of them refer to "general government," i.e., all levels of government combined.

GC = Government final consumption expenditures, p. 62.

SS = Social security transfers, p. 63.

GK = Total government outlays minus current disbursements, pp. 63–64.

GT = Total government outlays, p. 64.

GINT = Residual given by *GT – GK – GC – SS*, consisting mainly of interest payments on government debt and subsidies.

TAX = Current receipts of government, p. 64.

NLG = Net lending of government, p. 65.

DUC = Total unemployment benefits per unemployed as a percent of gross income of average production worker, change between 1972 and 1981 or latest available year, available for 12 countries, data obtained from OECD.[11]

All of the above variables except *NLG* and *DUC* have been defined in terms of both levels (annual averages for each period) and changes (the level in the last year of the period minus the level in the first year). The level variables preceded by D denote the corresponding change (e.g., *DTAX* is the change in *TAX* between the beginning and end of the period). Consequently, we have a maximum of 14 government-related variables, 7 in terms of levels and 7 in terms of changes.

In terms of the model of Appendix B, we wish to distinguish between effects of government on output growth for given employment growth (*GO* of equation (2.2)) and effects on the participation rate and employment rate (*G*1 and *G*2 of equations (2.4) and (2.5)). Referring to Table 3, the output growth effects operate through investment, saving, allocative efficiency, and the underground economy, while effects on participation rates and employment rates correspond to the labour supply effects of the table. In the case of output growth, it is conceivable that all of our government variables except *DUC* have roles to play, and a theoretical case can be made for entering these variables in either change or level form. The possibilities in terms of labour supply are much more limited — changes in participation rates may depend on changes in transfer payments or taxation, while changes in recorded employment rates (or unemployment rates) are likely to be most directly related to changes in unemployment compensation.

The result of this discussion is that the variables that may be included in our composite government-related terms GO, $G1$, and $G2$ include the following:

- Output growth (GO): all government-related variables except DUC
- Change in participation rate ($G1$): DSS and $DTAX$
- Change in employment rate ($G2$): DUC

The final item to be considered is the special interest group variable SIG. As noted in the text, we wish to test the sensitivity of the results to alternative measures of institutional sclerosis, and we also wish to include a unionization term as in Olson's tests based on the American states. The following variables were included:

- $SIG1$ = The Choi variable (his adjusted index B), which is a nonlinear function of the beginning year of "consolidation of modernizing leadership," adjusted for years of "major disruption."
- $SIG2$ = Beginning year of "consolidation of modernizing leadership" — Choi's raw data before his various manipulations.
- $SIG3$ = Beginning year of "economic and social transformation" — an alternative estimate of the first year of onset of institutional sclerosis.
- $SIG4$ = Year of first constitution — a second alternative estimate of initial year.
- $SIG5$ = Composite variable defined as $(a_0 + a_1 CB) UN$, where CB is the degree to which wage bargaining is centralized and UN is the percent of the work force unionized. Taking CB as a measure of "inclusiveness," the Olson thesis predicts $a_0 < 0$ and $a_1 > 0$ when the dependent variable is economic growth.

Data for $SIG1$ to $SIG4$ are from Choi (1983), and data for CB and UN are from Blyth (1979) and Crouch (forthcoming) respectively. Table 4 of the text sets out the data for the sclerosis index ($SIG1$), the unionization rate (UN), and the degree to which wage bargaining is centralized (CB). The strike and corporatism figures given in the last two columns of the table are taken from McCallum (1983b) and Crouch (forthcoming) respectively.

Appendix D
Regression Results

Regression results are discussed in three subsections: output growth equations, the post-1973 slowdown in economic growth, and employment growth equations.

Output Growth Equations

The first regressions to be reported are based on the output growth equation:

$$G = a_0 + a_1 GAP + a_2 SIG + a_3 GO + a_4 \dot{L} + a_5 D1 + a_6 D2$$

This is the same as equation (2) of the text except that we have now added two dummy variables, $D1$ and $D2$, to test for the possibility of changes in the constant term between time periods. $D1$ is set equal to one for all countries in the second time period, 1968–73, and zero otherwise, while $D2$ performs the same function for the third period, 1973–79. Further tests of structural breaks in the post-1973 period are reported below. The equation is estimated using two-stage least squares, with employment growth $\dot{L}$ treated as an endogenous variable.[12]

As observed in the text, the only government-related variables to be retained were the beginning-of-period level of social security payments adjusted for demographic factors (SSA) and the change in total government outlays (DGT). The regression containing GAP, $\dot{L}$, SSA, $D2$, and the constant term is reported in the first column of Table 6D-1. The dummy variable $D1$ was also included in this and all other reported regressions, but it has been omitted from the tables because the coefficient was always very close to zero. It can be seen that GAP, and $\dot{L}$, and SSA are highly significant, with the coefficient on $\dot{L}$ being quite close to labour's share in national income as expected. Not surprisingly, the coefficient on the 1973–79 dummy variable is negative and very significant. Column 2 adds the variable DGT to the estimated equation, with this variable treated as endogenous.

Turning now to the Olson thesis, the third column of the table adds the Choi variable $SIG1$, and it can be seen that this variable is correctly signed and highly significant. Note, however, that the coefficient on GAP becomes much weaker after the addition of $SIG1$. As noted in the text, GAP and the sclerosis variable are negatively correlated; but it can be seen nevertheless that the sclerosis variable adds materially to the explanatory power of the equation. Column 4 repeats the equation of column 3 except that the equation is estimated by ordinary least squares and the variables are now defined for the period 1960–79 as a whole — that is, there are now only 16 observations rather than 48. The results are very strong and generally similar to the previous equation, lending support to the robustness of the findings.

Three alternative measures of the Olson variable were also tested. These variables were defined as the first years of the onset of sclerosis ($SIG2$, $SIG3$, and $SIG4$) as defined in Appendix C. In all of these cases, the variables were significant at the 5 percent level, although they were consistently weaker than the results based on $SIG1$ as reported in the table. Column 5 of the table contains the unionization variable and

TABLE 6D-1 Output Growth Regressions

	1	2	3	4	5	6
Constant	1.94	2.33	4.88	3.80	2.98	6.30
	(4.25)	(4.60)	(6.58)	(7.27)	(4.21)	(6.24)
GAP	2.23	2.13	1.01	.80	2.14	1.51
	(4.47)	(4.25)	(2.04)	(2.36)	(4.23)	(2.27)
$\dot{L}$	0.66	0.57	0.61	0.56	0.60	0.77
	(5.08)	(4.40)	(5.53)	(6.60)	(4.61)	(4.36)
SSA	.113	.117	.100	.085	.128	.070
	(3.78)	(3.85)	(3.89)	(4.21)	(3.88)	(2.01)
SIG1			−.031	−.026		−.048
			(4.20)	(4.64)		(5.28)
UNION					−.021	
					(1.23)	
CB*UNION					.030	
					(2.05)	
DGT		−.045	−.066	−.011	0.122	−.133
		(0.95)	(1.66)	(1.32)	(1.71)	(2.34)
D2	−2.12	−2.22	−2.34		−2.36	−2.36
	(7.92)	(7.99)	(9.99)		(8.04)	(7.15)
No. of observations	48	48	48	16	48	51
Standard error	.661	.652	.546	.222	.641	.285
$\overline{R}^2$	.773	.779	.845	.860	.787	.798

interaction term as an alternative proxy for the Olson thesis, and the final column repeats the column 3 equation but with Japan included in the sample. Another point to note is that tests for nonlinearities yielded negative results, although there was a hint of a nonlinear relationship in the case of the social security variable SSA.

Table 6D-2 reports regressions testing the joint impact of the EEC and the social security variable. The dummy variable EEC is set equal to one for each of the five member countries in the first two subperiods (1960–68 and 1968–73) and zero otherwise. Column 1 repeats the basic equation from Table 6A-3; column 2 adds the EEC variable; column 3 contains EEC but not SSA; and column 4 is the basic equation but excluding the five EEC countries for the first two subperiods.

It can be seen that SSA remains statistically significant (but less so) when EEC is added, but that when EEC replaces SSA, the explanatory power of the equation in terms of R^2 does not drop very much. However, as indicated in column 4, SSA remains statistically significant at the 5 percent level when the original EEC members are excluded from the

TABLE 6D-2 Output Growth Regressions With EEC Variable

	1	2	3	4
Constant	4.88	4.89	5.30	5.36
	(6.58)	(6.56)	(6.83)	(6.00)
GAP	1.01	1.01	.85	.66
	(2.04)	(2.03)	(1.61)	(1.13)
$\dot{L}$	.61	.62	.63	.58
	(5.53)	(6.50)	(5.27)	(4.94)
SSA	.100	.087		.087
	(3.89)	(2.38)		(2.17)
DGT	−.066	−.061	−.018	−.066
	(4.20)	(4.15)	(4.05)	(4.02)
SIG1	−0.31	−0.31	−0.32	−0.35
	(4.20)	(4.15)	(4.05)	(4.02)
D2	−2.34	−2.23	−0.69	−2.28
	(9.99)	(6.91)	(6.89)	(6.59)
EEC		.16	.70	
		(0.51)	(2.93)	
No. of observations	48	48	48	38
Standard error	.546	.550	.587	.583
$\bar{R}^2$	.845	.843	.821	.825

regression for the first two subperiods. Furthermore, the coefficient on *EEC* when *SSA* is excluded implies a positive impact of the common market that is considerably greater than published estimates (e.g., Davenport 1982). This last point, together with the column 4 result, suggests that *SSA* is not merely serving as a proxy for the impact of the EEC.

The Post-1973 Slowdown in Economic Growth

On this issue one may ask two different sets of questions. First, taking the worldwide slowdown as a given, to what extent can these equations account for cross-country differences in the extent of the slowdown? Are the coefficients of the equations stable over time, or is there evidence of structural change after 1973? Clearly, the answer to this question is yes for the constant term, but have there been significant changes in the roles of the explanatory variables since 1973? A second set of issues relates to the reasons for the worldwide slowdown, a matter which we do not consider.

On the issue of stability, if we estimate the output growth equation separately for pre-1973 and post-1973 observations, then we find no

TABLE 6D-3 1973 Slowdown in Economic Growth

	Change in Aggregate Growth Rate[a]			Change in Productivity Growth[a]		
	Actual	Predicted[b]	Error	Actual	Predicted[b]	Error
	(percentage points)					
Australia	−2.7	−3.1	0.4	−0.9	−1.3	0.4
Austria	−2.1	−2.2	0.1	−2.5	−2.6	0.1
Belgium	−2.6	−2.9	0.3	−1.8	−2.1	0.3
Canada	−2.2	−2.1	−0.1	−2.2	−2.1	−0.1
Denmark	−2.3	−2.5	0.2	−2.0	−2.2	0.2
Finland	−2.7	−2.6	−0.1	−2.3	−2.0	−0.1
France	−2.4	−2.7	0.3	−2.0	−2.3	0.3
Germany	−2.1	−2.6	0.5	−1.3	−1.8	0.5
Ireland	−0.7	−1.0	0.3	−1.9	−2.2	0.3
Italy	−2.7	−1.7	−1.0	−4.3	−3.3	−1.0
Netherlands	−2.5	−1.7	−0.8	−2.2	−1.4	−0.8
Norway	+0.6	−0.7	1.3	−0.8	−2.1	1.3
Sweden	−2.2	−1.9	−0.3	−2.9	−2.6	−0.3
Switzerland	−4.8	−3.6	−1.2	−2.2	−1.0	−1.2
United Kingdom	−1.7	−1.6	−0.1	−1.6	−1.5	−0.1
United States	−1.3	−1.4	0.1	−1.8	−1.9	0.1

Source: See Appendix A, paragraph 1.
a. Growth rate of real GDP and real GDP per person employed, 1973–79 minus 1960–73.
b. Taken from equation reported in Column (3) of Table A-3. Predicted value includes the effect of the dummy variable D2, so that the errors may be regarded as deviations from the sixteen country mean 'error' of −2.34 percentage points.

evidence of instability. The Choi test F statistic is 0.89 as compared with a critical value of 2.23 at a 5 percent significance level. Furthermore, it is not possible to reject the hypothesis that all of the individual coefficients other than the constant term have remained stable. The estimated equations corresponding to the third column of Table 6D-1 were as follows for the two subperiods 1960–73 and 1973–79:

$$G = 4.48 - 1.18\,GAP + .105\,SSA - .063\,DGT + .538\,L - .025\,SIG1$$
$$(4.96)\quad(1.88)\qquad(3.29)\qquad(1.44)\qquad(3.74)\qquad(2.78)$$

$$N = 32 \qquad \text{Standard error} = .517 \qquad R^2 = .620$$

$$G = 3.38 - .50\,GAP + .088\,SSA - .072\,DGT + .776\,L - .041\,SIG1$$
$$(2.44)\quad(0.5)\qquad(1.74)\qquad(1.21)\qquad(4.72)\qquad(2.58)$$

$$N = 16 \qquad \text{Standard error} = .671 \qquad R^2 = .635$$

Table 6D-3 sets out the actual and predicted slowdown in aggregate growth and productivity growth between 1960–73 and 1973–79. It can be seen, first, that the magnitude of the productivity slowdown was quite similar in most countries — for example, 11 of the 16 countries experienced slowdowns in the −1.6 to −2.5 percentage point range. The prediction errors exceeded half a percentage point for four countries:

Norway's slowdown was 1.3 points smaller than predicted, while the drop in productivity growth was considerably larger than predicted for Switzerland (-1.2), Italy (-1.0), and the Netherlands (-0.8). For some of these cases there may be good explanations for extremely good or bad performance, but from the standpoint of this study, the key point to note is that there seems to be no obvious connection between the extent of a country's slowdown and the size or growth of the public sector.

Employment Growth

The results for the participation rate and employment rate (equations (2.4) and (2.5)) were in general very poor. That is, we could find no evidence of tax or transfer payment effects on the participation rate, nor of unemployment compensation effects on the unemployment rate. This is perhaps a puzzling result in the light of contrary findings in many country-level studies. We do not have any good explanation for this contradiction except to note that country-specific factors may create so much "noise" in our equations that we fail to detect effects that are apparent in studies of individual countries.

The equation for the participation rate was estimated as:[13]

$$\dot{PT} = .17 + .006\dot{PT_0} - 1.37GAP + 1.57\dot{E} + .28D1 + .88D2$$
$$(0.2) \quad (0.4) \qquad (4.6) \qquad (3.0) \quad (1.7) \quad (3.7)$$

No. of observations = 46   Standard error = .44
$$\overline{R}^2 = .41$$

The coefficient on $\dot{E}$ indicates that a one-point increase in the unemployment rate is associated with a drop of some 1.6 percentage points in the participation rate, giving support to the discouraged worker hypothesis. This figure, which implies that some 60 percent of any drop in employment shows up as a lower participation rate, and only 40 percent as a rise in the unemployment rate, seems rather high by Canadian standards. It may, however, be more realistic for European countries which make up the bulk of our sample. There was also a significant tendency for the more advanced countries (small values of GAP) to experience relatively large increases in their participation rates. But there was no evidence of convergence, as the coefficient on the initial period participation rate was very close to zero.

The results for the equation for $\dot{E}$ were even less positive, the only statistically significant variable being the post-1973 dummy variable $D2$. It would seem that other factors must be invoked if one is to explain cross-country differences in increases in unemployment rates, particularly in the post-1973 period. As noted in the text, evidence presented in McCallum (1983a) suggested that post-1973 differences in unemployment/inflation experience were closely related to differences in social consensus as proxied by a measure of long-run strike activity. If the strike variable is added to the $\dot{E}$ equation, one of the other explanatory variables (U_0) becomes significant, and the estimated equation is given by:

$$\dot{E} = .15 + .060U_0 - .059\,(1 + 1.60D2)\,LS - .063D1 + .139D2$$
$$\quad\;\;(1.99)\;(3.09)\qquad(3.70)\qquad\qquad\qquad(1.05)\qquad(.94)$$

$$\text{No. of observations} = 46 \qquad \text{Standard error} = .17$$
$$R^2 = .509$$

where LS is the logarithm of average working days lost per non-agricultural worker over the period 1950–1978. The equation now indicates a moderate tendency for unemployment rates to converge over time (at a rate of about 0.6 percentages points per decade), together with a tendency for high strike countries to experience larger increases in unemployment rates.

The estimated coefficient on the strike variable is $-.059$ for 1960–1973 and $-.154$ for 1978–79. The mean value of LS was 3.7 for the five lowest strike countries other than Switzerland (Austria, Germany, the Netherlands, Norway and Sweden) and 6.2 for the seven highest strike countries (Australia, Canada, Finland, Ireland, Italy, the United Kingdom and the United States). On average, then, the equation implies an additional 2.3 percentage point increase in the unemployment rate between 1973 and 1979 for this second group relative to the first group as a result of the strike variable.[14] This is consistent with the earlier results mentioned above. Furthermore, if one combines this result with the equation previously reported for $\dot{PT}$, the effect of the strike variable on employment is increased through the discouraged worker effect. While these results provide further support for the consensus hypothesis as applied to changes in the unemployment rate, they do not get us very far in terms of understanding the role of government, since none of the government-related variables turned out to be statistically significant.

Notes

This paper was completed in December 1984. We are grateful to Philippe Laheurte and Nour-Ed-Dine Barmaki for their research assistance and to Claude Felteau, David Laidler, Ross Preston, Craig Riddell, John Sargent, and Dan Usher, participants at a seminar at l'Université de Montréal, and two anonymous referees for their helpful comments.

1. Examples of such studies include Cameron (1982), Gould (1983), Keman (1984), Schmidt (1983), and unpublished reports prepared by the OECD. Landau (1983), on the other hand, conducts a test based on a sample of 96 countries and includes a "catch-up" variable in his equation for economic growth.

2. See, for example, Baily (1978), Boltho (1982), and Maddison (1964).

3. "Automatic stabilizers" consist of taxes that rise automatically as the economic expands, thereby dampening the expansion, and fall automatically as the economy contracts, thereby dampening the contraction. Payments of unemployment insurance are also automatic stabilizers because they automatically sustain purchasing power during times of high unemployment.

4. It could be argued that the exclusion of New Zealand is likely to bias the results in favour of a positive impact of government. Certainly New Zealand has had one of the lowest rates of growth, and that country also has a reputation as one of the more advanced welfare states. The problem is that data on New Zealand transfer payments are simply not available on a basis that is comparable with other countries. It may be noted, however, that to the extent one may draw any conclusions from the potentially noncomparable data contained in OECD (1976), New Zealand appears to have distinctly below average social expenditures (relative to GNP).

5. More precisely, SSA is defined as the sum of: (i) the pension component of SS multiplied by $\bar{d}/d$, where d is the proportion of the population aged 65 and over and $\bar{d}$ is the mean value of d for the 16 countries; and (ii) the nonpension component of SS.

6. The cross-country correlation coefficients between the various categories of government spending are consistently on the order of 0.3.

7. It might be recalled that the gap variable used in the regression equations is based on a logarithmic formulation and so is not identical to the figures shown in the table (see p. 26).

8. The variables shown in Figure 2 may be defined precisely as follows. Suppose that the following is the estimated regression equation:
$$G_{jt} = a_0 + a_1 SSA_{jt} + a_2 SIG_{jt} + \ldots + \epsilon_{jt}$$
   where G is the growth rate, SSA is social security payments as defined above, SIG is the Choi sclerosis variable, and ϵ is the error term. The horizontal axes measure the mean values of SSA_{jt} and SIG_{jt} over the three time periods. The vertical axes measure respectively $[a_1(SSA_{jt} - \overline{SSA}_t) + jt]$ and $[a_2(SIG_{jt} - \overline{SIG}_t) + \epsilon_{jt}]$, where a bar denotes the 16-country mean and again these variables are defined as the averages over the three periods.

9. One cannot, however, rule out the possibility that the relationship overstates the true influence of the United States on Canada, as it is likely that other factors, such as World War II, influenced both countries' growth rates in a similar fashion. If the roles of such other factors could be included in the relationship, then the estimated impact of the U.S. growth on Canada's growth would be reduced.

10. A test for structural stability over the two subperiods 1922–1939 and 1947–1983 yields an F-statistic of .66, as compared with a critical value of 2.58 at a 95 percent confidence level.

11. Notice that this variable does not capture the effects of the changes in the Canadian unemployment insurance system that occurred in 1971. The data were only available for the two years indicated.

12. The following variables were used as instruments in the two-stage least squares estimations: (1) government-related variables at the beginning of the period: SSA, GC, GK, GT, $GINT$, TAX: (2) alternative measures of institutional sclerosis; and (3) $P\dot{W}$ and PT_0. Also, in cases where additional exogenous variables were added (e.g., CB^*UNION), these were also included as instrumental variables.

13. Germany and Switzerland have been excluded from this regression for the third period 1973–1979 on the grounds that the large-scale repatriation of guest workers was likely to have affected participation rates. The equation containing these two countries had similar coefficients but much lower R^2.
14. This figure is obtained by the product of the difference between the average strike rates (2.5), the coefficient of LS (.154), and the number of years (6).

Bibliography

Abramovitz, Moses. 1983. "Notes on International Differences in Productivity Growth Rates." In *The Political Economy of Growth*, edited by Dennis C. Mueller. New Haven: Yale University Press.

Abramovitz, Moses. 1979. "Rapid Growth Potential and its Realization: The Experience of Capitalist Countries in the Postwar Period." In *Economic Growth and Resources*, edited by E. Malinvaud. London: Macmillan.

Baily, Martin Neil. 1978. "Stabilization Policy and Private Economic Behaviour." *Brookings Papers on Economic Activity*: 11–48.

Blyth, C.A. 1979. "The Interaction Between Collective Bargaining and Government Policies in Selected Member Countries" in *Collective Bargaining and Government Policies*. Paris: OECD.

Boltho, Andrew, ed. 1982. *The European Economy, Growth and Crises*. London: Oxford University Press.

Bruno, Michael, and Jeffrey Sachs. 1984. *Economics of Worldwide Stagflation*. Cambridge, Mass: Harvard University Press.

Cameron, David. 1982. "On the Limits of the Public Economy." *Annals of the American Academy of Political and Social Science* 459 (January): 46–63.

Castles, Francis G. 1982. "Introduction, Politics and Public Policy." In *The Impact of Parties: Politics and Policies in Democratic Capitalist States*, edited by Francis G. Castles. Beverly Hills: Sage.

Choi, Kwang. 1983. "A Statistical Test of Olson's Model." In *The Political Economy of Growth*, edited by Dennis C. Mueller. New Haven: Yale University Press.

Cornwall, John. 1977. *Modern Capitalism*. New York: Sharpe.

Crouch, Colin. 1985. "The Conditions for Trade Union Wage Restraint." In *The Politics of Inflation and Economic Stagnation*, edited by L. Lindberg and C.S. Maier. Washington, D.C.: Brookings Institution.

Davenport, M. 1982. "The Economic Impact of the EEC." In *The European Economy, Growth and Crisis*, edited by A. Boltho. London: Oxford University Press.

Ellman, Michael. "The Crisis of the Welfare State — The Dutch Experience." In *The Economics of Human Betterment* (forthcoming).

Gould, Frank. 1983. "The Development of Public Expenditures in Western Industrialized Countries: A Comparative Analysis." *Public Finance*: 38–69.

Gomulka, S. 1971. *Inventive Activity, Diffusion and the Stages of Economic Growth*. Aarhus: Aarhus University Press.

Hicks, J.R. 1969. *A Theory of Economic History*. New York: Oxford University Press.

Katz, Claudiov, Vincent A. Mahler, and Michael G. Franz. 1983. "The Impact of Taxes on Growth and Distribution in Developed Capitalist Countries: A Cross-National Study." *American Political Science Review* 77 (December).

Keman, A. Hans. 1984. "Politics, Policies and Consequences: A Cross-National Analysis of Public Policy Formation in Advanced Capitalist Democracies (1967–1981)." *European Journal of Political Research* 12 (July): 147–71.

King, Anthony. 1983. "The Political Consequences of the Welfare State." In *Evaluating the Welfare State: Social and Political Perspectives*, edited by S.E. Spiro and E. Yuchtman-Yaar. New York: Academic Press.

Kravis, I.P., R. Summers, and A. Heston. 1979. "International Comparisons of Real Product and Its Composition, 1950–77." *Review of Income and Wealth*: 19–66.

Landau, Daniel. 1983. "Government Expenditure and Economic Growth: A Cross-Country Study." *Southern Economic Journal* 49 (January): 783–92.

McCallum, John. 1983a. "Government Deficits: Historical Analysis and Present Policy Alternatives." In *Deficits: How Big and How Bad?*, edited by David W. Conklin and Thomas J. Courchene. Toronto: Ontario Economic Council.

———. 1983b. "Inflation and Social Consensus in the Seventies." *Economic Journal* (December).

Maddison, A. 1964. *Economic Growth in the West*. London: Norton.

Murrell, Peter. 1984. "An Explanation of the Factors Affecting the Formation of Interest Groups in OECD Countries." *Public Choice* 43: 151–71.

North, Douglass C. 1981. *Structure and Change in Economic History*. New York: Norton.

Organisation for Economic Co-operation and Development. 1976. *Dépenses publiques affectées aux programmes de garantie des ressources*. Paris: OECD.

———. 1983. *Historical Statistics 1960–61*. Paris: OECD.

Olson, Mancur. 1982. *The Rise and Decline of Nations: Economic Growth, Stagflation and Social Rigidities*. New York: Yale University Press.

Palaheimo, Heikki., ed. 1984. *Politics in The Era of Corporatism and Planning*. Tampere, Finland: Finnish Political Science Association.

Pryor, Frederic L. 1983. "A Quasi-Test of Olson's Hypotheses." In *The Political Economy of Growth*, edited by Dennis C. Mueller. New Haven: Yale University Press.

Rowthorn, R. 1975. "What Remains of Kaldor's Law?" *Economic Journal* (March): 10–19.

Scarfe, Brian L. 1977. *Cycles, Growth and Inflation*. New York: McGraw-Hill.

Schmidt, Manfred C. 1983. "The Welfare State and the Economy in Periods of Economic Crisis: A Comparative Study of the Twenty-Three Nations." *European Journal of Political Research* 11 (March): 1–27.

Statistics Canada. 1972. *Canadian Statistical Review, Historical Summary 1970*. Catalogue 11-505 Occasional. Ottawa: Statistics Canada.

Whiteley, Paul F. 1983. "The Political Economy of Economic Growth," *European Journal of Political Research* 11 (June): 197–213.

Wilensky, Harold L. 1983. "Political Legitimacy and Consensus: Missing Variables in the Assessment of Social Policy." In *Evaluating the Welfare State: Social and Political Perspectives*, edited by S.E. Spiro and E. Yuchtman-Yaar. New York: Academic Press.

7

Improving Productivity in the Government Sector:
The Role of Contracting Out

Robert L. Bish

Introduction

Increasing the productivity and adaptiveness to changing conditions of the Canadian economy is a major concern for citizens. This concern is reflected in many of the questions raised and reports prepared for this Royal Commission. One important question is whether the productivity and adaptiveness of government itself can be improved.

It has been long understood that competition in an economy encourages efficiency, responsiveness to consumers and economic growth. Recently in Canada there has been a considerable debate about introducing more competition through deregulation and freer trade. Closely related to this debate is the issue of whether or not competitive forces can also be introduced into the production of government services to increase their efficiency. One suggestion to introduce competitive forces is for governments to use competitive tenders to contract out the production of some services to private firms, voluntary agencies or other governments instead of relying only on the bureaucratic production of their own employees. While contracting out is only one of several strategies to increase the productivity of governments, it is an approach that directly introduces competition, and one that appears sufficiently promising to be worthy of detailed analysis. Information gained from such an analysis is relevant to both the larger forces in an economy and to inform government officials of practical approaches for improving the provision of government services.

Few independent studies of contracting for the provision of government services have been done in Canada; however, the results of recent ones are consistent with a large number of studies in the United States and Europe.[1] In British Columbia, an analysis of Burnaby's municipal solid waste collection compared to Surrey's contract collection indicates that Surrey's service is 18 percent cheaper per household; Coquitlam estimates a saving of 21.6 percent after its shift from a municipal to a private contract for solid waste collection 1982. The most dramatic results were obtained in Dr. Jim McDavid's study of Canadian cities with a population over 10,000. The analysis here showed that municipal collection in 1980 was 50.9 percent more expensive per household than private collection ($42.29 vs. $28.02). Yet another recent analysis of incentives in government contracting, prepared for the Ontario Economic Council by R. Preston McAfee and John McMillan, also indicates that properly designed contracts for service production can result in major cost savings to government.[2]

The evidence of potential cost savings by contracting out the production of government services has provoked a mixed reaction coloured by the old shibboleths of private greed versus the public good and private efficiency versus public sloth. Unfortunately these terms are used primarily as ideological masks, and they do not contribute any insight into actually improving the performance of governments.

There is evidence, however, that can be used to evaluate the potential use of contracting to increase the productivity and adaptability of the public sector. Existing research and experience also provide some guidelines to help managers take advantage of alternative arrangements for government service production in order to increase the effectiveness of their organization.

This report presents the theory and empirical evidence bearing on organizational arrangements which promote efficiency and adaptiveness in the production of government services. Specific emphasis is given to comparisons of bureaucractic in-house production with production done by private firms, nonprofit societies or other governments under contract. While the theory presented is general to all levels of government, most of the examples and empirical activities involve the direct production of services for local government residents where outputs can be identified and measured. This is because the large number of local governments with diverse production arrangements permits empirical analysis of large sample sizes as well as case studies. Such a research environment is less available for analyzing provincial or federal government activities, although contracting to improve production efficiency is important for these governments too.

The analysis of alternative arrangements for producing government services is only beginning to be a focus of research in Canada,[3] although the findings from the work that has been done are consistent with those of work done in the United States and Europe. In this report, empirical evidence from those areas will be used to supplement Canadian-based analyses.

To present the theory and evidence of alternative arrangements for producing government services, the approach will be to discuss first the nature of production problems faced by governments, and then proceed to a review and analysis of contracting out — including history, theory, evidence and examples. In the concluding section the implications of the evidence for increasing efficiency and adaptiveness of government service production will be drawn. The lessons from this evidence should provide some clear guidelines for increasing the productivity of the government services sector of the economy.

Separating Demand and Supply

Most analyses of government deal with its political processes: voting, elections, and the policy making of parliament, legislatures, councils and boards. These are the demand-articulating processes, i.e., the processes through which citizens indicate preferences and through which policies regarding services are decided upon.

Conceptually distinct from politics and policy making, however, is the production or supply of goods and services after they have been decided upon through political processes. For the most part, it is assumed that the same organization that does the policy making also organizes and manages production, but there is nothing that binds one to such an assumption. There is no reason, for example, why production cannot be undertaken by a private firm, a nonprofit society, or another government under contract to the policy-making organization, as well by its own bureaucracy. Recognizing the potential for separating demand and supply is not the same as an earlier distinction made in public administration between politics and administration, where policy makers made policy and administrators mechanically carried out those policies. Suppliers *do* influence the kinds and quality of services provided, for better or worse, and matching supply to demand is a problem in the public sector just as it is in private markets.

Explicitly recognizing that the supply of politically decided-upon goods and services does not need to be done by the demand-articulating organization is critically important for understanding how different supply arrangements can be matched to demand so as to obtain more efficient and adaptive production than that obtained by limiting production to government itself. Such recognition enables one to look more closely at the kinds of goods and services that are demanded and the problems of matching supply to demand. This examination is necessary to sort out how alternative production arrangements can be used for different activities.

The Nature of Government Services and Bureaucratic Production

Government services are typically produced by a bureau or department of the government organization through which demands are articulated and policies made. This approach to production, while typical, poses some problems that are the result of four related causes. First, federal, provincial and municipal governments undertake many different activities. Second, outputs of many government services are hard to measure so that management to produce such services is very difficult. Third, it is hard to introduce penalties and rewards into government organizations both because of the difficulty of measuring and evaluating outputs and because the organizations are "public." Fourth, because of the diverse range of activities and the difficulty of managing them by measuring outputs or subjecting subordinates to performance-based rewards and penalties, managers become overloaded and simply do not have the time to do a good job. Each of these problems will be briefly described here and each will be treated in more detail when examining the potential role of contracting out government service production.

Table 7-1 provides an example of the variety of activities a municipal government may become involved in. The range of activities for the provincial government and federal government is equally extensive.

Though no municipality undertakes all of the functions listed in Table 7-1, the range of services provided by any municipality except the smallest is greater than the range of products produced by virtually any private firm. Furthermore, many of the functions themselves comprise several distinct activities, each of which has different production characteristics. Such activities are most efficiently performed at different scales of activity. For example, key activities making up policing include patrol, criminal investigation, traffic control, crime lab analysis, detention, radio dispatching and information systems. Recreation activities may range from neighbourhood-oriented summer activities for preschoolers to metropolitan-wide opera houses and arenas. The result of this diversity in functions and the multitude of separable activities which comprise them is that no single organization is the appropriate size to produce all of the activities efficiently.

The second difficulty with producing government services is that many of the services have no clear measures of output. Without such measures, it is extremely difficult to determine the right amounts and combinations of inputs being used for the output desired. Combining inputs efficiently is made even more difficult because many outputs that are in fact measurable, such as the participation rate in recreation programs or use of a library, are difficult to evaluate qualitatively. Thus it is very difficult to assess whether benefits exceed costs, let alone determine efficient input mixes in production processes.

The problem of measuring and evaluating outputs makes it extremely difficult to design reward and penalty systems within organizations producing government services so that employees and managers face direct incentives to manage as efficiently as possible. This difficulty is compounded by the multiple attribute nature of most services, where to

TABLE 7-1 Municipal Functions

Airports	Planning and zoning
Animal regulations	Police protection
Building inspection	Public health regulation
Business licensing	Public transit
Cemeteries	Public works
Civil defence and emergency measures	Recreation facilities
Control of firearms	Recreation programs
Economic development	Refuse collection and disposal
Elections	Regulation of nuisances
Electricity generation and distribution	Sewage collection and treatment
Fire protection	Social welfare administration
General administration — purchasing,	Soil fill and removal regulations
contracting, labour relations, etc.	Storm drainage
House numbering	Streets, curbs and sidewalks,
Industrial parks	lighting
Irrigation and flood control	Subdivision control
Land purchase and development	Tax collections
Libraries	Telephone service
Museums	Television rebroadcasting
Noise control	Water supply and distribution
Parks	Weed control

Source: Robert L. Bish, *Local Government in British Columbia* (Victoria, B.C.: University of Victoria, School of Public Administration, 1984), p. 35.

reward a person for some measurable output may result in negative consequences elsewhere. For example, it is sometimes suggested that police departments be evaluated on the basis of crime rates, yet the easiest way to reduce reported crime rates is for police to reclassify incidents reported as crimes and not follow up on citizen complaints. The result will be fewer reported crimes but police-citizen relationships will deteriorate and actual crime will go unmeasured.

Another difficulty with designing reward and penalty systems is that government organizations often develop an egalitarian civil service ethic where "professionals" are expected to work in the public interest and where sanctions for poor performance are so time-consuming to use that many managers ignore substandard performance rather than try to do anything about it. The net result is a work environment where organizations continue along habitual lines with little innovation or adaptive behaviour unless they are subjected to major externally generated shocks. Such organizations are likely to lag, rather than lead, in innovation and productivity increases.

Finally, the problem of management overload is simply the cumulative result of all these difficulties. When an organization is attempting to undertake many diverse functions and activities, when many outputs are unmeasurable and difficult to evaluate, and where it is difficult to develop incentive systems to reward superior performance and penalize inadequate performance, management is very difficult. Managers will have neither sufficient time nor expertise in all functional areas to manage their organization effectively. Thus, while crises may be attended to, routine activities may continue using excess resources or obsolete technologies long after adaptations are made elsewhere in the economy.

One should note that the production difficulties faced in governments are not due to slothful employees or a lack of interest in being efficient. The problems faced are extremely difficult to overcome because of the nature and diversity of the functions performed. Given these problems and the objective that government services be provided efficiently, it is useful to examine how governments can obtain more efficient production of some of their services by contracting them to private firms, nonprofit societies and other governments.

Contracting

Contracting to have government services produced can be examined from several perspectives. Three will underlie this analysis. One perspective will focus on the consequences for citizens, ie., can the use of contracting result in having demanded government services provided more efficiently? A second viewpoint will focus on how managers can manage[4] the production and delivery of the diverse range of activities in which governments are engaged without having to administer all of them in their own organization. Guidelines will be provided to help managers decide whether they can get better results from contracting out certain production activities instead of administering them in-house.

The third perspective will examine a very important issue. What are the broader effects on responsiveness and adaptiveness to changing conditions that can result from the widespread use of contracting for the production of government services in contrast to relying on in-house production for most government activities? While this latter question is more difficult to answer definitively, empirical evidence from at least one major study does draw conclusions on this important question.

The Extent and Variety of Contracting

Contracting with the private sector or other governments for the production and delivery of government services in North America has a long history. In the past two decades, however, contracting out has moved beyond the traditional purchase of typewriters, police cars and buildings to include virtually every function of local government and many provincial and federal government activities. For example, of the 121 Canadian cities with a population over 10,000 responding to Professor McDavid's survey of municipal administrators, 82 percent contracted out some services. A Bureau of Municipal Research survey of 47 cities with populations ranging from 35,000 to 500,000 indicated 87 percent contracted out some services.[5] Four municipalities in the Vancouver area have switched from municipal to contracted residential solid waste collection during the past three years. A wide variety of local government services, in fact, are provided under contract in both Canada and the United States (see Table 7-2). Contracting out local government service production is also common in Great Britain, Europe and Japan. In Switzerland, for example, more than 30 villages and townships contract with a private company, Securities, for police services.[6]

As previously indicated, contracting for service production is also undertaken by many provincial governments as well as the federal government. For example, the British Columbia Ministry of Human Resources contracts for the production of special care homes, hostels, transition houses, child care, rehabilitation services and other human services.

McAfee and McMillan, in their study for the Ontario Economic Council, also cite many studies of contracting by other governments in Canada, but there does not seem to be any systematic compilation of the range of activities for which the provincial and federal governments contract.

While the range of services for which contracting is used is wide, as indicated by Table 7-2, the diversity of production activities necessary to provide all these services implies a diversity of contract arrangements.[7]

As far as may be gathered from the evidence available, early contracts tended to be either for entire functions (i.e., solid waste collection, water supply, etc.) where the contractor was paid to organize all aspects of production and delivery; or for support services, such as providing detention facilities for a police department or payroll processing for all city employees.

While these kinds of contracts continue, the variety of contract arrangements has also expanded. Much of this expansion appears to be related to the increased variety and scale of local government activities.

The most important kinds of contracting arrangements include:
1. *Purchase of an entire function from a single producer.* Examples of this kind of contracting include solid waste collection where the contractor owns the equipment and is fully responsible for all aspects of collection.
2. *Purchase of an entire function from several producers.* Contracts for solid waste collection are let to different companies for different areas to maintain a more competitive environment. Montreal contracts in this manner for solid waste collection.
3. *Purchase of provision of a service but capital plant and equipment are owned by the government.* Examples include hiring firms to manage a sanitary land fill, a recreation centre, or hospitals where the physical facility in each case is owned by the government. The separation of ownership of the capital facility from management recognizes the

TABLE 7-2 Contracted Local Government Services

1. Central Services

Assessing
Computer services
Document destruction
Election administration
Equipment maintenance
Food services for government
  employees
Grounds maintenance
Janitorial services
Labour negotiations
Legal services
Microfilm services
Payroll
Personnel services
Printing
Public relations
Records maintenance
Registration of voters
Tax collection
Treasury functions
Utility billing
Vehicle maintenance

2. Development

Building and mechanical
  inspection
Electrical and plumbing
  inspection
Engineering services
General development
Housing
Industrial development
Land development
Licensing
Mapping
Planning urban renewal
Tourist information center
Zoning and subdivision
  control

3. Human Resources

a) Education
   Daycare for children
   Schools
   School crossing guards
   School lunches
   School bussing
b) Health
   All public health services

Alcoholic rehabilitation
Ambulance services
Animal control
Cemeteries
Homes for the aged
Hospitals
Hospital maintenance
Mental health
Mosquito control
Nursing services
Pest control
c) Recreation
   Libraries
   Museums
   Parks
   Park maintenance
   Recreation facilities
   Sports programs
d) Pollution Control
   Air pollution statement
   Noise abatement
   Water pollution abatement
e) Public Transportation
   Special transportation service
   Management service for
     publicly owned transit
   Transit systems
   Seaplane base management
   Selected transit routes
f) Welfare services

4. Public Safety Services

a) Civil Defence
   All civil defence
   Civil defence communications
   Civil defence training
b) Fire Services
   All fire services
   Fire communications
   Fire prevention
   Training of firefighters
c) Police Services
   All police services
   Crime laboratory
   Criminal investigations
   Jails and detention homes
   Juvenile delinquency programs
   Parking meter patrol
   Patrol services
   Police communications
   Police training
   Probation and parole

different scales of those activities and maintains a more competitive climate for management firms. Various divisions of ownership and management for such facilities is possible depending on the activity involved.

4. *Contracting for the physical facilities of an in-house operation.* The best example of this kind of contracting is when a government rents building space from private owners rather than constructing its own buildings; further examples include the leasing of automobiles, computers and other office equipment.

5. *Contracting for part of a service and manage part in-house.* Contracting out part of a service is a way to stimulate competition in part of the market, against which in-house performance can be continually compared. This approach is followed in Edmonton and Winnipeg for solid waste collection. It appears to have led to the increased efficiency of the government organizations.

6. *Contracting for support services only.* Most government functions involve services to citizens and services to the department providing the service to citizens. For example, a small city may want to provide police patrol, but contract for dispatching, detention facilities, or police car maintenance; or it may want to contract for such support services as payroll processing, janitorial services or legal services. Support services are an area where multinational corporations are actively involved in contracting through franchises or branch operations, because these services have historically received less attention from public officials than those delivered directly to citizens. Hence it has been relatively easy for private firms to develop more efficient production techniques.

7. *Contracting for management only.* In the areas of hospital and transit system management, municipalities are buying management services only — while retaining ownership of the physical plant and equipment and continuing to be the employer of the non-management employees. This is a clear case of large companies providing specialized management expertise, enabling them to manage more efficiently than in-house managers. In some cases there are also economies of scale involved, when managers may use their relationship with a large company to make quantity purchases at lower cost or even borrow capital funds at more favourable terms than those available to the local government.

The simple identification of the diverse services for which contracting is used indicates that many government officials have concluded that contracting out is an effective way to get government services produced. In addition, the development of a wide variety of contracting arrangements indicates that there is unlikely to be any one best way to engage in contracting out. However, in order to draw conclusions on the consequences of the use of contracting and make practical recommendations for using it effectively, it is necessary to look more closely at the historical, theoretical and empirical analysis of the use of contracting.

History: Contract Cities[8]

When one looks at the history and analyses of contracting, it is clear that public officials were engaged in contracting for major public services long before academics discovered that it could have major implications for the operation of government. And yet, it is only with academic scholarship begun by a few political scientists working with economists in the 1950s and 1960s, that major theoretical breakthroughs began. Their scholarship has led to considerable academic analysis of alternative ways to produce local government services.[9] To place this work in perspective, it is useful to provide first a very brief history of the development of the contract cities in Southern California — a phenomenon which gave rise to the early scholarship — and then an examination of subsequent theory and empirical research.

In 1954, as an outgrowth of the conflict over the tax subsidization of heavily populated but unincorporated suburban areas in Los Angeles County, a new city form was created. Specific areas became new, fully legal cities, but instead of hiring large numbers of employees and going into debt to provide a city hall and the other equipment necessary to deliver local government services, they purchased services from the county government. This gave citizens political control over their own area without incurring associated start-up costs of a new city.

The first of these cities was Lakewood. The area continued its membership in special districts for fire protection, sewers, street lighting, schools and recreation, and entered into contracts with the county government for 15 other services, including policing, engineering, street construction and maintenance. The city itself hired a manager, a city attorney, a city clerk and several secretaries whose responsibilities were primarily contract management. County officials were appointed to fill all other statutory positions.

By 1960, 25 additional cities were incorporated in Los Angeles County. Some were large, some small; some were diversified, some specialized. What they all had in common, however, was a desire to control their own areas while receiving local government services as efficiently as possible. Equally important, because they lacked established bureaucracies, they were free to choose the most efficient production arrangement without the political constraint of existing organizations.

As one might imagine, contracting with a large county bureaucracy did not prove ideal. As city officials gained experience, they discovered activities where county costs were higher than they thought necessary, and they found it difficult to bargain with and obtain accommodations from an organization that acted like a large monopolistic bureaucracy.

Instead of simply assuming responsibility for their own production of local services, however, the Association of Contract Cities was formed with the specific objective of balancing the county government's monopoly power and seeking alternative suppliers. What followed was the development of a vast network of producers and contract arrangements where cities buy and sell to one another, where private firms compete actively among themselves and with government producers for contracts, and where the county has decentralized its production bureaucracies to compete with other suppliers. With this response, the county's role was greatly reduced. What emerged has been characterized in the major study of the development of contract cities as a "market-model" of government service production.[10]

The characteristics of the "market-model" described by Robert Warren include important implications for problems of government service production. First, producing organizations can be more specialized, so that by selling to different sized markets they can adjust to efficient sizes. Secondly, when drafting a contract, the outputs and pricing methods have to be specified very carefully. In spite of the difficulty of measuring the outputs of many government services, greater degrees of measurement have thus been developed than those of traditional government budgeting processes. Third, the competitive tendering process introduces incentives to be efficient and innovative to obtain the contracts. Most important in this regard is Warren's observation that government departments producing to sell to other governments could compete with private firms and, in so doing, become more efficient for their own citizens as well. Thus, the variable affecting incentive to be efficient was not whether the producer was public or private, it was whether the producer was producing for sale in a competitive market rather than as a monopolist.

In his study Warren did not deal with management overload specifically; however, he characterized the role of municipal managers very differently — as purchasers for a consumer cooperative instead of as administrators of a bureaucracy. This new role, Warren concluded, also gave managers the perspective of the consumer-citizen instead of that of the producer, which is characteristic of managers whose main day-to-day responsibilities are administering production organizations. Warren concluded that systems of local government production characterized by extensive competitive contracting would be more efficient and more oriented to citizens and consumers than systems comprised primarily of bureaucratic monopolies. The logic of Warren's conclusions has also been developed within the context of economic theory,[11] and an integration of Warren's insights and economic theory has also been published.[12] A recent empirical analysis of the contract cities indicates that they also continue to receive services at lower cost than the non-contract cities in Los Angeles County.[13]

Of equal importance to the emergence of contract cities was the intellectual challenge the development posed for traditional public administrators. Since the 1920s at least, administrators had been taught and continue to teach that local governments should be consolidated and organized into neat hierarchies with a single treasury to be allocated by council members, who would then turn over the administration to a city manager who would manage the producing bureaucracies.[14] The development of contract cities with competitive contracting did not fit the traditional bureaucratic model of government for a metropolitan region, and scholars began to examine critically both the theory and evidence regarding government organization and service production.[15]

These scholars noted the importance of elected local government officials making decisions on what kinds and levels of services they wished to provide and how they were to be financed to resolve problems of large-group public goods and collective action. Beyond that, however, they observed that it was not critical that the governments themselves hire employees to undertake production. Instead, local managers could choose to hire employees for some activities. But they could also enter into joint agreements for sharing the supervision of production with another government, could contract with either another government or a private firm, or could issue franchises to private firms for user-charge financed services. Different production arrangements appeared appropriate for different local government activities.

Furthermore, once the question of contracting was raised, everywhere they looked they observed that contracting for the production of local government services went on — not just in contract cities. Local administrators had not heeded advice from scholars on contracting. Instead, in a variety of circumstances, elected and appointed officials decided that contracting out was an easier or less costly way to get local government services produced. It is since the intellectual challenges posed by contract cities, however, that significant and serious scholarly attention has been given to contracting and its broader implications.

The Potential Role of Contracting — Theory and Concepts

How can the production and delivery of local government goods and services be accomplished to provide the greatest net benefit to citizens? As net benefits are related to quality and responsiveness to citizen preferences, as well as cost, both benefits and costs must be kept in mind as alternative arrangements are evaluated.

In order to develop guidelines for considering when and where contracting to improve efficiency may be appropriate, the major problems of government service production in relation to contracting are discussed more fully below.

ECONOMIES AND DISECONOMIES OF SCALE

Economies of scale are decreases in the average cost of production as output increases. They are usually due to the spreading of the costs of indivisible capital equipment over larger and larger outputs, and they are usually associated with capital intensive activities such as sewage treatment and mass transit systems. Diseconomies of scale, on the other hand, occur when increasing output causes average costs to rise. Diseconomies are usually due to disproportionate increases in the cost of management in organizations with large numbers of employees whose work must be supervised. Costs increase with size: as the organization grows an increasing proportion of the total workforce must be devoted to supervision instead of direct service delivery. Diseconomies of scale are associated with activities such as education or police patrol (a small department will have 90 percent of patrol officers in the street while a large department will have 50 percent of its patrol-related officers supervising the 50 percent who are in the street).

In addition to considerations of capital investment and management costs, scale problems also arise when a service requires expensive equipment or highly skilled people — but the need for the service only arises infrequently. For example, even though most small cities will occasionally need an efficient homicide squad and crime laboratory for a criminal investigation, it is unlikely that they would require such services often enough to justify the costs of maintaining a squad and laboratory in their own police departments. Thus, because of the periodic demand for the service, it is more efficient to arrange for an organization that serves a large population to provide the service, as with any other activity with economies of scale.

Furthermore, the research and development of innovative techniques for the management of service production and delivery has economies of scale. Only a very large organization can justify its expenses on research and development because it can spread the costs over very large outputs. The best examples of economies of scale with this rationale are the development of more efficient equipment and techniques for solid waste collection by multinational companies, for hospital management by American Medical International, or for school lunch programs by an increasing number of very large suppliers. These firms then make their techniques available to decentralized branches or local organizations on a franchise basis, and the local organizations in turn contract for local government service production. It is becoming increasingly clear that local organizations that receive their training and expertise under franchise agreements from such companies can provide services that are as responsive and efficient as those provided by many local governments or traditional small-scale producers who are not large enough to make comparable investments in research and development.

A government undertakes many diverse activities. It is impossible for a government to be at an efficient scale of production for all its activities if it alone produces all of them. A city of 10,000, for example, may be able to provide police patrol services most efficiently, but it is unlikely to be able to provide a crime lab or run a large capital-intensive recreational complex for its citizens as efficiently as a city of 100,000.

There are two common problems with adjustments to scale. One is to use different technology to get the services provided (i.e., rent school space for recreation instead of constructing a separate recreation facility) or enter into a contract or joint agreement so that the producing organization can be either smaller, larger, or provide more expertise than the city purchasing its services. Making efforts to achieve scale adjustments is an obvious reason for contracting out.

INCENTIVES AND MONOPOLIES

If the efficient production and delivery of public services is to be achieved, it is important that managers and employees face incentives which reward them for efficient performance and penalize them for inefficient performance. Structuring such incentives in organizations, however, is extremely difficult.

The ideal environment to promote efficiency is one where consumers can easily evaluate products and choose among producers. Producers in turn face the positive incentive of profits if they can provide what consumers want efficiently, and the negative incentive of losses and going out of business if they cannot. Similarly, the managers of such organizations also have an incentive to try to manage efficiently and in truly competitive environments even lower-level employees recognize that their performance makes a contribution to the long-term viability of the organization. In summary, government organizations, like private firms, respond to competitive environments.

Governmental producing organizations, however, do not usually face the same incentives as a private firm in a competitive environment. The government may be a monopolist where managers and employees are neither rewarded for efficient performance nor threatened with going out of business if performance is poor.[16] To complicate matters further, it is likely to be more difficult to measure the efficiency of organizations producing many government goods and services, and hence such organizations are likely to be much more difficult to manage than a private firm which produces a measurable product.[17]

The combination of monopoly characteristics of many government bureaucracies and the difficulties of managing the production of unmeasurable goods and services, provides an environment where one should not anticipate especially efficient production. When management incentives are further affected by asymmetrical treatment of innovations (managers are seldom rewarded for successful innovations but may be terminated for failed ones) and management is constrained by civil service rules and union contracts, it is surprising that public sector managers do as well as they do.

Contracting through competitive tendering is a major way to deal with incentive problems in the public sector. One must recognize, however, that the critical variable is not public vs. private. Instead, the contractor faces positive incentives to be efficient and negative sanctions if he is not. These conditions can also exist for a government that sells to other governments, and for nonprofit and voluntary organizations, as well as private firms. Furthermore, when purchasing managers can exercise positive rewards and negative sanctions in contract renewals or terminations, they can exercise at least as much, if not greater, control over the output of the contractor than they generally can over the output of a government bureaucracy.

While competitive tendering can be used to overcome problems of monopoly and incentives, not all local government services can be contracted because of the difficulty of defining, measuring, or monitoring service outputs. Although some contracts are paid in terms of inputs (legal fees and engineering services, for example, are often billed on a per hour of input basis), the best results are achieved when contracts are written in terms of outputs, thereby freeing the contractor to organize to achieve those outputs most efficiently. Thus, contracts are much more feasible when outputs can be measured, as in the case of solid waste collection, water supply, sewage treatment, prisoner days, laboratory tests performed, or number of assessments performed. With the ability to measure, it is also much easier to monitor the quality of output so that the government can be sure that citizens receive what has been paid for. Still, one must also be aware that there will be an incentive to do a good job beyond any strict interpretation of contract terms only if the contractor is interested in going beyond the current contract — just as a retailer may do a little extra to obtain repeat sales.

Information and measurement are necessary to draft enforceable contracts. Nevertheless, it has been observed that even when contract specification is not perfect, the information and specificity generated during the tendering and contract-drafting process is much greater and much more useful for management decision making than the information generated in traditional government budgeting processes.[18] Thus, one must recognize the need and ability to define outputs before a contract can be used. But one must also recognize that output specification need not be perfect to get more efficient performance under contracting than under regular budgeting processes.

One final note on incentives and monopoly is appropriate. It is very important when tendering for there to be more than one potential supplier in addition to the government going into production for itself.[19] This is because the step to utilize in-house production is often irreversible and should not be taken lightly. The way to be sure of potential alternative suppliers is to examine the market closely and pay special attention to just what is demanded in a tendering process. For example, if one is calling for solid waste collection in a city with a population of 100,000, it is probably better to issue four separate tenders for areas of 25,000 people each than it is to issue one large tender. It is also useful to separate the construction of capital facilities from management to avoid being locked into a long-term management contract just because an organization could offer a lower price on the initial construction.

Finally, in the case of an in-house production, the organization may be able to provide incentives to be more efficient by contracting out part of the production and then comparing the performance of the two organizations. When this was done for solid waste collection in Minneapolis, the private firm was at first much more efficient than the municipal crew, but over time the municipal crew improved its efficiency. Similar internal competition between private contractors and municipal employees is used in Montreal and Edmonton.

Contracts can be used to create incentives for the efficient production of government services. Remember, however, that contracting is not a passive process, but rather one where managers must pay very careful attention to the specification of the services desired, the tendering process and monitoring results. Simply issuing a tender to a private monopoly because it is private is unlikely to produce successful results.

LOAD SHEDDING

Since governments undertake a diverse range of activities, it is impossible for top managers to be experts in every one. At the same time, few governments find it efficient to hire experts in every area, and if they did, the span of control problem for the manager would still be a major constraint on effective management. In addition, because of the unmeasurability and political sensitivity of some government activities, a manager's job is often more difficult than that of a private sector manager in a comparably sized organization.

One response to the diverse range of municipal activities and the difficulty of managing some of them is load shedding. This means contracting out some activities because the tendering process, including the supervision of performance, may require less time and effort for managers than the direct supervision of in-house production. The greater the number of activities that can be tendered out, the more time managers will have to supervise those activities that are unsuitable for tendering and especially difficult to manage. The top management staff is thereby kept small and efficient.

Benefits from load shedding can be in addition to any cost-saving benefits from contracting. For example, school principals are trained to run educational programs — not cafeterias, janitorial staffs, landscaping and bus systems. Other managers have similar limitations. A manager's time is scarce. Managers, then, should always keep in mind that they need to be able to call on a variety of arrangements to get services produced, including contracting.

EMPIRICAL STUDIES

The implications of economic theory for government production are that net benefits can be anticipated from contracting if contracting out permits better adjustment to economies or diseconomies of scale, creates a better environment to reward efficiency or penalize inefficiency, or results in a net reduction in manager's workloads so that they can concentrate their time and energy on other different management activities. It is necessary to undertake an empirical analysis, however, to be sure that the results expected from a theoretical analysis actually do occur.

There are several ways to analyze empirically the actual or potential results of contracting out relative to in-house production. When government officials undertake such studies, they generally focus on comparisons of their operation with other organizations or with proposals. Academics, in contrast, try to collect data on larger sample sizes and then analyze the data to determine what variation in cost is attributable to the institutional arrangements for production when other variables are also accounted for in the analysis. Some independent academic analysis has also begun on case studies where a change in arrangements has taken place. In addition to these cost-oriented studies, there have also been surveys of public officials to determine their attitudes, reasons and preferences with regard to contracting and bureaucratic production.

The kind of study undertaken is determined by its purpose. However, particular problems arise with studies that focus on comparative costs. Governments seldom keep records in a way that lets an analyst calculate the full cost of any given activity. One may get data on payroll, for example, but fringe benefits may or may not be included. Data on capital equipment, depreciation, utilities, the value of buildings, and administrative overhead seldom exist. Thus, there is a systematic bias toward underestimating the costs of bureaucratic production unless a thorough effort is made to make a full accounting, including estimates of costs for which no systematic records are kept.

There are different problems with cost data for contracts. Detailed cost breakdowns are rarely available because the information is the property of the producing firm. This is not a major problem if one is interested only in the price of the contract to the contracting government. It is a limitation, though, if one is trying to discover why cost differences exist between different organizations. One must also be sure that when calculating costs to the government, any contract supervision and monitoring costs are added to the price of the contract to provide a full-cost measure for the activity. Some studies of contracted production have neglected this cost component and hence have understated the real costs of the contract.

It is useful to examine several studies, keeping in mind that different kinds of studies serve different purposes and that studies must be fully described to assure the reader of complete and unbiassed cost data.

FIRE SERVICES[20]

Along with policing and street building and maintenance, fire services are one of the three most expensive functions undertaken by general local governments. This is also a service dominated by bureaucratic production where there has been relatively little innovation. In 1971, one of the first statistical studies, undertaken by Roger Ahlbrandt, compared the production of fire services by a private firm under contract to those by traditional bureaucratic production.[21] It is especially interesting because it examined the routine processes and included a case study of the private company.

Ahlbrandt's study was done by constructing an expenditure function to predict costs for traditional fire departments to service different areas in Washington State. The items taken into account included population, area served, assessed valuation, firemen's wages, the use of volunteers, the number of full-time employees, the number of fire stations and first-aid cars, housing conditions, and fire insurance ratings — the latter being a standardized but less than perfect measure of the quality of services. The coefficient of multiple determination for the function was .96. This means that 96 percent of the variance in the cost of providing fire protection by traditional fire departments was explained by the variables included in the regression analysis.

Following the construction of the expenditure function, information on the same variables for a sample of Arizona departments was analyzed. It was concluded that they were consistent with the original samples. Variables for Scottsdale, Arizona, were then inserted into the function to predict what the costs would be if Scottsdale were served by a traditional public fire department. The prediction indicated an expected cost of $475,000 or $7.10 per capita.

Scottsdale, however, is not served by a traditional fire department. The City of Scottsdale with the Rural-Metropolitan Fire Protection Company, which also serves several other cities and unincorporated areas in Arizona. The actual contract cost for the provision of fire protection to Scottsdale by Rural-Metro was $252,000 or $3.78 per capita, a cost 47 percent lower than that predicted if the area were served in the traditional manner.

Because these cost savings were quite dramatic, an effort was made to identify the specific areas of cost saving within the Rural-Metropolitan Fire Protection Company. The innovations that were identified included the use of part-time but fully trained fire fighters to supplement full-time employees, the use of smaller trucks and other modern equipment.

In addition to cost savings, a comparison between Rural-Metro's annual reports and those furnished by traditional fire departments indicated that the private company provided city officials with better information on the costs and potential benefits of different types and levels of fire protection than did traditional fire departments. Thus, Rural-Metro was shown to be both more efficient and more responsive than traditional departments in providing its users with the services they prefer.

Rural-Metro is an independently owned company regulated by the Arizona State Utilities Commission. Since company profits are limited to seven percent of sales, the only way the owner can raise total profits is to raise total sales. He does this by providing fire protection at a lower cost than cities could provide for themselves through traditionally organized fire departments. The company also has a profit-sharing plan for employees, which the owner-manager feels contributes to high morale and a search for improved efficiency.

Ahlbrandt's study is a careful one, but two cost-affecting variables are missing. Neither the costs of the administrative overhead for traditional companies nor the costs of the contract administration by Scottsdale were included. Thus, the costs of both the traditional and the contract departments were slightly understated. The inclusion of these costs, however, would not change the conclusions of the study.

SOLID WASTE COLLECTION

There have been at least nine major statistical studies of residential solid waste collection, two of which have been supplemented with a variety of case study analyses. They include studies in Switzerland,[22] the United States,[23] and Canada.[24] The results of all but one study are consistent and serious methodological problems exist in that one.[25]

Professor Jim McDavid of the University of Victoria has begun major studies of the provision of police and fire services, and residential solid waste collection in all cities in Canada, excluding Quebec, with populations over 10,000. The statistical portion of the component on residential solid waste collection has been completed, and research is continuing on several case studies.

In 1981, McDavid surveyed a total of 205 Canadian cities. The response rate for the solid waste questionnaire, including telephone follow-up, was 126 cities or 61 percent. In this sample, 26 (20.6 percent) use exclusive bureaucratic production within the city for residential solid waste collection, 53 (42.1 percent) use exclusive private collection, and 47 (37.3 percent) use both bureaucratic and private collection.

TABLE 7-3 Residential Solid Waste Collection Costs
by Collection Arrangement

Collection Arrangement	Operating Cost Per Household
Exclusive public collection	$42.29
Exclusive private collection	28.02
Public collection in mixed systems	31.31

McDavid's data base consists not only of complete cost data (including bureaucratic overhead, and contract administration and supervision costs) but also details of service conditions, services provided, and technologies used for collection.

The overall collection costs are shown in Table 7-3.

These data indicate that the average cost per household of exclusively public collection systems is 50.9 percent higher than that of private contract arrangements. One should note, however, that when public collection is undertaken in a city which also has private contract collection, public system costs are very close to those incurred in exclusively private systems — only 11.7 percent higher.[26]

Because of his large data base, McDavid was able to examine not only cost differences between bureaucratic and contracted production, but also how the two kinds of organizations vary in collection technologies and wages paid. There is a difference in wages paid by private and public collectors ($17,441 for private and $19,272 for public). There are also major differences in technologies used and in productivity. Private companies employ smaller crews, use larger and newer trucks, and offer a significantly greater number of incentives to increase the productivity of their employees. As a result, their employees collect an average of 1.25 tonnes per hour compared to .64 tonnes per hour collected by municipal employees. This productivity difference of 92 percent — not the difference in wages (10.5 percent) — is the major reason contract collection is so much cheaper.

McDavid's analysis is of a large sample of Canadian cities operating on a routine basis. It includes some efficient municipalities and some very expensive private contracts (not all contracts are let through competitive tenders). But it also shows that on average public management has not responded to new technologies — such as buying larger trucks — as have private companies, nor does public management design routes, rationalize crew sizes, and provide incentives for its employees. Because the study drew upon a wide sample of cities and was carefully executed, it provides a unique and important comparison of public and private government service production in Canada. Its findings point to serious deficiencies in the public production of this service.

During the past three years, four municipalities in the greater Vancouver region (Coquitlam, Richmond, City of North Vancouver and

District of West Vancouver) have switched from municipal to contracted solid waste collection with private firms. These changes are not routine in nature; in fact, these changes have been vigorously criticized by municipal unions affiliated with CUPE. Nevertheless, they provide an opportunity to examine before and after costs, together with the analytical and political processes that led to each decision. Although the study is still going on, it is possible to draw some conclusions on the basis of the interviews with public officials and a preliminary examination of cost data.[27]

The initiatives for the switches came from private firms that submitted unsolicited proposals to city councils. These unsolicited bids were lower than city costs, but not especially low compared to McDavid's Canadian-wide average of $28.02 per household (in 1980). Each municipality asked its own solid waste collection department or a consultant to cost out its service provision and make recommendations for improvements. Inefficiencies were discovered in all four cases. After accepting the improvements, however, it was determined that municipal costs could approach contract costs very closely, depending on one important factor: that municipal management could count on the willingness of unions to cooperate with major changes in crew sizes and route configuration. Unions in each municipality opposed the switch to contract collection as well as changes in internal management. The municipal councils, in spite of the union opposition, decided to contract out the service because they apparently doubted they could get sufficient union cooperation to increase productivity, thereby making their costs comparable with those offered by private contractors. From the municipal managers' perspective, contracting out the collection service had a major impact on their workload, because they would not have to spend time negotiating productivity improvements with reluctant unions. Net cost savings also appear to have been significant. In the case of Richmond, where data analysis has been completed, its municipally run residential solid waste collection cost $46.24 per household in 1982. With the contract arrangement, costs fell to $30.63 in 1983, including contract administration and enforcement costs, and all overhead.[28] The contract was also written to ensure a very high quality of service, with financial penalties for deficiencies in quality.

The results from preliminary examinations of the four cases in British Columbia are consistent with the conclusions from McDavid's statistical analysis of Canadian cities. Each municipality, upon analysis, recognized that the cost of its collection was higher than necessary. Each also concluded that with cooperation from employees it could produce at a cost very close to that of a private contractor. Such results prompt the following question: Why do municipalities continue routinely to produce solid waste collection at a cost that is approximately 50 percent higher than that obtained by good management? Of course, a similar question could be raised regarding municipal solid waste collection in the United

States and Switzerland, although the cost differences between public and contract collection there are less than those identified in the Canadian study.

While large differences in cost have been identified between exclusively public and exclusively contract systems, public collection in mixed systems has proved almost as efficient as private contract collection. The possibility of dividing up a city into separate collection zones, with some areas being cleared by a private firm and others by the government's own organization, has been recognized for some time. Indeed, several cities, including Edmonton, Winnipeg and Montreal use this strategy to maintain a presence in the collection process while introducing explicit competitive comparisons and pressures to get efficient service. The most widely studied example of a mixed system is that of Minneapolis where, upon the initial division, the private contract was much less costly, but over time the municipal organization was able to achieve comparable production costs.[29] This particular study has been used to conclude that the public collection of solid waste can be as efficient as the private collection. This conclusion is valid, however, only if the public organization is subject to competitive pressure. Municipal monopolies simply have not proven as efficient as organizatons subject to competition, regardless of whether they are public or private.

OTHER STUDIES

The above studies all deal specifically with the different effects realized when service production is contracted out. The services under discussion here are reasonably easy to measure, draft contracts for, and monitor. Many activities of government, though, do not meet these conditions. Accordingly, two Canadian experiences associated with contracting for different kinds of activities deserve mention. One is the federal government's attempt to use contracting to stimulate private sector research and development.[30] The other concerns the province of British Columbia's grants to nonprofit agencies to provide social services.

After governments set policy, a specific performance-related contract can be used to obtain production of the service from another organization. This contracting process requires the ability to specify closely what is expected and how it is to be priced. Yet the very nature of research and development, with all of its uncertainties, would appear to be incongruous with the use of contracting as conceptualized in this report. It is perhaps possible to define some costs and outputs of a research and development effort and engage in competitive tendering, but it is more likely to expect that contracting would turn into sole-source negotiations with pricing resembling cost-plus. Such an incentive system is exactly the opposite of the one that appears to make the contracted production of government services more efficient. It is the kind of contracting that has been heavily criticized in the United States.[31] One must avoid generalizing about other forms of contracting because of the poor results from one particular process.

Along with the use of contracted government service production has come the use of nonprofit agencies to deliver social services. Social service agencies usually differ from contract suppliers, however. Even though government funds are involved, the agency has a major voice in deciding not only the service delivery processes but also the policies surrounding the services. Thus, the public funding resembles a grant more than a contract, where the organization awarded the contract uses the funds as if they are a grant to accomplish what it has determined to be important. The tension created by the uncertain policy role of the nonprofit agency when the distinction between a grant and a contract is clouded has been the focus of considerable analysis.[32]

A recent study in British Columbia by John W. Langford identified approximately 900 social service agencies, with a total of 6,000 employees, that received $150 million in public funds from the province in 1983-84.[33] These organizations, Langford observes, face neither the profit motivation of the private sector nor any government incentive to encourage efficiency, and therefore no one really knows if they are making good use of taxpayers' funds. Langford also observes that many of the organizations appear to be run by their professional staff — their independent volunteer boards play an insignificant role. The professional staff members often receive much higher salaries than the senior regional manager of the ministry that funds their agencies. Langford is likewise unable to identify any clear lines of accountability for the uses of public funds by these agencies. He does not conclude that they are inefficient. Instead he points out that no one knows if they are indeed efficient and no obvious incentives exist to encourage them to be efficient.

While grants to social service agencies may appear to resemble a form of contracting, they are unlikely to meet the conditions under which contracted service production has been identified to be efficient and adaptive. These conditions stipulate that the output must be specified and monitored in a contract that is let in a competitive tendering process. The cost savings and adaptability to changing conditions come as a result because the contractors are then free to organize their production process as efficiently as possible. A clear policy is set by government, and production operates under conditions similar to those found in private competitive markets.

In British Columbia, the dual recognition of the potential efficiency of using small producing organizations to deliver services — such as child care, day care, and rehabilitation services — and the weaknesses of the contracts as grants system has resulted in the development of an exceptionally sophisticated Purchase of Services Policy and Procedures Manual by the B.C. Ministry of Human Resources.[34] If the recommended decision-making, negotiating and evaluation processes specified in this manual are fully utilized, much will be learned about the usefulness of contracting for services that are more difficult to measure than those for which evidence of the effectiveness of contracting already exists. Major productivity increases in producing human services would make a significant contribution to resolving the increasing-cost problems of these services.[35] Innovative contracting for human services would also contribute to more innovative arrangements for producing education and health services, two other very costly government activities.[36]

Observations on Empirical Studies

Many studies of contracting out have been done in the past decade. Most, however, consist of particular case studies, usually examining a change from bureaucratic production to a contract, and conclude that contracting is a superior production arrangement. While these studies are useful, however, they generally do not deal with ongoing arrangements run in a routine manner from which generalizations with greater validity can be drawn. However, the large-scale statistical studies discussed earlier in this paper both examine ongoing systems and have striking results. They indicate that having services produced under contract does result in considerable cost savings for comparable service levels (to the extent they are measurable) compared to the performance of in-house bureaucracies. Furthermore, the lower costs of production are a consequence of higher productivity, not simply lower wages for contract employees. This evidence, combined with the theory developed to explain the operation of non-market institutions, indicates that there is considerable potential for improvement in the operation of governments by contracting out service production.

Attitudes to Contracting Out

Decisions on arrangements to produce government services are related to considerations other than efficiency. For example, the Ontario Bureau of Municipal Research study concluded that elected officials from business backgrounds were more likely to support contracting out production of services than elected officials from professional backgrounds.[37] Only two cities were included in the study, however, and one must be very careful when generalizing from such a small sample.

Large-scale surveys of the attitudes of elected officials have been undertaken in the United States. Results from a survey of managers from 87 local governments in California on perceived advantages, disadvantages and problems associated with contracting are summarized in Table 7-4.[38]

TABLE 7-4 Contracting: Advantages, Disadvantages and Problems

	Responses (of 87)	
	Number	**Percent**
Advantages		
Availability of special equipment and skilled personnel	66	76
Reduced cost	60	69
Avoidance of start-up costs to provide services	50	57
Ease in adjusting program size	46	53
Improved service	36	41
Ease in measuring and monitoring contractor performance	21	24
Disadvantages		
Difficulty in monitoring contract	35	40
Unreliability of contractor	29	33
Poorer service	16	18
Increased costs	15	17
Displacement of employees	10	11
Problems		
Legislative constraints	22	25
Union or other employee organizations	18	21
Public to be served	13	15

Source: "Contracting Out Local Government Services in California", California Tax Foundation (May, 1981), p. 9.

As the survey indicates, managers' attitudes regarding the advantages of contracting support the theory presented earlier in this paper. In addition, 41 percent of the managers thought that contracting out services that are difficult to measure improved their quality; only 18 percent thought that the arrangement resulted in lowering the quality. Empirical studies have generally not observed systematic quality differences between municipal and contract production, although individual examples of better or poorer service for either kind of production can be identified. It is also important to note, however, that difficulties in monitoring contracts can occur and unreliable contractors do appear, and that the monitoring difficulty is most severe when a government hasn't developed procedures to monitor its own production.

Another survey of California city managers concluded that city managers felt they had less control over service production with contracting than with production managed in-house.[39] The survey, however, does not indicate whether managers felt they had less control over the processes — which clearly occurs — or over outputs. A different analysis has concluded that managers often overestimate their actual control over their own employees, and that careful contract can be used to have more, rather than less, control over actual outputs.[40]

Of lesser importance in the California survey cited above, but of major importance in Canada are labour union attitudes toward government contracting. The major local government union, the Canadian Union of Public Employees (CUPE) has adopted a simple "no contracting" position without any regard to production efficiency. The Canadian Labour Congress has also considered recommending that its members not contribute to charitable campaigns such as United Way, because some of its recipient organizations undertake service production under contract to governments. In some provinces, especially in British Columbia, union attitudes have been inflamed by provincial government legislation that reduced the provincial government's workforce by approximately 25 percent in two years, and where many services formerly produced by government employees are now provided under contract.

While it is difficult to generalize about the relation between rules of employment which have evolved in union contracts, there are many examples where the rules do result in much higher costs than necessary to produce government services. Examples include restrictions on the use of part-time drivers to provide peak-load service in public transit systems, and overtime payments for court reporters who take depositions in the evening or on weekends for the convenience of witnesses. Increasing flexibility in these situations provides for more efficient service. But if unions are unwilling to agree to productivity-increased changes, they can expect increasing pressures to contract out, as has occurred in the previously described changes to solid waste collection contracts. In these cases, even though the cities had estimated they could organize solid-waste collection internally with union employees as efficiently as they could with a private contractor, the unions refused to cooperate on work-rule changes, which ultimately led to contracting out. It should also be noted that contracting out does occur in spite of no-contracting clauses in union contracts. The government simply switches to a contract to purchase services at the expiration of the union contract period.

While union opposition to contracting may slow its development in some governments, an anti-contracting position combined with opposition to more efficient internal working rules is unlikely to be sustainable over the long run. Unions representing solid-waste collection employees in the City of Vancouver and the District of North Vancouver recognized this and cooperated with city governments in an attempt to make their solid waste collection as efficient as the contract collection in adjacent municipalities. This union strategy is likely to be much more beneficial to both unions and citizens.

One aspect of contracting that has not received significant attention since Robert Warren's study of contract cities in California is the contracting among governments. Some of this contracting is for services deemed unsuitable for a private firm — such as general police services — but most of it is for a variety of services that are also contracted to private firms. For example, municipalities in British Columbia often sell fire protection services to fire districts adjacent to the muncipality. Such a contract should be mutually beneficial, because the municipality can spread its overhead and the fire district does not have to invest in capital equipment to have the service provided. Thus, savings occur from adjustments to more efficient scales of production. It would also be interesting to know if the municipal fire department has become more efficient because it now falls under the scrutiny of fire district trustees. Similar questions have yet to be systematically analyzed regarding other intergovernmental contracting.

A wide variety of contracting arrangements exist for an extensive range of government services. The attitudes of elected and administrative officials toward contracting vary. Some view it as an efficient way to get government services produced; others perceive it as involving serious problems. Either position can be supported by individual case studies.

Adapting to the Future

Governments have at their disposal alternatives for organizing the production of goods and services. The alternatives include not only in-house production but also a variety of contracting arrangements. The important characteristics of each kind of production have been discussed and these observations noted: contracting may be relatively more efficient when governments must adjust to economies or diseconomies of scale, when better incentives for efficient production are needed, and when it enables managers to shed part of their day-to-day management responsibility so that they can concentrate on more difficult-to-manage activities. All of these considerations, however, focus primarily on efficient production at a given point in time.

· The world is not static. Problems perceived by the public change just as the technology of production processes changes. For example, many of the recommendations for consolidating local governments in urban areas arose when the major concern was building a physical infrastructure where economies of scale existed. More recent agitation for decentralization has revolved around the diseconomies of scale and the unsatisfactory services provided by large social service bureaucracies. And of course, we have the complete cycle brought about by computerization. Take, for example, what has occurred in records and data processing. In the beginning, bookkeeping ledgers were considered best and there were no economies of scale. Then large mainframe computers were introduced for record keeping and data processing, and they did possess economies of scale. Now micro computers have been found to be the most efficient means of keeping records and processing data.

Such changes in both perceived problems and technology should be anticipated in the future.

Responding to changing conditions is not easy for organizations, but one of the observed characteristics of contracting systems is that it is relatively easy to integrate new technologies and take advantage of, rather than resist, productivity-enhancing changes. This is because tenders are issued in terms of outputs, and competitive bidders will be those who adopt the most efficient techniques of production. If technologies change to create economies of scale, successful bidders will tend to be large organizations which can take advantage of such economies. In contrast, if technological change makes small firms more efficient, they will be the successful competitive bidders. The incentives inherent in the competitive bidding process seem to have produced a situation where much, if not most, of the innovation and productivity increases in public sector production are being initiated by private firms contracting to governments. Of course not all innovations are adopted by governments — including such obvious things as differentially staffing fire houses in relation to fire incidence or the use of large side-loading trucks for solid waste collection. It is resistance to, or simply a lack of interest in, productivity-enhancing changes which is one of the greatest weaknesses in government production of services.

Lack of innovation and slowness to adapt to technological change are not unique to governments. The Economic Council of Canada has observed that the diffusion of technological change into and throughout Canada tends to be slower than that in other Western countries, and it is slowest in the service sector.[41] A major part of the service sector is government. Research on contracting, however, indicates that it may also be important to differentiate services provided under competitive conditions from those provided by government monopolies, where incentives for improving productivity may simply not exist.

In dealing with this monopoly problem, the first step would be to encourage the use of competitive tendering for the supply of government services, and to create mechanisms to produce and disseminate information on comparative performance, making it easy for citizens and elected officials to compare the performance of their government with that of other governments. Although the Economic Council did not consider contracting the production of government services, it did recommend that provincial governments provide information to speed up the use of new technologies in their non-market sectors, especially hospitals, education and public administration. The council also recommended that the federal government reinstate productivity comparisons among departments across the country in a renewed effort to spread best-practice administration throughout the government.[42] The assumption seems to be that if information is available, organizations will improve.

While one cannot be sure that information alone will produce improvements, carefully prepared documents on comparative performance, published on a regular basis, could provide an incentive to managers of the least efficient operations. For example, a provincial government could contract with an independent organization to select a sample of municipalities or school districts within the province and develop careful cost and output measures for a particular function, such as solid waste collection, school busing or building maintenance costs. The results could be published with accompanying information on examples of best performance so that citizens, and also elected and appointed officials, could easily compare their organization with the examples. This would not be an expensive task. If it were done for a different activity two to four times a year, major activities could be covered over a three- to five-year cycle. Such a project could lead to considerable improvement among the most inefficient producers. If an analysis included contract production as well as in-house production, it would also be possible to identify new technologies and create rivalry for improved performance. This kind of general approach would be consistent with what is known about both technological change and the use of contracting in government — that competition can encourage improved performance. Competition could be fostered among cities, as well as among producing organizations that seek contracts. Such competition would also encourage contracting out to adapt to different economies of scale in production. Some governments might not welcome such scrutiny. However, elected and appointed officials who are truly interested in improved performance would welcome such a data base to help them improve the performance of their own organizations.

Conclusions and Observations

The purpose of this paper has been to present the broader considerations for deciding whether or not contracting may be an efficient way to get government goods and services produced. While the concepts advanced here have been derived by analyzing considerable research on contracting, only a few of many empirical studies have been described. Other books are available, including those by Robert Pool, E.S. Savas, Harry Hatry, and the International City Managers Association, which provide such summaries.[43] Those studies, along with the concepts presented above, should provide some ideas to get managers started on the path toward more efficient and flexible production strategies for the future. The Hatry, ICMA and previously mentioned *Contract Services Handbook* from the U.S. Department of the Interior also provide specific guidelines for analyzing and undertaking contracting.

A consideration of contracting implies several cautionary steps. First, in order to determine whether contracting is efficient, one must have reliable data on the existing costs of government production. This involves having a cost accounting system in which the costs are accurately presented — including the costs of fringe benefits for employees, the rental value of physical facilities and utilities, and administrative overhead. Only with such cost data can sound decisions be made.

Second, changing from in-house production to contracting involves labour relations and politics. The labour relations issues are complicated by the fact that employees themselves are seldom solely responsible for low productivity. Low productivity is more likely caused by government managers who do not organize effectively, past decisions which entrenched obsolete work practices into union contracts, or the reluctance of councils or legislatures to budget for the purchase of new productivity enhancing equipment. In most cases where a shift from bureaucratic to contract production has occurred, governments have assumed an obligation to accommodate their employees who were displaced, usually by transferring them to employment with the contractor or by moving them elsewhere in the city government. In respect to labour relations, it should be noted that contractors as well as governments may employ union labour. The difference, however, is that a contract can be written with default conditions so that a strike and elimination of service can lead to termination of the contract and the jobs of the striking workers. This incentive has resulted in very few strikes among contractors' employees.

Keeping in mind that one's own cost accounting systems must be in order, and that politics and labour relations will also be important, decisions to contract, like decisions to improve efficiency must balance multiple criteria. Since any single case is likely to have some unique characteristics, it is difficult to predict just what should, or should not, be contracted out rather than produced in-house.

The concepts and problems presented in this paper suggest some sources of potential cost savings. They can be summarized briefly in this manner.

- Scale Adjustments   Is an in-house production organization too big or too small to adjust to high capital costs, high management costs, periodic demands or lack of expertise?
- Incentives   Can we specify what we want in a tender and contract, and have more than one potential producer interested in contracting?
- Load Shedding   Can a manager supervise an activity through a tender and thus devote more time and energy to other management problems?
- Response to Change   Is our internal organization too rigid to innovate and adopt new technologies and more efficient production methods over time?

If any one of these questions elicits an affirmative answer, it may be useful to examine that activity in more detail to see if contracting would be efficient. Obviously, if the questions prompt several affirmative answers, it is likely that contracting will lead to savings for the government.

Contracting is not a panacea for problems of efficient government service production and delivery. It is, however, a technique that offers solutions to major problems of scale adjustments, administrative overload, adaptation to change and incentives to be efficient. As such it deserves careful consideration as part of the normal management process. Carefully used, contracting service production can increase the productivity of resources and adaptiveness of the government sector of the Canadian economy.

Notes

This study was completed in December 1984.

I wish to thank colleagues who assisted in the development of this paper. Dr. Jim McDavid of the University of Victoria provided unpublished data from his survey of local government service production and many useful comments on earlier drafts of the paper. Trish Richard of Victoria and the Local Government Center of the Reason Foundations, Santa Barbara, California, provided assitance in gathering material on government contracting; and Dr. David Laidler and members of the Commission's Social and Economic Ideas Research Advisory Group provided comment and discussion on earlier drafts of the paper.

1. Apparently the earliest Canadian study is the one Kitchen did in 1976 of 48 Canadian cities with a population over 10,000. It concluded that municipally run refuse collection was more expensive than contract collection. See Kitchen (1976). The recent Candian studies are summarized in Bish (1984, chap. 8). Other studies are presented in Savas (1982); Poole (1980); Hatry (1983); International City Management Association (1984).

2. See McAfee and McMillan (1986).

3. For example, the most recent Canadian text on local government does not include *any* analysis of the production of local services, let alone any analysis of alternative production arrangements. See Tindal and Tindal (1984).

4. Note that the term "manage" is used in a problem and program context — where management includes using contracts or other kinds of agreements with different organizations to accomplish their objectives efficiently. Management in this sense is differentiated from the traditional term "administration," which refers to legalistically supervising one's own bureaucracy. Given the diversity of contemporary government activities, viewing management in a broader context is critical for evaluating the efficiency and responsiveness of the government's performance.

5. See McDavid (1984). The data is based on an ongoing study of the local government at the University of Victoria, School of Public Administration. See Lynch and Wright (1981).

6. See Poole (1982a, 1982b).

7. A useful analysis of various kinds of contracts is presented in Kolderie (1983).

8. A history and analysis of the evolution of contract cities in Southern California is presented in Warren (1966).

9. The major theoretical analysis of the potential for contracting-out service production was based on Ostrom, Tiebout and Warren (1961). It stimulated major research efforts in the United States. Academic research on contracting out in Canada is very limited.

McDavid is doing the first large-scale research on local service delivery (See note 24) and the Bureau of Municipal Research has published one paper, referred to above. This empirical work has been supplemented by McAfee and McMillan's excellent theoretical analysis for the Ontario Economic Council but most popular debate in Canada still concerns ideology rather than management effectiveness. See, for example, Crooks (1982).

10. See Warren (1964).
11. See Bish (1971).
12. Bish and Warren (1972).
13. See Deacon (1979).
14. For an analysis of political reform movements see Warren (1966), chaps. 1–3, and Bish and Ostrom (1973).
15. The classic article challenging the consolidation tradition is Ostrom, Tiebout and Warren (1961).
16. Tullock (1965); Niskanen (1971); Borcherding (1977); Breton (1974); Leibenstein (1979).
17. Ostrom (1973), pp. 93 – 112.
18. Warren made this observation in his original analysis of contract cities in California. Ahlbrandt (1973), analyzed this hypothesis and drew the same conclusion.
19. Crooks (1982), emphasizes potential problems of monopolization and price fixing among bidders. McAfee and McMillan also point out problems of price fixing, but cite considerable evidence that the more bidders there are on a contract, the lower the lowest price offered. See McAfee and McMillan (1985, chap. 5).
20. This summary is taken from Bish and Ostrom (1973, pp. 47–49).
21. See Ahlbrandt (1973).
22. See Pommerehne and Frey (1977).
23. See Savas (1977a).
24. See McDavid (1984).
25. An analysis of studies completed prior to 1979 is presented in Savas (1979).
26. A regression analysis was done which includes variables for institutional arrangements, frequency of collection, place of pickup, spring/fall clean-up, average crew size, percentage of 32 cubic-yard packers, average age of vehicles, tonnes collected per household, population density, distance to the dump or transfer station, precipitation, and annual temperature variation. The results indicate that exclusive public collection is $10.34 more expensive (per household) than either private or mixed collection. In addition, exclusive private collection is $3.06 less expensive than either mixed or public collection. The wage differences between public and private collectors are not statistically significant in the analysis. These results are very similar to the bivariate comparison of simple average costs per household under alternative institutional arrangements.
27. These preliminary conclusions are drawn from student interviews with officials involved in the changes. The data and description of Richmond's change are included in the McDavid (1984) study.
28. See McDavid, Richards and Doughton (1984).
29. This study is reported in the Bureau of Municipal Research study. The research was done and originally reported in Savas (1977b). Further development of this idea is presented in Savas (1981).
30. Several analyses of federal contracting policy for research and development have been undertaken. One recent analysis is that by Supapol and McFetridge (1982).
31. See Hanrahan (1983).
32. A good survey of issue is presented by Wedel (1976).
33. See Langford (1983).
34. See Province of British Columbia (1984).
35. For a broader analysis see Blomqvist (1985).

36. Experience with direct contracting of elementary and secondary education is very limited, but it is common to contract for the production of specialized training programs. The kind of contracting in education that would appear most effective would be permitting students and their parents to choose their schools from among both public and private providers, with public financing available to both public and private schools based on the number of students enrolled. Such a policy with partial payment to private schools, exists in British Columbia. Given the very large differences in the costs of public and private schools (in 1982–83, private schools in British Columbia were 55 percent as costly per pupil as public schools; $4,179 vs. $2,283), any shifts to the private sector would be cost reducing, and may even encourage public schools to become more cost effective.

Many health care services are already delivered under contract, in the sense that the government reimburses suppliers for services. More attention needs to be paid to the structure of the contracting arrangements to introduce incentives for productivity increases instead of cost pass-through.
37. See Lynch and Wright (1981).
38. See Hatry (1983).
39. Sonnenblum, Kirlin, Ries (1977).
40. United States Department of the Interior (1979).
41. Economic Council of Canada (1983, p. 61). Also see Conklin (1985).
42. Economic Council, ibid., p. 139.
43. See note 1.

Bibliography

Ahlbrandt, Roger S. Jr. 1973. *Municipal Fire Protection Services: Comparison of Alternative Organizational Forms*. Beverly Hills: Sage Publications.

Bish, Robert L. 1984. *Local Government in British Columbia*. Victoria, B.C.: University of Victoria, School of Public Administration.

———. 1971. *The Public Economy of Metropolitan Areas*. Chicago: Markham/Rand McNally.

Bish, Robert L., and Vincent Ostrom. 1973. *Understanding Urban Government: Metropolitan Reform Reconsidered*. Washington, D.C.: American Enterprise Institute.

Bish, Robert L., and Robert Warren. 1972. *Urban Affairs Quarterly* (September): 97–122.

Blomqvist, A.G. 1985. "Political Economy of the Canadian Welfare State." In *Approaches to Economic Well-Being*, volume 26 of the research studies prepared for the Royal Commission on the Economic Union and Development Prospects for Canada. Toronto: University of Toronto Press.

Borcherding, Thomas E., ed. 1977. *Budgets and Bureaucrats*. Durham, N.C.: Duke University Press.

Breton, Albert. 1974. *The Economic Theory of Representative Government*. Chicago: Aldine.

Conklin, David W. 1985. "Entrepreneurship, Innovation and Economic Changes." In *Responses to Economic Change*, volume 27 of the research studies prepared for the Royal Commission on the Economic Union and Development Prospects for Canada. Toronto: University of Toronto Press.

Crooks, Harold. 1982. *Dirty Business: An Inside Look at the Garbage Industry in Canada*. Toronto: James Lorimer.

Deacon, R.T. 1979. "The Expenditure Effects of Alternative Public Supply Institutions." *Public Choice* 34: 381–97.

Economic Council of Canada. 1983. *The Bottom Line: Technology, Trade and Income Growth*. Ottawa: Minister of Supply and Services Canada.

Hanrahan, John D. 1983. *Government by Contract*. New York: Norton.

Hatry, Harry P. 1983. *A Review of Private Approaches for Delivery of Public Services*. Washington, D.C.: The Urban Institute.

International City Management Association. 1984. *Rethinking Local Services: Examining Alternative Delivery Approaches*. Washington, D.C.: ICMA (March).

Kitchen, Harry M. 1976. "A Statistical Estimation of the Operating Cost Function for Municipal Refuse Collection." *Public Finance Quarterly* 4 (January): 56–76.

Kolderie, Ted. 1983. "Contracting as an Approach to Management." Public Services Redesign Project. Minneapolis: University of Minnesota, Humphrey Institute.

Langford, John W. 1983. The Question of Quangos: Quasi-Public Service Agencies in British Columbia." *Canadian Public Administration* 26 (Winter): 563–76.

Leibenstein, Harvey. 1979. *General X-Efficiency Theory and Economic Development*. New York: Oxford University Press.

Lynch, Mary, and Ute Wright. 1981. "Providing Municipal Services — Methods, Costs, and Trade-Offs." Toronto: The Bureau of Municipal Research (February).

McAfee, R. Preston, and John McMillan. 1986. *Incentives in Government Contracting*. Study prepared for the Ontario Economic Council. Toronto (forthcoming).

McDavid, James. 1984. "Residential Solid Waste Collection Services in Canadian Municipalities." Victoria, B.C.: University of Victoria School of Public Administration (April). Mimeographed.

McDavid, James, P.L. Richards, and B.E. Doughton. 1984. "Privatization of Residential Solid Waste Collection in Richmond, British Columbia." Victoria, B.C.: University of Victoria, School of Public Administration (May). Mimeographed.

Niskanen, William A. 1971. *Bureaucracy and Representative Government*. Chicago: Aldine.

Ostrom, Elinor. 1973. "On the Meaning and Measurement of Output and Efficiency in the Provision of Urban Police Services." *Journal of Criminal Justice* 1: 93–112.

Ostrom, Vincent, Charles Tiebout, and Robert Warren. 1961. "The Organization of Government in Metropolitan Regions: A Theoretical Inquiry." *American Political Science Review* 55 (December): 831–42.

Pommerehne, Werner W., and Bruno S. Frey. 1977. "Public vs. Private Production Efficiency in Switzerland: A Theoretical and Empirical Comparison." In *Comparing Urban Service Delivery Systems: Structure and Performance*, Urban Affairs Annual Reviews, vol. 12, edited by Vincent Ostrom and Frances Pennel Bish, pp. 221–42. Beverly Hills: Sage.

Poole, Robert W., Jr. 1980. *Cutting Back City Hall*. New York: Universe Press.

———. 1982a. "Contracting Out — Around the World." *Fiscal Watchdog* 68 (June). Santa Barbara, Cal.: Local Government Center, a non-profit research foundation.

———. 1982b. "Why not Contract Policing?" *Fiscal Watchdog* 72 (October). Santa Barbara Cal.: Local Government Center, a non-profit research foundation.

Province of British Columbia. Ministry of Human Resources. 1984. *Purchase of Service Policy and Procedures Manual*.

Savas, E.S. 1977a. *The Organization and Efficiency of Solid Waste Collection*. Lexington, Mass.: Lexington Books.

———. 1977b. "An Empirical Study of Competition in Municipal Service Delivery." *Public Administration Review* 37 (November/December 1977): 717–24.

———. 1979. "Public vs. Private Refuse Collection: A Critical Review of the Evidence." "*Journal of Urban Analysis* 6: 1–13.

———. 1981. "IntraCity Competition Between Public and Private Service Delivery." *Public Administration Review* 41 (January/February): 46–52.

———. 1982. *Privatizing the Public Sector*. Chatham, New Jersey: Chatham House.

Sonnenblum, Sidney, J.J. Kirlin, and J.C. Ries. 1977. *How Cities Provide Services: An Evaluation of Alternative Delivery Structures*. Cambridge, Mass.: Ballinger.

Supapol, A.B., and D.G. McFetridge. 1982. *An Analysis of the Federal Make-or-Buy Policy.* Discussion Paper 217. Ottawa: Economic Council of Canada.

Tindal, C.R., and S. Nobes Tindal. 1984. *Local Government in Canada.* Toronto: McGraw-Hill Ryerson.

Tullock, Gordon. 1965. *The Politics of Bureaucracy.* Washington, D.C.: Public Affairs Press.

U.S. Department of the Interior. Heritage Conservation and Recreation Service. 1979. *Contract Services Handbook.* Washington, D.C.: USDOI (October).

Warren, Robert, 1964. "A Municipal Services Market Model of Metropolitan Organization." *Journal of the American Institute of Planners* 30 (August): 193–214.

_____. 1966. *Government in Metropolitan Regions: A Reappraisal of Fractionated Political Organization.* Davis, Cal.: University of California, Institute of Governmental Affairs.

Wedel, Kenneth R. 1976. "Government Contracting for Purchase of Service." *Social Work* 21 (March): 101–105.

Robert L. Bish is Professor in the School of Public Administration and in the Department of Economics, University of Victoria.

André Blais is Professor in the Department of Political Science, Université de Montréal, and is Research Coordinator for the Industrial Policy section, which is part of the Politics and Political Institutions Research Area, Royal Commission on the Economic Union and Development Prospects for Canada.

David W. Conklin is Executive Director of the Ontario Economic Council, Toronto.

C. Knick Harley is Professor in the Department of Economics, University of Western Ontario, London.

John C.R. McCallum is Associate Professor in the Department of Economics, University of Quebec at Montreal.

Claude Montmarquette is Professor in the Department of Economics, University of Montreal.

Charles K. Rowley is Professor of Economics, Centre for Study of Public Choice, George Mason University, Fairfax, Virginia, and is an Honorary Research Associate, Centre for Socio-Legal Studies, Wolfson College, Oxford, England.

Dan Usher is Professor in the Department of Economics, Queen's University, Kingston.

THE COLLECTED RESEARCH STUDIES

Royal Commission on the Economic Union and Development Prospects for Canada

ECONOMICS

Income Distribution and Economic Security in Canada (Vol.1), *François Vaillancourt, Research Coordinator*

Vol. 1 Income Distribution and Economic Security in Canada, *F. Vaillancourt* (C)*

Industrial Structure (Vols. 2-8), *Donald G. McFetridge, Research Coordinator*

Vol. 2 Canadian Industry in Transition, *D.G. McFetridge* (C)
Vol. 3 Technological Change in Canadian Industry, *D.G. McFetridge* (C)
Vol. 4 Canadian Industrial Policy in Action, *D.G. McFetridge* (C)
Vol. 5 Economics of Industrial Policy and Strategy, *D.G. McFetridge* (C)
Vol. 6 The Role of Scale in Canada–US Productivity Differences, *J.R. Baldwin and P.K. Gorecki* (M)
Vol. 7 Competition Policy and Vertical Exchange, *F. Mathewson and R. Winter* (M)
Vol. 8 The Political Economy of Economic Adjustment, *M. Trebilcock* (M)

International Trade (Vols. 9-14), *John Whalley, Research Coordinator*

Vol. 9 Canadian Trade Policies and the World Economy, *J. Whalley with C. Hamilton and R. Hill* (M)
Vol. 10 Canada and the Multilateral Trading System, *J. Whalley* (M)
Vol. 11 Canada–United States Free Trade, *J. Whalley* (C)
Vol. 12 Domestic Policies and the International Economic Environment, *J. Whalley* (C)
Vol. 13 Trade, Industrial Policy and International Competition, *R. Harris* (M)
Vol. 14 Canada's Resource Industries and Water Export Policy, *J. Whalley* (C)

Labour Markets and Labour Relations (Vols. 15-18), *Craig Riddell, Research Coordinator*

Vol. 15 Labour-Management Cooperation in Canada, *C. Riddell* (C)
Vol. 16 Canadian Labour Relations, *C. Riddell* (C)
Vol. 17 Work and Pay. The Canadian Labour Market, *C. Riddell* (C)
Vol. 18 Adapting to Change: Labour Market Adjustment in Canada, *C. Riddell* (C)

Macroeconomics (Vols. 19-25), *John Sargent, Research Coordinator*

Vol. 19 Macroeconomic Performance and Policy Issues: Overviews, *J. Sargent* (M)
Vol. 20 Post-War Macroeconomic Developments, *J. Sargent* (C)
Vol. 21 Fiscal and Monetary Policy, *J. Sargent* (C)
Vol. 22 Economic Growth: Prospects and Determinants, *J. Sargent* (C)
Vol. 23 Long-Term Economic Prospects for Canada: A Symposium, *J. Sargent* (C)
Vol. 24 Foreign Macroeconomic Experience: A Symposium, *J. Sargent* (C)
Vol. 25 Dealing with Inflation and Unemployment in Canada, *C. Riddell* (M)

Economic Ideas and Social Issues (Vols. 26 and 27), *David Laidler, Research Coordinator*

Vol. 26 Approaches to Economic Well-Being, *D. Laidler* (C)
Vol. 27 Responses to Economic Change, *D. Laidler* (C)

* (C) denotes a Collection of studies by various authors coordinated by the person named.
  (M) denotes a Monograph.

POLITICS AND INSTITUTIONS OF GOVERNMENT

Canada and the International Political Economy (Vols. 28-30), *Denis Stairs and Gilbert R. Winham, Research Coordinators*

Vol. 28 Canada and the International Political/Economic Environment, *D. Stairs and G.R. Winham* (C)
Vol. 29 The Politics of Canada's Economic Relationship with the United States, *D. Stairs and G.R. Winham* (C)
Vol. 30 Selected Problems in Formulating Foreign Economic Policy, *D. Stairs and G.R. Winham* (C)

State and Society in the Modern Era (Vols. 31 and 32), *Keith Banting, Research Coordinator*

Vol. 31 State and Society: Canada in Comparative Perspective, *K. Banting* (C)
Vol. 32 The State and Economic Interests, *K. Banting* (C)

Constitutionalism, Citizenship and Society (Vols. 33-35), *Alan Cairns and Cynthia Williams, Research Coordinators*

Vol. 33 Constitutionalism, Citizenship and Society in Canada, *A. Cairns and C. Williams* (C)
Vol. 34 The Politics of Gender, Ethnicity and Language in Canada, *A. Cairns and C. Williams* (C)
Vol. 35 Public Opinion and Public Policy in Canada, *R. Johnston* (M)

Representative Institutions (Vols. 36-39), *Peter Aucoin, Research Coordinator*

Vol. 36 Party Government and Regional Representation in Canada, *P. Aucoin* (C)
Vol. 37 Regional Responsiveness and the National Administrative State, *P. Aucoin* (C)
Vol. 38 Institutional Reforms for Representative Government, *P. Aucoin* (C)
Vol. 39 Intrastate Federalism in Canada, *D.V. Smiley and R.L. Watts* (M)

The Politics of Economic Policy (Vols. 40-43), *G. Bruce Doern, Research Coordinator*

Vol. 40 The Politics of Economic Policy, *G.B. Doern* (C)
Vol. 41 Federal and Provincial Budgeting, *A.M. Maslove, M.J. Prince and G.B. Doern* (M)
Vol. 42 Economic Regulation and the Federal System, *R. Schultz and A. Alexandroff* (M)
Vol. 43 Bureaucracy in Canada: Control and Reform, *S.L. Sutherland and G.B. Doern* (M)

Industrial Policy (Vols. 44 and 45), *André Blais, Research Coordinator*

Vol. 44 Industrial Policy, *A. Blais* (C)
Vol. 45 The Political Sociology of Industrial Policy, *A. Blais* (M)

LAW AND CONSTITUTIONAL ISSUES

Law, Society and the Economy (Vols. 46-51), *Ivan Bernier and Andrée Lajoie, Research Coordinators*

Vol. 46 Law, Society and the Economy, *I. Bernier and A. Lajoie* (C)
Vol. 47 The Supreme Court of Canada as an Instrument of Political Change, *I. Bernier and A. Lajoie* (C)
Vol. 48 Regulations, Crown Corporations and Administrative Tribunals, *I. Bernier and A. Lajoie* (C)
Vol. 49 Family Law and Social Welfare Legislation in Canada, *I. Bernier and A. Lajoie* (C)
Vol. 50 Consumer Protection, Environmental Law and Corporate Power, *I. Bernier and A. Lajoie* (C)
Vol. 51 Labour Law and Urban Law in Canada, *I. Bernier and A. Lajoie* (C)

The International Legal Environment (Vols. 52-54), *John Quinn, Research Coordinator*

Vol. 52 The International Legal Environment, *J. Quinn* (C)
Vol. 53 Canadian Economic Development and the International Trading System, *M.M. Hart* (M)
Vol. 54 Canada and the New International Law of the Sea, *D.M. Johnston* (M)

Harmonization of Laws in Canada (Vols. 55 and 56), *Ronald C.C. Cuming, Research Coordinator*

Vol. 55 Perspectives on the Harmonization of Law in Canada, *R. Cuming* (C)
Vol. 56 Harmonization of Business Law in Canada, *R. Cuming* (C)

Institutional and Constitutional Arrangements (Vols. 57 and 58), *Clare F. Beckton and A. Wayne MacKay, Research Coordinators*

Vol. 57 Recurring Issues in Canadian Federalism, *C.F. Beckton and A.W. MacKay* (C)
Vol. 58 The Courts and The Charter, *C.F. Beckton and A.W. MacKay* (C)

FEDERALISM AND THE ECONOMIC UNION

Federalism and The Economic Union (Vols. 58-72), *Mark Krasnick, Kenneth Norrie and Richard Simeon, Research Coordinators*

Vol. 59 Federalism and Economic Union in Canada, *K. Norrie, R. Simeon and M. Krasnick* (M)
Vol. 60 Perspectives on the Canadian Economic Union, *M. Krasnick* (C)
Vol. 61 Division of Powers and Public Policy, *R. Simeon* (C)
Vol. 62 Case Studies in the Division of Powers, *M. Krasnick* (C)
Vol. 63 Intergovernmental Relations, *R. Simeon* (C)
Vol. 64 Disparities and Interregional Adjustment, *K. Norrie* (C)
Vol. 65 Fiscal Federalism, *M. Krasnick* (C)
Vol. 66 Mobility of Capital in the Canadian Economic Union, *N. Roy* (M)
Vol. 67 Economic Management and the Division of Powers, *T.J. Courchene* (M)
Vol. 68 Regional Aspects of Confederation, *J. Whalley* (M)
Vol. 69 Interest Groups in the Canadian Federal System, *H.G. Thorburn* (M)
Vol. 70 Canada and Quebec, Past and Future: An Essay, *D. Latouche* (M)
Vol. 71 The Political Economy of Canadian Federalism: 1940–1984, *R. Simeon and I. Robinson* (M)

THE NORTH

Vol. 72 The North, *Michael S. Whittington, Coordinator* (C)

COMMISSION ORGANIZATION

Chairman

Donald S. Macdonald

Commissioners

Clarence L. Barber	William M. Hamilton	Daryl K. Seaman
Albert Breton	John R. Messer	Thomas K. Shoyama
M. Angela Cantwell Peters	Laurent Picard	Jean Casselman-Wadds
E. Gérard Docquier	Michel Robert	Catherine T. Wallace

Senior Officers

Executive Director
J. Gerald Godsoe

Director of Policy	*Senior Advisors*	*Directors of Research*
Alan Nymark	David Ablett	Ivan Bernier
	Victor Clarke	Alan Cairns
Secretary	Carl Goldenberg	David C. Smith
Michel Rochon	Harry Stewart	
Director of Administration	*Director of Publishing*	*Co-Directors of Research*
Sheila-Marie Cook	Ed Matheson	Kenneth Norrie
		John Sargent

Research Program Organization

Economics	Politics and the Institutions of Government	Law and Constitutional Issues
Research Director	*Research Director*	*Research Director*
David C. Smith	Alan Cairns	Ivan Bernier
Executive Assistant & Assistant Director (Research Services)	*Executive Assistant*	*Executive Assistant & Research Program Administrator*
I. Lilla Connidis	Karen Jackson	Jacques J.M. Shore
Coordinators	*Coordinators*	*Coordinators*
David Laidler	Peter Aucoin	Clare F. Beckton
Donald G. McFetridge	Keith Banting	Ronald C.C. Cuming
Kenneth Norrie*	André Blais	Mark Krasnick
Craig Riddell	Bruce Doern	Andrée Lajoie
John Sargent*	Richard Simeon	A. Wayne MacKay
François Vaillancourt	Denis Stairs	John J. Quinn
John Whalley	Cynthia Williams	
	Gilbert R. Winham	
Research Analysts	*Research Analysts*	*Administrative and Research Assistant*
Caroline Digby	Claude Desranleau	Nicolas Roy
Mireille Ethier	Ian Robinson	
Judith Gold		
Douglas S. Green	*Office Administration*	*Research Analyst*
Colleen Hamilton	Donna Stebbing	Nola Silzer
Roderick Hill		
Joyce Martin		

*Kenneth Norrie and John Sargent co-directed the final phase of Economics Research with David Smith